PRACTICAL CARRIAGE BUILDING

COMPILED BY M.T. RICHARDSON

Combining
Volumes I and II

THE ASTRAGAL PRESS
Mendham, New Jersey 07945-0239

Library of Congress Catalog Card Number: 94-70620
International Standard Book Number: 1-879335-50-6

Published by
THE ASTRAGAL PRESS
5 Cold Hill Road, Suite #12
Mendham, New Jersey 07945-0239

Manufactured in the United States of America

PRACTICAL

Carriage Building:

COMPRISING

NUMEROUS SHORT PRACTICAL ARTICLES UPON CARRIAGE AND
WAGON WOODWORK; PLANS FOR FACTORIES; SHOP AND
BENCH TOOLS; CONVENIENT APPLIANCES FOR REPAIR
WORK; METHODS OF WORKING; PECULIARITIES
OF BENT TIMBER; CONSTRUCTION OF CAR-
RIAGE PARTS; REPAIRING WHEELS;
FORMS OF TENONS AND MORTISES;
TOGETHER WITH A VARIETY OF
USEFUL HINTS AND SUG-
GESTIONS TO WOOD-
WORKERS.

COMPILED BY M. T. RICHARDSON,

EDITOR OF

"THE BLACKSMITH AND WHEELWRIGHT," "PRACTICAL BLACKSMITHING," "PRACTICAL
HORSESHOEING," ETC.

PROFUSELY ILLUSTRATED.

VOL. I.

NEW YORK:
M. T. RICHARDSON CO., PUBLISHERS,
1892.

CONTENTS.

CHAPTER I.

CHAPTER II.

CHAPTER III.

PREFACE.

WITH a view to furnishing, in a condensed form, practical information upon all minor matters pertaining to carriage making, the publisher of PRACTICAL CARRIAGE BUILDING has caused to be compiled a great variety of short articles bearing directly upon the Woodwork Department, and has so arranged and classified them as to afford a convenient and reliable book of reference to the worker. Abstruse theory and complicated rules are made secondary to practical instruction. This volume is, in fact, an epitome of the principal methods of construction, as expressed by workmen who have gained their knowledge from every-day experience. In this respect it differs from any previous publication, in that it represents no one man's views upon any one subject. As is natural in such cases, it will be found that there are apparent contradictions regarding methods; but as no two authorities follow the same course throughout, the contradictions are more apparent than real.

One advantage in thus giving the results attained by different workmen is that they meet a variety of conditions; and the man who is desirous of learning new ways will find conditions that meet the immediate situation.

To the young workman these directions must prove valuable, as they are given in the simplest language that will serve to make clear the object of the authors.

The profuse use of illustrations places each individual subject before the reader in a much clearer light than could have been done by words alone.

Not the least among the subjects of interest is the description of numerous appliances for labor-saving—appliances of simple forms and construction, which bring them within the range of the workman's skill to produce.

Workmen as a rule read too little on topics pertaining to their business. This is due in great part to the fact that the treatment of the subjects is from a scholarly rather than a shop standpoint, and practical mechanics is subordinated to elegance in phraseology, and the practical man who has but few hours for study, tires before he has learned what the writer is trying to teach. Articles written for shop men by shop men carry a weight that the most skillfully written essays by professors cannot command.

There is a kinship in thought as well as in blood, and nowhere is this more clearly shown than in practical mechanics. Plain, simple, correct language, stripped of all redundance of words or of style, which serve simply as polish, is easily understood, and in the treatment of practical questions is much to be preferred to the polished expressions so essential to classical literature.

In mechanics as in science there is a primary and a higher grade; but most works are prepared for the higher, and by them they invite the student to neglect the simpler for the more advanced studies—a mistake similar to teaching a child to read as soon as it has learned its letters. A mechanic well versed in the rudiments finds little difficulty in working out intricate problems, and is thoroughly fitted to grasp the higher principles of his art. To acquire this rudimental knowledge the instruction must be in language that can be understood and the teachers must be many. Books of instruction therefore, like PRACTICAL CARRIAGE BUILDING, become of the first value both to the student and the man whose opportunities have been few.

With us the well being of the country is in the hands of the masses, and it becomes important that they be educated up to a higher standpoint where they are prepared to analyze facts and prove them from practice. This holds good in every department of life, and in none more than in the mechanical. The practical man, with a mind properly trained, works out results clean-cut, and secures success while the theorizer is harping on the old saw, "That is in opposition to mechanical laws." It is not to be understood that theory is to be ignored; but theory unsupported by practice is a barrier to all advancement; whereas the two combined lead to success.

To know how to work in our country is to be able to command high wages. We are less hampered by arbitrary laws, made under conditions not now existing, than the people of other nations. Our workmen are more manly, more thoughtful, and more energetic. But they should read and study more. Therefore this little volume of nuggets, gathered from the workshop of the practical, has been prepared for and is respectfully dedicated to them by

THE PUBLISHER.

NEW YORK, December, 1891.

PRACTICAL CARRIAGE BUILDING.

CHAPTER I.

Introductory remarks regarding Timber, Plans for a Carriage Shop, Tools, Floor and Bench, and Woodworking Appliances.

THERE are so many matters pertaining to the arrangement of the carriage shop—the timber used, plans of shop, tools, &c.—that it is but fitting that the opening chapter should be devoted to the consideration of these subjects.

To the carriage woodworker the quality and character of the timber used is a matter of prime importance, and how to secure it is quite as well worth considering as is the style of the vehicle he is to build. The subject is too extended to permit its being treated in detail herein, but a brief review may suffice to interest and lead to more extended study.

The hard woods used are hickory, oak, ash, elm, locust, beech, gum, cherry, and black walnut; the two last mentioned, however, have become too expensive for general use. Whitewood, basswood, and pine are the soft woods, their importance ranking in the order named.

When such a variety is used, economy suggests that the selections be made with care. In the first place, seasoned timber is an absolute necessity, and as there must always be a stock ripening, the storage rooms should be so arranged that the seasoned and unseasoned are separate. Then too plank must be piled in a manner that will reduce handling to a minimum, particularly if thin stock. There are certain pieces that can be sawed out in large quantities and piled up in a manner that will permit their seasoning without losing shape, and also make them accessible. All that is required is to carefully assort the various sizes and kinds before piling. Axle beds, spring bars, perches, head blocks, side bars, poles, shafts, cross bars, and a great variety of straight stock, as well as such body stuff as door and standing pillars, top rails and curves, and often top rails, arm pieces, and even rockers and bottom sides, may be sawed and stacked up in separate piles or racks. Small manufacturers who do not have power of their own, but send all plank to the mill to be sawed, will find it not only convenient but also economical to mark up the entire plank into such strips or forms as will be needed, in addition to the original pieces. It costs no more to keep sawed stock than it does to keep the plank, and much time can be saved by having pieces ready for use.

Hickory, oak, ash, and locust for carriage parts can be sawed before the plank is thoroughly seasoned, and then racked up in a well ventilated loft. When free from excessive heat or moisture, they will dry out without being attacked by insects or injured by the changes in the atmosphere. Soft stock, such as panels, seat ends and backs, bottom boards and roofing, can be sawed up in lengths, racked up in accordance to width, in a manner that will insure their not warping, and where loss from handling may be avoided entirely. It is almost impossible to handle thin stock in long boards without splitting, but if cut up as directed, the loss will be trifling.

Convenient tools for general shop use are essential, and the manufacturer who fails to provide these, acts against his own interest. The journeyman is expected to furnish his bench tools, but not such articles as wood or iron clamps, wood or iron hand screws, glue pots, saw horses, trustles, and draft boards. If the supply of these is ample, it will facilitate work and prevent much discontent among workmen. Wood hand screws should be in three sizes. The complement for each bench will consist of four twenty-inch, one dozen twelve inch, and half a dozen six-inch. There should be two long clamps to each bench, and not less than one dozen and a half thumb screws, one glue pot—not less than quart size. One white lead pot, two glue and one lead brush are also needed to each bench.

Convenient grind stones, propelled by power whenever possible, and when not, by foot gearing, should be in a convenient location. A small hand or jig saw, propelled by power, will be found profitable in shops where other machinery is not used.

A store room, no matter how small the factory, wherein can be kept screws, files, bolts, sand paper, &c., should be provided.

Cleanliness is an important feature, and once a week at least, the wood shop should be thoroughly swept and the windows cleaned. Glue pots should be cleaned daily during warm weather. Unless this is done, the glue will decompose and its strength will be lost. Decomposition is decay, and the slightest taint indicating its presence should act as a warning against its use. Even in cold weather it is a poor plan to make up more glue at one time than will be needed for two days' use, as reheating weakens it as surely as does decomposition, but not quite so quickly.

Sinks, water closets, and lockers for clothes all tend to promote cleanliness and to administer to the comfort of the workmen. They cost but little to erect and should be provided unhesitatingly.

A Well Appointed Carriage Shop.

Every hamlet and village in the land is supplied with its repair shop and wagon shop, even if it cannot boast of its carriage shop. Every town of considerable size has not only its wagon shops, but from one to a half dozen concerns known as carriage shops or carriage repositories. Among these establishments a well appointed factory, one which is supplied with every necessary tool, one in which the arrangements are such that work is moved among its several departments with the least possible handling, and in which there is good light and ventilation, is indeed a rarity. It frequently happens that the smaller shops in the large cities, in which people generally expect to find the best of everything, are but little better arranged than the so-called country shop of corresponding size.

We propose here to describe a well appointed small shop. Large concerns are conducted perhaps on even better methods, but it is to be remembered always that systems applicable to large establishments are seldom suited to small ones.

It is a fact well known to experts, although not in all cases admitted, that many concerns doing a small business, the mechanical operations in which in part only are adapted to the use of steam power, frequently execute their work at a greater expense by the employment of power than would be required if power were not used. This is especially true of carriage shops. There are but few of the operations in carriage making in which steam power can be advantageously employed, and a very large business is essential to warrant its use. Therefore in small establishments the expense of a steam engine very frequently entails a loss.

A model establishment, illustrated herewith, occupies four floors and a basement. The basement is used as a blacksmith shop. The first floor contains the office and a delivery and receiving room. The second floor is the repository. The third floor contains the body shop and trimming room, while the paint shop and the varnishing and finishing rooms are on the fourth floor. The main building is supplemented by an extension of the roof, which is placed at a level with the second floor, and which is furnished with large skylights and a ventilator of sufficient capacity for carrying off the smoke and gases from the smith shop. It will be seen by examination of the plan, Fig. 1, that the first floor does not ex-

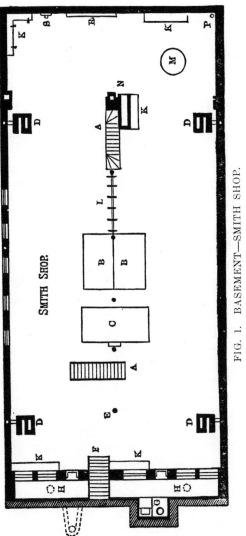

FIG. 1. BASEMENT—SMITH SHOP.

A, Stairs to first floor. *B*, Coal bins. *C*, Carriage elevator. *D*, Forges. *E*, Tire setter fastened to post. *F*, Stairs to sidewalk. *G*, Water closet. *H*, Cess pools. *K*, Benches. *L*, Rack for spring and axle iron. *M*, Tire platform. *N*, Tire oven. *P*, Hydrant. *R*, Rack. *S*, Drill.

tend through this addition across the rear of the building.
A fence or guard terminates the room at the rear, in which
is placed a gate or opening for the convenience of handling
work to and from the smith shop. This arrangement affords
ample light and air in the blacksmith shop, especially in the
rear part, where most of the drilling, vise work, bench work,
tire setting, &c., is performed. At the same time this arrangement affords light and ventilation to the first floor in a
very desirable manner.

The blacksmith shop contains four forges, located in the
four corners of the room, and each provided with its own
proper flue in the wall. The entrance to the blacksmith
shop from the front or sidewalk is by a broad stairway, head-
room for which is provided by a platform or a raised floor in
the office. This raised platform also affords sufficient hight
for the window placed alongside the stairway, and which affords ample light to a bench placed in front of it, as shown
in the plan. Under the sidewalk and along the front of the
basement, is the usual area provided for city building, from
which opens the door to a water closet, all of which is shown
upon the plan. Besides the stairway leading to the sidewalk
there are two other stairways from the blacksmith shop
leading to the first floor, the location of which is clearly
shown in the engraving. The girder running lengthwise
through the center of the building is supported in the basement by iron columns, against the front one of which is fastened a tire-setting machine, indicated by E in Fig. 2. The
carriage elevator is shown in the plan of the smith shop,
coming between the second and third of the iron columns.
A coal bin is placed just in the rear of the carriage elevator
and about the center of the shop, thus making it equally
convenient to each of the several forges. The construction
and arrangement of this coal bin is something unique and
something to which the attention of many employers may
well be given. It is filled through trap doors placed in the
first floor. A cart or wagon of coal may be driven through

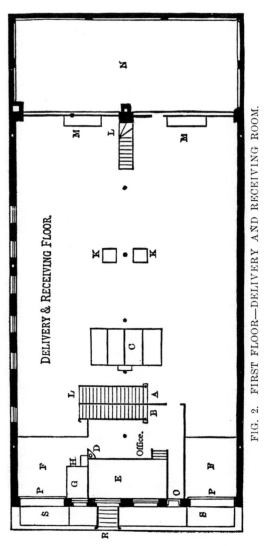

FIG. 2. FIRST FLOOR—DELIVERY AND RECEIVING ROOM.

A, Stairs from delivery room to second floor. B, Stairs from office to second floor. C, Carriage elevator. D, Washstand in office. E, Raised platform in office, to afford head room to door to basement. F, Inclined floor. G, Hardware closet. H, Bench with vise. K, Scuttle holes to coal bins. L, Stairs to basement. M, Benches. N, Opening over smith shop. O, Door into office. P, Doors for receiving and delivering carriages. R, Outside entrance to basement. S, Sidewalk area.

either of the two large doors in the front of the first story and dumped directly over one of these trap holes, most of the coal by its own weight finding its way into the bin, thus requiring very little shoveling. The coal is taken from the bin at the bottom, an arrangement resulting in the least possible handling of it, and consequently making the least possible dirt about the premises. Between the coal bin and the back stairs in the smith shop, and supported by two of the iron columns carrying the girder, is a rack for spring and axle, iron and steel. The arrangement of this rack and its location is such as to commend it to the approval of intelligent shop superintendents. The tire oven is located near the middle of the back part of the shop, and is in convenient proximity to a flue built in the pier which supports the center of the rear wall. Its location and general arrangement may be seen by referring to the plan, Fig. 2. Inspection of the same engraving will show the location of the tire platform, the hydrant, benches, racks, &c.

Entering the first floor we find in the center of the front of the building the office, consisting of two general divisions. The floor of the rear part is on a common level with the receiving room back of it, while the floor of the front is elevated to accommodate the stairway and window of the basement already described. An incline in the floor upon either side of the office facilitates the delivery and receiving of carriages, &c. A hardware closet is located just to the left of the office, lighted by one of the front windows, and back of it in the corner against the office door is a small bench with a vise, provided with wrenches and such other tools as are frequently in demand at the last moment when a vehicle is being sent out. Along the wall above the inclined floor on the left a pole rack is provided.

There are two flights of stairs leading from the first floor to the second floor, or rather a broad flight is divided by a partition so as to admit of a direct passage both from the office and from the receiving room. This is a matter of convenience.

Underneath the stairs in the office a closet is provided. A washstand occupies a corner between the raised platform and the door entering from the left. There are no other special features in connection with the first floor that require special attention. The location of the carriage elevator, the trap doors to the coal bin, benches, &c., are all clearly shown in Fig. 1.

Ascending now to the second story, which is occupied as a repository, one finds in the front corner, on the right, a wash floor. This floor is raised a trifle above the common level, is provided with a gutter all around leading to a waste pipe, and is so calked and painted as to be water tight. All necessary washing of buggies and carriages may be done here with the same security as though it were being done upon the ground floor. By examining the rear of the second story, as shown in Fig. 3, the position of the skylights and ventilators already referred to in the description of the blacksmith shop may be seen.

The front of the third story is occupied as a trimming room. A speaking tube leads from this room direct to the office, the pipe following down the posts which support the girders. Benches are located across the front in places where the light is the best, while a closet for holding trimming material is placed against the wall at the right hand end. Between it and the partition separating the trimming room from the body shop is placed a set of shelves for cushions, &c. This trimming room, as arranged, has accommodations for five men. The body shop occupies the rear of the same floor. The location of benches is clearly shown in Fig. 4. It needs no special description other than that given in the caption under the engraving.

The fourth or upper floor, as is usual in many shops, is occupied as a paint shop. The finishing and varnishing rooms are located in the front and are separated from the paint shop by a close partition fitted with sliding doors. In addition to the light supplied by the front and side windows,

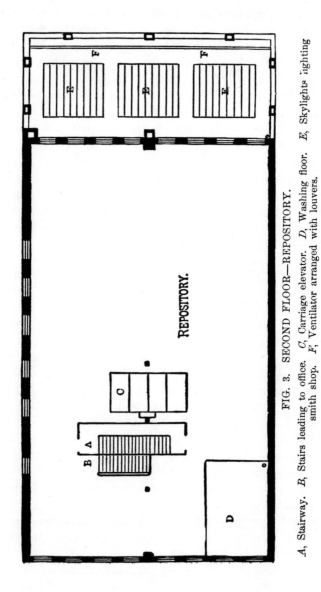

FIG. 3. SECOND FLOOR—REPOSITORY.

A, Stairway. *B*, Stairs leading to office. *C*, Carriage elevator. *D*, Washing floor. *E*, Skylights lighting smith shop. *F*, Ventilator arranged with louvers.

this part is also lighted by a skylight, thus rendering it in every way desirable for the purpose for which it is used. Closets for lamps, &c., are provided, as may be seen in Fig. 5. A case for glass frames, indicated by *E* in the same engraving, occupies a space under the partition separating the varnishing and finishing rooms. This feature is something of a novelty. The case is provided with movable shelves or slides, upon which the frames can be placed. It is also furnished with doors for closing against dust, &c. The floor of both the finishing and varnishing rooms is made water tight and is provided with a gutter and a connection with a waste pipe so as to prevent damage in the rooms below, in case anything is spilled or water is used. In the front right hand corner of the paint shop may be noticed a urinal and a wash sink. A similar convenience is also provided on the other floors. A skylight covers the space occupied by the carriage elevator, thus throwing an abundance of light upon it at whatever elevation it may be in the building. In the rear left hand corner of the paint shop is located the paint bench.

The cost of the building described, exclusive of the ground it occupies, was $16,000. Roughly estimated, it provides for the employment of about fifty-five men, divided something as follows: Fifteen in blacksmith shop, fifteen woodworkers, five trimmers, and about twenty in the paint shop and varnishing and finishing rooms.

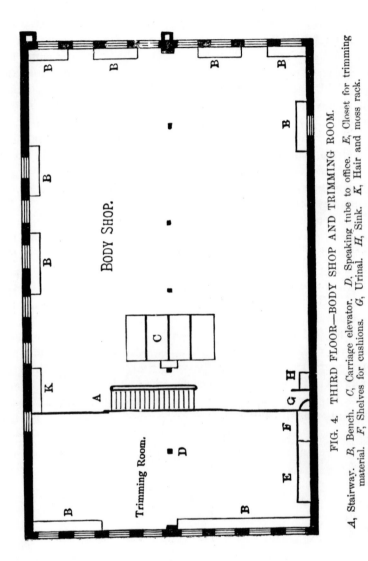

FIG. 4. THIRD FLOOR—BODY SHOP AND TRIMMING ROOM.

A, Stairway. B, Bench. C, Carriage elevator. D, Speaking tube to office. E, Closet for trimming material. F, Shelves for cushions. G, Urinal. H, Sink. K, Hair and moss rack.

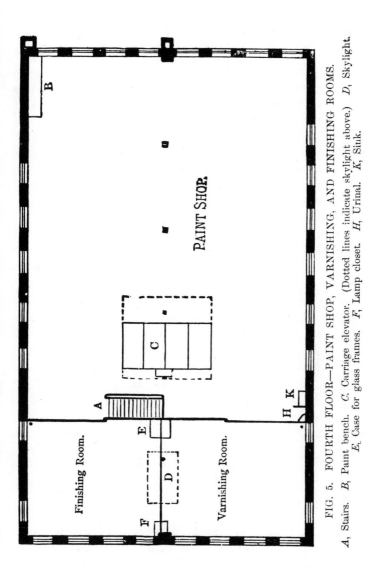

FIG. 5. FOURTH FLOOR—PAINT SHOP, VARNISHING, AND FINISHING ROOMS.
A, Stairs. B, Paint bench. C, Carriage elevator. (Dotted lines indicate skylight above.) D, Skylight. E, Case for glass frames. F, Lamp closet. H, Urinal. K, Sink.

Power vs. Hand Work.—Plan of a Wheelwright's Shop.

I have had power in my shop for more than three years, and have found that it is as good as an extra man. I began with little machinery, but have added to my stock of tools and appliances as the money came in to enable me to do so. I have now a circular saw, a band and a buzz saw, a Daniels, and a side wheel planer, a rounding and a polishing machine, a turning lathe, a boring and a mortising machine. They have not cost a great deal of money, and as I bought them from time to time, the money paid for them has not been missed. The cost of running them is but trifling; they have saved a great deal of hard labor and have improved the qual-'ty and increased the quantity of the work done in my shop. Moreover by having these machines I have largely increased my business by securing jobs that could not have been obtained if I had used hand labor only. Another advantage gained by machinery is the saving of time when it is desired to have work done in a hurry. In these days of sharp competition men with small shops need all the help that machinery can give them.

Fig. 6 represents my shop and yard. The plan shows the location of each machine and the general arrangement of the benches, &c. The shop is thirty feet by fifty feet, and is two stories in hight. The first story is the wood shop. It is ten feet high, which enables me to turn over express shafts, &c. The second story is the paint shop, and the attic is used for storage. It will be noticed that the shop is square and has no jogs. This is the best way to build for room and convenience.

While I fully believe in power, yet if any do not have it, and cannot get it, much can be done by hand. I worked for years with a hand band-saw and spoke tenoning and boring machine.—*By* J. D. S.

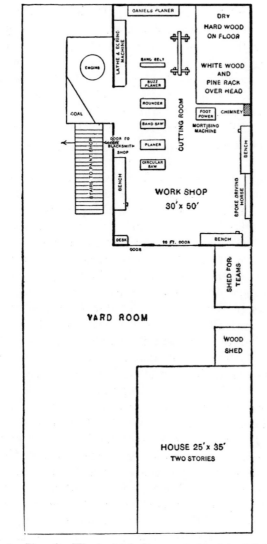

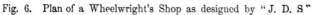

Fig. 6. Plan of a Wheelwright's Shop as designed by "J. D. S"

Large vs. Small Carriage Shops.

One of the greatest mistakes often made in small shops is in copying the methods and styles of big ones with the idea of putting on the road a carriage having the appearance of being the outcome of the big shop. If the small manufacturers would try to lead, instead of following, the result of their labors would no doubt be a hundred per cent. better than it is. There is no reason why they should be afraid to take the lead. A man can shape and put together wood, iron, and leather with the ordinary tools of a shop, if he be a mechanic, in as neat and perfect a manner as the man who works with machinery. In fact, a good mechanic can sometimes make a good job with a few tools. Machines may shape material in a quick and easy manner, but the same work may be done equally as well without the machines, provided the workman fully understands his business. The writer can remember a small shop in Baltimore where all the work was done by two or three men, with no machinery, and that shop had the reputation of doing the best work in the State. In style, durability, and finish it could not be equaled by any other establishment in Maryland, and even in prices the large factories were unable to undersell it. For many years Thomas Goddard, the well-known carriage builder of Boston, enjoyed an enviable reputation in building buggies. All his work was done with primitive appliances, and yet he secured higher prices than any big Boston shop would dare to ask. This goes to show that the best policy of the small manufacturer is in maintaining independence in the production of his work by not copying others. Let him do good work with the aid of men who can bring experience and judgment to bear in every department—men who are not, as most hands are in the big shops, mere machines, able to do only one thing, knowing nothing of what had been done or what would afterward be done by others.

There are facilities possessed by the large concern that the small manufacturer can easily secure, particularly in the paint shop. The finish of a carriage is looked upon by most men as deciding the general workmanship of the whole, provided the style, proportions, fit, and correct adjustment of the parts which go to make up a carriage are as they should be. A good painter is he who can take a job from the smith shop to the repository, through the many operations necessary; and he will be better able to judge of the proper degree of dryness in each coat, of the materials used and their manipulation, the effects of atmospheric changes, &c., than the man who knows but one thing about the work. The paint shop then is one of the most important places in a factory, and it should be fitted up with every facility for doing work well. It needs a perfectly tight and well ventilated varnish room, a clean paint room, as good a means for heating as can be found (and for small shops the self-feeding stove has no equal), and, last of all, a painter who knows the whole art, not a city-bred specialist.

There are a few other points I might mention, and one is that, in the hurry to make room in a small shop for other work, there is a great mistake made, and that mistake is the very thing that often spoils the entire work. I speak of the washing of a job when it comes from the varnish room. In large shops a job is hung up and run into the fitting-up room, where irons are put on, top fixed, straps buckled, &c., and it may stay there for two or three days—perhaps longer —before a drop of water is allowed to touch it. In small shops the job is hung up, run on to the washing floor, the hose, with a good head of water, is turned on, and all before the varnish is thoroughly dry. The varnish hardens on the outside, but absorbs moisture underneath, and when this moisture evaporates, the outer surface is dulled or made flat and devoid of brilliancy. The large shop job becomes dry before it is washed, and presents a brilliancy far superior to the job the small concern hurried into use by sousing the varnish with cold water to harden it. If the small carriage maker would depend more upon himself, and give more attention to details in his work, he would have no cause to complain that he could not compete with the big factory.— FRITZ SCRIBER.

Advice to Small Carriage Makers.

I think a good workman need never fail in his business if he will only attend to it himself. If a man starts a shop, he cannot expect to have everything to his mind at the first, but if he is accommodating, uses good stock, does good work, and, last but not least, completes his job at the time agreed upon, the community will soon notice these facts, and his business will begin to improve. A man, to be successful, should be on time, have a place for every tool, and every tool in its place; what tools he buys should be the best. There is as much difference in tools as there is in men. Poor tools and poor lumber a good workman has no use for. I like to select my lumber as it stands; but every one is not located so that he can do this. I think the best ash grows on ground that is rather moist. It can be cut any time between August and March. The quicker it is sawed and stacked after being cut, the better. It should be stacked under cover, in a cool place, where the sun cannot touch it. If timber is seasoned in a warm, dry place, it is liable to be hard and brittle. It is better to take the bark off when it is sawed.—*By* W. L. P.

Carriage Woodwork Tools.

All workers in wood require good tools, but none more so than bodymakers. Theirs must be of a form and quality that will cut the hardest as well as the softest wood, and either with or across the grain. The bench tools absolutely necessary are one single-iron jack, one double iron jack, one twenty-four-inch joiner, one smoothing and one door plane, three draw knives, one rabbet knife, one set of framer chisels, six socket mortise chisels, one set of flat gouges, one light iron brace, one ratchet, adjustable brace, half dozen auger bits, half dozen pod bits, half dozen center bits, half dozen German gimlet bits, three brace screw drivers, two hand screw drivers, two try squares, one bevel square, one pair compasses, one callipers, one scratch awl, one cutting marker, half dozen brad awls, one scraper, two T planes, three rabbet planes, one claw hammer, one riveting hammer, one large oil stone, two small oil stones, one small and one large hack saw, one sixteen-inch straight cut, one large ripping and one large cross cut saw, one whip saw frame, three blades, one keyhole saw, one spoke shave, one double and two single routers, and one set of punches.

Armed with these, a good workman is fairly equipped, but there are a score or more tools which are absolutely necessary .f work is to be done rapidly. Many of the special tools have been made for specific uses, but scarcely one comes amiss on the bodymaker's bench nowadays.

Carriage Woodwork Tools. Fig. 7. Cross section of Draw Knife with flat face.

One of the most important tools is the draw knife, and the workman who has a good variety, properly ground, is able to perform his work more easily and better than the one poorly equipped in this respect. Five knives can be used to an advantage, two for dressing up broad hard wood, one having a flat face, as shown by the cross section, Fig. 7, two concaved, as shown by Figs. 7a and 8. These should not be less than one and three-eighths inch wide on the face. If for use on hard and soft wood alike, the bevel should be as shown by Fig. 7a; if for hard wood only, a shorter bevel, as shown by Fig. 7; if for soft wood only, then the bevel should be long, as shown by Fig. 8.

The next size knife should have a face about one and one-eighth inch wide, perfectly flat, or slightly concaved, with the back ground, as shown by Fig. 8. A fifth knife should have a short blade, not to exceed seven inches long on the cutting edge, one-half inch wide on the face, ground short bevel, as shown by Fig. 7, and ground round on the back.

The large knives should be heavy, so that they will not spring when used on the heaviest work. The cutting edges should have a true sweep of one-quarter of an inch to the foot, and in all cases there must be metal enough back of the face to give a support; ground as shown by Figs. 7, 7*a*, and 8.

The hang of the blade is an important matter, but as no

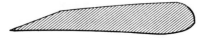

Fig. 7*a*.   Cross section of Draw Knife with concave face.

two workmen grasp the handles alike, it is impossible to give an angle that would suit all parties. Then too the angle for a heavy knife for dressing up would not be the angle desired for smaller knives for general work. The best guide for determining the angle is to lay the face of the blade flat upon a piece of wood secured in the vise on a line horizontal

Fig. 8.   Cross section of Draw Knife with concave face and beveled back.

with the top of the bench, grasp the handles firmly with both hands, the arms in a natural, easy position, without bending the wrist. When this can be done without bending the wrist, or changing the position of the face of the blade, the angle is all right. For general use on all kinds of timber the edge should hang a little lower than for dressing up.

The question is often asked, " Why is it that one man, who

apparently works no harder than his neighbor, can accomplish so much more?" An examination of the drawing knives will answer the question. The quick workman has a good assortment, all properly ground, so that when working the edge "bites" and the cut. is clean and true. There are men who will dress up a pair of four-inch ash bottom sides with a knife as true as most men will with a plane, and in half the time.

Planes are important tools and they must be kept in good order. I have a strong leaning toward good beechwood planes, notwithstanding the improvements made in iron planes. The wood plane works more smoothly, and is less tiresome to handle. The iron plane has an advantage over the old-fashioned wood plane in the mechanism which adjusts the blade; but wood planes fitted with a patent iron throat, as

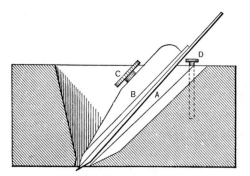

Fig. 9. Mechanism of Plane.

shown by Fig. 9, the parts of which are *A*, an adjustable wedge, to change the angle of the blade; *B*, securing wedge; *C*, set screw; *D*, set screw for wedge *A*, have all the advantages of the metal planes and none of the disadvantages.

The single blade plane is a roughing tool, which, owing to the general use of machine-planed timber, is less called for than formerly; but it is a handy tool. The bit should be ground to a short bevel, the cutting edge ground to the segment of a six-inch circle. The edge of all other plane bits must be ground square, but, to prevent scratching, the corners should be beveled off so as to remove the sharp angles at the cutting edge and about one-eighth of an inch at the back corner of the bevel.

It is absolutely necessary that the face of the cutting blade be perfectly true, so that the cap shall fit close, whether near or far from the edge. When once trued, there is no need of touching the face with the grind or oil stone.

In grinding, have the stone revolve toward the cutting edge, as the steel that is worn away is removed more easily than when cutting toward the edge, and the grinder can tell when he reaches the edge. The cutting edge of planes and other tools of like character for cutting soft wood, should be twenty to thirty degrees; for hard wood, forty to eighty degrees.

Chisels come next in order. A full set of framing chisels consists of one dozen in all; the smallest, one-eighth inch, graded by eighths up to one inch, and then by quarters up to two inches. In purchasing these, test the faces carefully, as it is almost impossible to find a set in which the faces are not warped to a greater or less extent. It pays, when the face is warped, to have it trued.

Bodymakers are getting to use turned handles, probably because they are less troublesome to procure than the octagon handles. The latter are preferable, and I recommend that the bodymaker should put on the handles. It is a nice piece of work to put them on properly; but it pays. Select close, fine grained hickory; split out the blocks so as to insure straight grain; cut the longest handle six inches long, the shortest five, and grade all others between these two lengths. If a taper bit can be procured with the correct taper for the shank, bore a hole with a small twist bit and rim out with the taper. Drive the blocks on the shanks to within one-eighth of an inch of the shoulders; then dress up. First strike a line through the center of the blade and block, as shown by A, Fig. 10; then measure off on line X the width required for the handle at that point, and strike lines B and C. Dress off to these lines at right angles with the face of the blade and strike a center line, as shown by

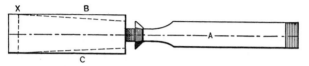

Fig. 10. How to put a Handle on a Chisel. Front view.

A, Fig. 10. This line, as will be seen, begins at the cutting edge and intersects the middle of the shank at the shoulder. Extend the line up the handle, as shown; then draw lines B and C. Dress off to these lines. This will give a perfectly square handle. Remove the block, having first marked it so as to designate the face. Procure a thin piece of sole leather, punch a hole through it, dampen it and force it over the shank down to the shoulder. Fill the shank hole in the

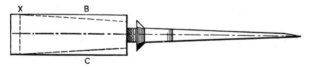

Fig. 11. How to put a handle on a Chisel. Side view.

handle with water, allowing it to remain thereon five minutes. Then nick the corners of the shank, turning a few spurs upward, and drive on the handle. The leather will act as a cushion, to prevent rebounding, and the moisture in the hole will soften the wood so that the corners of the shank will cut their way without splitting; the nicks will assist to keep the handle on, after being worn for a time. When the leather and wood are dry, finish the handles by removing the corners so as to make an octagon. Round up the top to a fullness of one-fourth of an inch. When the handles are completed, dip them in warm, raw linseed oil down to the leather. Allow them to remain in the oil one night; then remove them and set them aside until the oil is absorbed. A second dipping will do no harm. After the oil has thoroughly gone into the wood, burnish the entire surface with a bone or steel burnisher, and the handles are completed. A set made in this way will last as long as the chisels will.

For mortising, every bodymaker should have at least half a dozen socket chisels. They are long and rigid and will not spring. Grind chisels with a long bevel and perfectly square cutting edges. Never grind on the face. It is impossible to make a perfectly true tenon or mortise with badly ground chisels.

Saws next claim attention. These, no matter whether hack or otherwise, should be in good order. For the bodymaker, large saws are of less value than formerly; but a good, large cross-cut and a rip saw should be included in every kit. The cross-cut should have about eight teeth to the inch, the rip about seven. The cross-cut should be filed with teeth having about one-thirty-second inch dip and a cross angle of forty degrees. The rip should have the face of tooth at right angles with the face line of the points, and file straight across. For ordinary use, the 'set' should not exceed one-third the thickness of the blade. Back saws should have cross-cut teeth, but with little 'set.'

The handy saw is a twenty-two-inch blade, about seven inches at the handle and two and a quarter at the end, ten teeth to the inch—the teeth filed at the same angle as the cross-cut, but straight across, as with the rip. This saw is a general utility tool. If the blade is good but not heavy, it answers as both a rip and cross-cut, taking the place of the back saw for tenon shoulders and for sawed tenons. If kept in good order it cuts smooth and quickly, and will be called into use five times to either or all these others once.

A good supply of bits is necessary. These should consist of a variety of sizes of auger bits. Cook's concavo-convex is the best, but spur bits, if kept in order, are good. Both kinds of auger bits must be sharpened from the top—Cook's with a rat-tail file, and the lip bit with a smooth mill file. Center bits are convenient, but they should be fitted up, as when purchased the center point is not equi-distant from the spur. To correct this, grind away the spur. The bit for all work is the twist bit. It is the most complete boring tool in the market. It is easily kept sharp, will cut straight any way of the grain of the wood, and will not split. For taper holes use the 'German gimlet,' a taper pod bit, having a screw point.

A small set of gouges should be on every bench, and one or two framer chisels, ground with round cutting edges, will be found useful.

The screw driver is an important tool, but there are few that are properly ground. Most bodymakers grind them wedge shape, and then wonder why they cannot "send the screw home." If they will look at the slot in the screw head, they will see that it is as broad at the bottom as at the top, and that if a screw driver is to hold well, it must be ground to fit the slot. If ground that way, and then roughened by a few lines across the faces, it will hold the screw and will not split the head, as is often done by the wedge-shaped screw

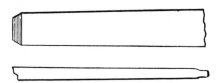

Figs. 12 and 13. The proper form for a Screw Driver Point.

driver. Figs. 12 and 13 show the proper form for a screw driver point.

Hand screw drivers are always needed. The remarks regarding grinding them are as pertinent as to the brace screw driver bit.

Braces receive too little consideration from the bodymaker. So long as they hold the bit, they are made to answer, even though of the most inferior quality. The old-fashioned wood brace is convenient for light work, but the bits must be well fitted. The patent 'compressed sleeve' iron brace is the most convenient. There is no trouble fitting any bit, and it is sure to hold. For general use it should have about six-inch crank. The 'compressed sleeve' and 'reversible ratchet' braces are indispensable, as with them holes can be bored at almost any point, for the sweep of the crank can be got out of the way so that a hole can be bored in corners or elsewhere. If the bodymaker cannot afford to have but one brace, that one should be the 'reversible ratchet.'

In addition to the regular lines of tools mentioned, there are others equally necessary, many of which cannot be purchased at the toolmakers', unless made to order, and as a rule better results are attained by the bodymaker making them for himself than when made by the toolmaker. Those of metal throughout must be made by the toolmaker, but

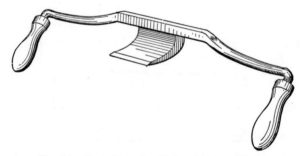

Fig. 14.   Best shape for Blade of Rabbet Knife.

the bodymaker must provide a perfect model. The rabbet knife is of the latter class. It is a tool that cannot be dispensed with. There are numerous forms, but for general use one with a blade as shown by Fig. 14 will be found the most satisfactory. The arms should be bow-shaped and heavy enough to work without springing. The bit should not be less than two and a quarter inches on the cutting edge. As will be noticed, the bevel is ground on the upper side, the face being true and edge low so as to bite quickly. The form of the face is such that the knife works well upon straight and concave surfaces, and in the absence of another pattern, can be used on convex surfaces. The arms should not be less than eight inches long in the clear between the handle and the blade.

A second knife should have a straight slotted arm about

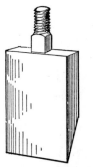
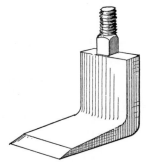

Fig. 15. Adjustable Blade of Rab-   Fig. 16.   Another form of Blade of Rabbet
bet Knife.   Knife.

Fig. 17.   Convex face of Blade of Rabbet Knife.

eighteen inches long, into which blades of various sizes and forms can be put, and which permits their being adjusted to different points, the bits, four or five in number, varying in size from one-quarter to one and a half inch. The forms of blades may be used as designated by Figs. 15, 16, and 17 respectively.

The 'double' or panel router is at best an awkward tool, and it requires much skill on the part of the workman to enable him to cut a smooth groove. The common shape of the cutter blade is shown by Fig. 18. A better cutter is shown by Fig. 19. This has a cutting spur and a smooth face, which protects the molding from being damaged by the cutter. It is a troublesome tool to grind, but it cuts smooth and works easy.

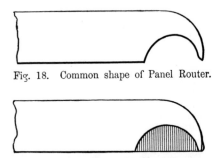

Fig. 18.   Common shape of Panel Router.

Fig. 19.   Best shape for Panel Router.

Planes and tools for rounding and finishing moldings are necessary. Some of the most convenient have awkward forms, but they can be handled easily. Planes shaped like Fig. 20 (page 37), may be fitted with faces and cutters to work on any part of the body. Ample provision must be made in all cases for free discharge of chips. Each form should have a convex and straight face, and be in right and left pairs. Beading tools, and others with handles of like form, are necessary for working in places that cannot be reached by the planes. The faces and guards of these should be narrow and rounded so as not to scratch. Concave and convex face planes, smoothing plane form, but with a T iron and an open throat, are convenient tools for cleaning off body panels. Fig.

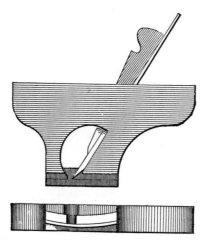

Fig. 20.   Good shape for a Molding Plane.

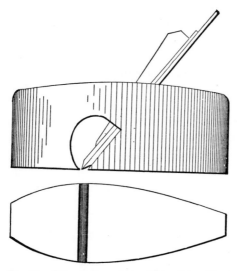

Fig. 21.   Side or face view of Smoothing Plane.

21 shows one of these planes, also a face view of the same.

The advantage of this plane over the ones in general use is
that the iron is flush with the sides, and can be worked close
up to moldings, &c. If the sides are well rounded, as shown
by face view, access can be had to points that cannot be

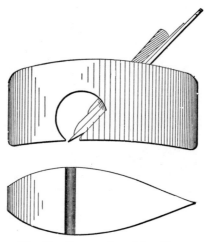

Fig. 22.   Concave Smoothing Plane.

reached by the ordinary form.   Fig. 22 shows one of these
planes with a concave face.

A full set of rabbet planes, seven-eighth-inch across the
face, is necessary.   There should be at least four with convex and four with concave faces.   One or more straight, concave, and convex rabbet planes, with guards, as shown by
Fig. 23 (page 39), will be found useful.   The guards should
be secured by set screws, so that they can be raised or lowered.

The scraper is a little tool, and one that should be used
more than it is by bodymakers.   It is a great labor saver,
and there is nothing that operates so successfully as a flexi-
ble scraper for removing file scratches and other blemishes
upon panels.   The steel in these must be of the finest quality, and the sides polished very smooth.   The edge must be

trued upon an oil stone, and the edge turned by a triangular steel burnisher. The turning of the edge requires skill and care, but it can be turned to cut almost as true a shaving as a plane. The first operation is to rub down the flat sides. To do this, lay the steel upon a flat, true surface and rub

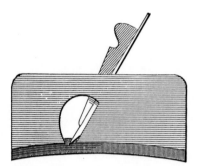

Fig. 23. Rabbet Plane with concave face.

the burnisher rapidly the whole length of the scraper. Repeat this until the edge is very smooth; then turn the scraper up on end and pass the burnisher down or up—but never both ways—on the edge bearing outward. This will turn a fine, true edge that will cut smooth, and heavy enough not to roll off.

It is not necessary to say that bodymakers need files, as all must use them. But there are few bodymakers who have a good set of files. They generally content themselves with one or two flat bastard and a half-round, and so long as they cut away the wood, they are apparently satisfied. Owing to a desire to cheapen files, many of them are not properly faced. The true face is a taper both ways from the center, but many are made thick at the tang and tapered to the points. With this form the heel is sure to scratch when filing large surfaces. Recut files should never be used by bodymakers, as they invariably scratch, and weak points break off. This is due to the fact that, notwithstanding the old teeth have been ground out, yet there is an embrasure which reveals itself when recutting.

In addition to the large files commonly in use, the body-maker should have a set of stubs of different forms, and large files with smooth edges. Stubs are always handy. They should be about five inches long, three-eighths of an inch thick in the center, and the face slightly rounded. The cut

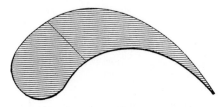

Fig. 24. Convenient form for File Stub.

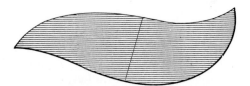

Fig. 25. Another convenient form for File Stub.

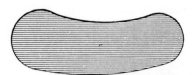

Fig. 26. A third form for File Stub.

should be from both ends, for convenience. Figs. 24, 25, and 26 show good forms for stubs. With these almost any point can be reached and filed. By having them quite thick, the workman can grasp them firmly and use them without handles.

Another class of files almost as useful as stubs are rifflers—flat, round, square, and triangular—cut on sides and edges. Fig. 27 shows a flat, bent riffler, Fig. 28 a square, Fig. 29 a half-round, and Fig. 30 a round rasp. These should be fitted with handles in all cases. They cost but little, and the time

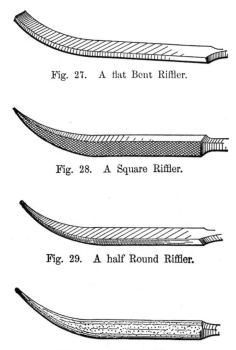

Fig. 27.   A flat Bent Riffler.

Fig. 28.   A Square Riffler.

Fig. 29.   A half Round Riffler.

Fig. 30.   A Round Rasp.

saved by their use on one large body will more than compensate for the cost.

It may not be amiss to speak in this connection of a little article that should be on every workman's bench—the file-cleaner. This can be made of a small piece of wire-card cloth, secured to a piece of wood. It costs little, and is thoroughly efficacious.

Files are easily damaged by coming in contact with one another; and to prevent injury from that cause a file rack should be made, having a recess for each file.

In addition to bench tools there are a number of articles that are needed. These are: A dozen or more thumb-screws, a set of vise jaw-blocks (half dozen at least); small wood hand screws, a good trestle, and a small hand vise.

In most shops the thumb and hand screws, as well as tres-tles, are furnished by the employer, but the bodymaker who owns a good set of clamps of all kinds is independent of his neighbors.

OLD VETERAN.

Poorly Made Tools.

My son recently began his apprenticeship, and I bought him a complete kit of tools. I did not haggle about the price, but paid what was asked, supposing I would get value for my money. But the fact turns out quite differently. Some of the chisels are soft on one side and too hard on the other, and as the temper color is polished off, I don't know whether the error was in the hardening or the tempering. I am in favor of leaving the temper color on, so that if there is any part left too hard, it can be tempered down without hardening the whole chisel over again. I believe it would pay to make first-class tools, notwithstanding the keen com-petition.

Now let me run over some of the faults I find these tools possess.

First, the compasses in Fig. 31 (page 43). The screw A an the nut B are almost stripped of their threads already. The segment C holds in some places but not in others, and the spring D has lost a great part of its set.

Next, the bit, Fig. 32. has a crooked spiral from S to S, and a crooked flute at F. The bits in Fig. 33 have too much clearance at A but not enough at B, so one edge does all the cutting.

Some of the brad awls, Fig. 34, have more spread at C than at D. When we come to the auger bits, Fig. 35, we find one cutting edge, A, is lower than the other, B. The screw S is oval. One spur, W, is higher than the other, and the edges C are of different depths.

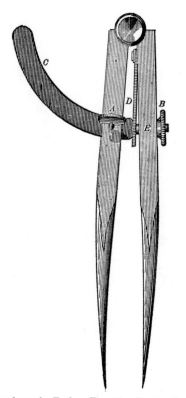

Poorly-made Tools. Fig. 31. Faulty Compasses.

The small auger bits, Fig. 36, are the best tools of the whole lot, although some of their screws have very shallow threads

I have among the lot a brace that holds the bits by a spring catch, and the notches at N, Fig. 37, are cut so deep that the catch does not hold.

Now I don't think that it is at all necessary to sacrifice quality for price in order to make sales, and I believe that if the manufacturers were to make really first-class tools and charge a fair price for them, no workman would object to pay it.—*By* M. E.

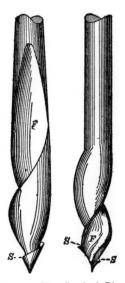

Fig. 32. The Crooked Bit.

Fig. 33. Other faults in Bits.

Fig. 34. Brad Awls with an imperfect spread.

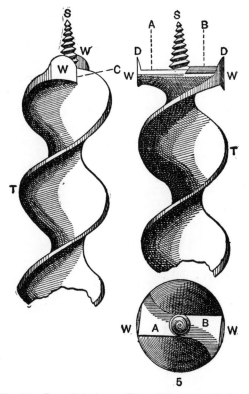

Fig. 35.   Imperfect Auger Bits.   Side and end views.

Fig. 36.   A Bit with threads too shallow.

Fig. 37.   Another defective Bit.

Screwdrivers.

The correct form for a screwdriver is a matter of much importance, but no matter what the form, experience in its use is a great aid in keeping the lip from slipping. An amount of pressure must be brought to bear upon the driver equal to that expended in turning the screw, otherwise the power spent in turning being greater than the pressure, forces the lip from the slot. It is also necessary that the driver should be at all times held at right angles with the plane of the head of the screw.

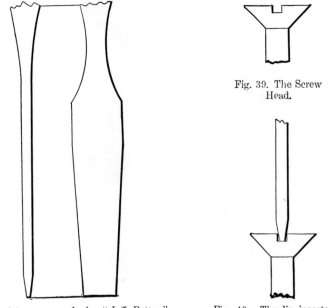

Fig. 39. The Screw Head.

Fig. 40. The lip inserted in the Slot.

Screwdrivers as made by "Jeff. Potter." Fig. 38. Usual shape.

The majority of drivers are shaped like Fig. 38. The lip is wedge-shaped, while the two sides of the slot in the screw are parallel and at right angles with the plane of the screw head (Fig. 39), and when the screwdriver is inserted in the slot the appearance is similar to that of Fig. 40. It will be observed that this is wrong in principle, but is very convenient when one screwdriver answers for several sizes of screws. It is better—in fact, necessary—to have different sized drivers. I have at least a half dozen, having occasion to use screws ranging from three-eighths inch, No. 4, to five inches, No. 24.

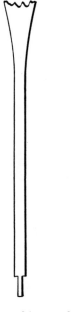

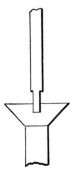

Fig. 41. Screwdriver used by Jeff. Potter.

Fig. 42. The Screwdriver inserted in the Slot.

I give to the lips of my screwdrivers the shape represented in Fig. 41. When the lip is inserted in the slot it appears as shown in Fig. 42; and if properly used a screwdriver of this shape will never slip from the slot.—*By* JEFF. POTTER.

The Saw—Its Uses and Management.

The saw, critically considered, is a series of knives set on a line. Each tooth is a knife which cuts and carries away a small portion of material. Each individual tooth is kept from cutting too deeply by the teeth which immediately precede and follow it. When the saw is properly constructed, each tooth cuts its own allotted portion and carries the chip or slice of material along to the edge and drops it on the outside. Saws used for special purposes or employed upon specific materials, require to be constructed upon different principles, as well as managed in different ways.

The cross-cut saw, embracing those which require two men to operate them, and those commonly used for cutting off boards and small timbers by hand, is perhaps in most general use of the various forms in which the saw is made. The rip-saws of the mills probably do a larger amount of cutting, but mechanics generally have more to do with the class of saws here named. To understand the cross-cut saw, first consider just what it is expected to perform, and this can best be done by examining the end of a log or timber which is

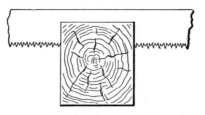

Fig. 43.   End view of a timber, showing the grain or fiber which is cut by the saw.

to be cut. In Fig. 43 is presented the end view of such a piece of wood, showing the ends of the fibers. The grain, as it is frequently called, consists more or less of minute fibers and threads, which must be severed in the process of cutting. As the material is non-elastic and unyielding, the fibers must be cut; they cannot be pushed to one side. Since, from the shape and construction of the saw, it is necessary to leave a small space between the two parts of the timber, technically known as the kerf, the saw must be made to cut the wood in a way to provide the channel in which it runs. This it does by cutting the fibers which constitute the structure of the wood in two places; that is, it cuts them at points corresponding to the sides of the kerf. The intervening wood or portions of fiber are rasped or scraped away by the teeth of the saw as it is worked back and forth in the process of

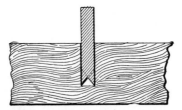

Fig. 44. Longitudinal section through log, and saw, showing the actual operation of the teeth.

cutting still deeper. This action of the saw is clearly illustrated in Fig. 44.

The question of the shape of the teeth and the pitch or bevel which they should have in order to best accomplish this result, next comes up.

Fig. 45. Section through a cut made by a saw, the teeth of which are in proper order.

Fig. 46. Section through a saw, the several teeth forming a groove, as shown.

Fig. 45 shows a section through the cut made by a saw,

The bottom of the cut s'iould be square, as shown in the illustration. It will not do for it to be in shape like the groove formed in the edge of a saw by the teeth; or, in other words, to be the reverse of the shape shown in Fig. 46. The saw, to operate in the best manner, must be managed in such a way that those portions of wood lying between the cuts made along the sides of the kerf will crumble away readily and be removed from the channel of the saw without any appreciable labor.

Now, the sharper each tooth is, that is, the more bevel it has on the point, the deeper it will cut. But, for reasons just explained, it must not be allowed to cut deeper into the wood than will readily crumble out across the groove from the point of one tooth to the point of the other. A section through a saw is as shown in Fig. 46, and when it is properly filed the angular groove will be so true that a fine needle will slide along the entire length from one end to the other without falling off. The cutting, as has been explained, is all done by the outside edge of the tooth. The actual operation of the teeth is as shown in Fig. 44, already referred to. The wood is cut by the point of the tooth along the sides of the kerf, and the portion between the cuts crumbles out.

The effect of different bevels in the teeth of saws is to cut

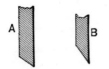

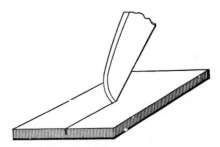

Fig. 47. Effect of different bevels in the teeth of saws. *A* will not cut as deep as *B*,

Fig. 48. A knife held in this manner will cut deeply, and at the same time easily.

to different depths. A tooth of the bevel shown at *B*, Fig.
47, will cut into the wood deeper than a tooth of the bevel
shown at *A*. It follows then that with very soft woods in
which cutting may be done very rapidly, a tooth calculated
to cut deep into the wood is best, while for hard woods less
bevel must be employed. The bevel of the cutting edge of
the tooth should be the same for all saws, but the bevel of
the point which is governed by the angle at which the file
is held, is to be varied as circumstances require.

The philosophy of some saws cutting better than others is
easily explained, and may be illustrated in a very familiar
manner. Suppose it is desired to cut across a board with a
knife or other sharp pointed instrument. If the knife is held
as shown in Fig. 48, the point will cut deeper and at the

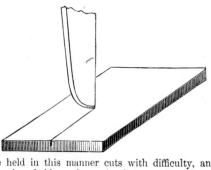

Fig. 49. A knife held in this manner cuts with difficulty, and not so deeply
as when held as shown in the preceding figure.

Fig. 50. Correct shape for the cutting
edges of teeth in a cross-cut saw.

Fig. 51. A common fault in cross-cut
saws is to make the teeth too
" hooking."

same time easier than if it is held as shown in Fig. 49. Hence it follows that the cutting edge of the tooth in a saw should incline forward after the manner of the knife shown in Fig. 48; or, in other words, that its shape should be as indicated in Fig. 50, rather than of the kind shown in Fig. 51. If the bevel of the cutting edge of the tooth—the bevel of the point in relation to the material to be cut—and the pitch or inclination of the cutting edge be carefully considered and properly combined, a perfect tooth will be obtained.

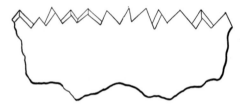

Fig. 52.   The saw as frequently filed by unscientific and inexperienced persons.

Fig. 52 shows the teeth of a saw, not at all exaggerated, as it is sometimes found in use among men who have neither genius nor knowledge in filing. Such a saw will undoubtedly scratch its way through a piece of timber, and in course of time a log or board may be cut in two by it; but how much better will a saw cut which is filed in a scientific manner.

It holds to reason that the teeth of a saw, both in their size and in the manner in which they are filed, should be adapted to the wood they are intended to cut. A tooth appropriate for very soft wood is not the best for very hard wood, and a tooth that cuts hard wood to advantage will not work very satisfactorily upon quite soft wood. Hence the necessity of considering the nature of the material to be cut before selecting a saw and before undertaking to put it in order.

The first thing to be done in filing a cross-cut hand saw is to see that the teeth are perfectly straight upon the edge, or, if anything, a little higher in the middle than at the end,

This is very important, for if any tooth is shorter than the next, it will not cut at all, and is therefore worse than useless, because it gives the next tooth more than its fair share of the work to do, rendering the cut imperfectly made.

A cross-cut saw for very soft wood should have about six teeth to the inch. The bevel to be observed in filing is

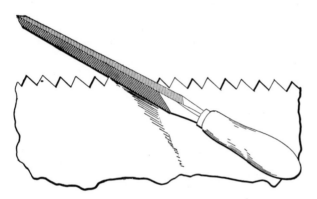

Fig. 53.   A cross-cut saw with six teeth to the inch, suitable for very soft wood. The position of the file shows the bevel to be obtained in filing.

shown in Fig. 53. The teeth should have a full set, and the sides should be jointed thoroughly. About setting, however, something will be said further on. In this figure, as well as in the others in this paper, the point of the saw is supposed to be on the left hand side of the filer. A good sized file, say four and a half or five inches in length, should be used. There is no difference in the angle between a large and a small file. The only point therefore to be considered is the cut of the file—whether it is fine or coarse. A fine cut, with sharp corners, is much to be preferred in this class of work. By soft wood, in this connection, is meant such as basswood, pine, and cedar. Fig. 54 shows the shape of teeth to a scale somewhat larger than natural size. It also shows the bevel of the point of the tooth in a saw adapted to soft

woods. The bevel on the point is consequent upon the bevel
of the file and the bevel of the back of the tooth.

Fig. 54.   The shape of tooth (shown larger than natural size) and bevel of
point of tooth, in a saw adapted to soft woods.

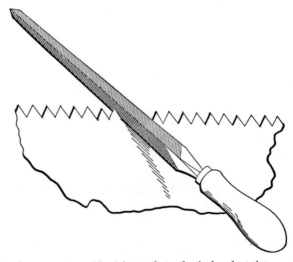

Fig. 55.   Cross-cut saw with eight teeth to the inch, adapted to cutting wood
of medium hardness.   The position of the file shows the proper bevel to
be observed in filing.

Fig. 55 shows a cross-cut saw with eight teeth to the inch,
which is adapted to medium woods, and Fig. 57 shows one
with ten teeth to the inch, adapted to hard woods. The
position of the file to be observed in filing is shown in each
engraving. Figs. 56 and 58 show the shape of the teeth
upon an enlarged scale, and sections through the points of

the teeth in the saws shown in the two preceding cuts respectively. By medium woods is meant such as black walnut, cherry, chestnut, &c. Hard woods include such as hickory, oak, ash, maple, beech, &c.

Fig. 56. Shape of tooth and bevel of point of tooth (more than full size) in a saw adapted to cutting medium woods.

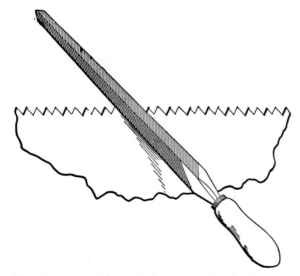

Fig. 57. A cross-cut saw with ten teeth to the inch, adapted to cutting hard wood. The bevel to be observed in filing is indicated by the position of the file.

By observing the directions above given it will be seen that the bevel on the pitch or cutting edge of the tooth is the same in all; but the bevel of the point looking the length of the saw is quite a different thing. The angle of the pitch of the cutting edge of the tooth has been considered already.

As already stated in the examples here given, the end of the saw is supposed to be to the left of the filer; or, in other words, the point of the saw is supposed to be in the direction toward which the point of the file is directed in the cuts. Some may object to this, contending that the saw should be filed toward the handle, because in so doing it prevents a feather edge on the teeth of the saw. A feather edge cannot be considered a serious objection, since every saw, after filing, should be laid down flat—first on one side, then the other—and jointed or planed down until every tooth is exactly in line. For this purpose a long whetstone or fine-cut file with straight edges should be used. Such an operation takes off all of the feather, makes a finer edge, and affords more cutting surface. If a saw is newly set and not jointed as above recommended after filing, all the cutting surfaces will be at the extreme point of the teeth, which only scratch and do not cut. The operation of such a tool may be likened to marking across a board with the point of a

Fig. 58. Shape and bevel of point of tooth (more than full size) in a saw adapted to cutting hard woods.

Fig. 59. The point of tooth as shown at *A* is as left after filing. *B* represents same tooth after joining the sides, which makes a real knife edge of it—not a mere scratching point.

pin. In Fig. 59 *A* represents the point of a tooth as it is left after filing, while *B* represents the same tooth after it has been jointed. It will be seen by comparison that the operation of jointing gives the tooth a real knife edge.

Hand Wood Turning.

While the march of improvement has made metal turning by hand almost a rarity, hand turning for wood is almost as much in vogue as ever. Indeed the pattern maker—who must be one

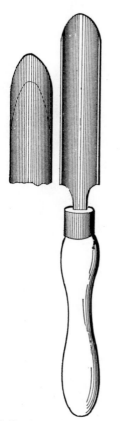

Hand Wood Turning.   Fig. 60.   The Gouge.

of the most skillful of woodworkers—relies wholly on hand tools in getting out his lathe work. Then too a very few tools will serve for wood turning, whereas for metal turning

the variety is great.   But these few tools require much skill
and dexterity in their use.

Beginning with the gouge, shown in Fig. 60, it may be
said that it is the custom to reduce the work in the lathe to
nearly the required form by this tool, the finishing tools being, with one exception, simply scraping tools, and not, properly speaking, cutting tools.   Hence it is evidently inadvisa-
ble to leave much for them to take off.

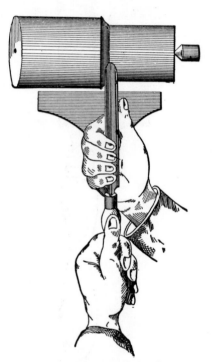

Fig. 61.   How to hold the Gouge.

The manner of holding the gouge is shown in Fig. 61.
One hand grasps the handle near the end, while the other
grasps the gouge near the cutting point—that is to say, as

near as the hand-rest will permit. It is, however, sometimes necessary to slightly vary the manner of holding, by passing the forefinger of one hand around the hand-rest, while the gouge is confined between the thumb and forefinger, thus gripping the gouge end to the rest.

This is advisable when turning a piece of work that is not completely round, as, for instance, tipping off the teeth of a gear wheel, in which case gripping the gouge to the hand-rest will steady it and prevent it from digging into the work.

The gouge is shown in Fig. 61 to be cutting from right to left. It will, however, cut equally well if used from left to right, in which case the position of the hands must be reversed, the left hand gripping the gouge near the cutting edge. In either case, however, the gouge is not held horizontally level, but is tilted to one side, the lower side being the cutting one; otherwise the tool would rip into the work.

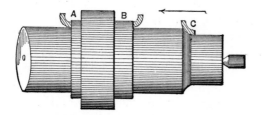

Fig. 62.   Tilt of tool in cutting from right to left and from left to right.

Fig. 62 shows, at *B*, the section of the tool and the tilt of the tool when cutting from right to left, while the tool at *A* shows the tilt when cutting from left to right. The reasons for this are as follows :

The face of the gouge, on its hollow side and near the cutting edge, receives the strain which is necessary to curl the shaving and force it out of the straight line.

But if the gouge is placed in the position shown in Fig. 62, at *C*, the whole of this strain would be upon the gouge, tending to force it forward and into the cut, as denoted by the direction of the arrow, and as a consequence the gouge would run forward and dig into the work, in spite of all endeavors to prevent it.

When, however, the gouge is held in the positions relative to its line of travel to its cut, shown in Fig. 62 at A and B, there is but little tendency for it to run forward, and it can be fed easily to its cut.

In addition to its use as a roughing tool, the gouge makes a very efficient finishing tool for hollows, though it is not so often employed as such by pattern makers. In this case, however, great care must be taken in controlling its position to the work, as illustrated in Fig. 62.

For finishing plain work, there is the tool shown in Fig. 63 (page 61), which is the exception noted previously as being a finishing and at the same time a cutting tool. It is called a 'skew chisel,' because its cutting edge is ground at an angle, or askew to the center line of its length.

Furthermore, it is beveled at the cutting end on both sides —as shown in the end view—being ground very keen.

It is employed for finishing straight or parallel surfaces and for dressing down the ends or down the sides of a collar or shoulder. When used for finishing straight or parallel surfaces, it performs the cutting in the center of the length of its cutting edge only, as shown at A, Fig. 63. When it is nicely sharpened, it leaves a polish unlike other finishing tools. But even with these advantages, it has a drawback, and a serious one, to learners, as it seems to have a terrible propensity for tearing into the work, whether it is used on the circumference or facing the shoulders of the work.

This fault can only be overcome by practice, and the reason lies in the difficulty of learning how to handle the tool with dexterity. It must be held almost flat to the work; and yet if it should get quite flat against it, the cutting edge would cut along its whole length, and the pressure of the cut would be sufficient to force the tool edge deeper into the work than is intended, which process would continue, causing the tool to rip in and spoil the work. The face of the chisel nearest to the face of the work being operated upon,

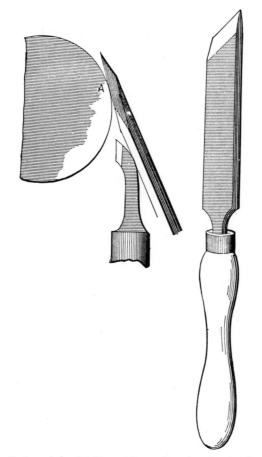

Fig. 63. Tool used for finishing plain work; also showing how to cut in finishing straight or parallel surfaces.

stands almost parallel, with just sufficient tilt of the tool to let the cutting edge meet the work in advance of the inside face of the tool; or, in other words, the amount of the tilt should be about that of the intended depth of the cut, so that when the cutting edge of the tool has entered the wood to the requisite depth, the flat face will bear against the work and form a guide to the cutting edge.

The corner of the chisel which is not cutting must be

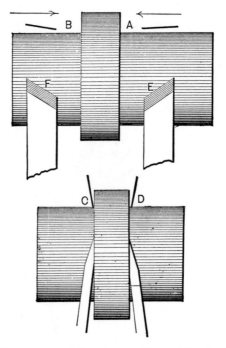

Fig. 64. Showing various positions of the chisel.

kept clear of the work. Fig. 64 will convey the idea, the arrows showing the direction in which the chisel is supposed to be traveling in each case.

The short lines *A* and *B* under the arrows, and those touching the collar at *C* and *D,* show the tilt or incline of the chisel to the work. In turning the circumference, the ob-

tuse corner of the chisel is the cutting one; while in turning down a side face it is the acute angle. Most pattern
makers, however, do not often use the skew chisel for finishing straight cylindrical work, because it is liable to make
the surface of the work more or less wavy.

It is, however, almost always used for cutting off and for
cutting down shoulders, for which purpose it is highly advantageous. For circumferential work on cylindrical surfaces
an ordinary chisel is mostly employed, the position in which
it is held to the work causing it to scrape rather than cut.

A worn-out paring chisel is as good as any. Such a chisel,

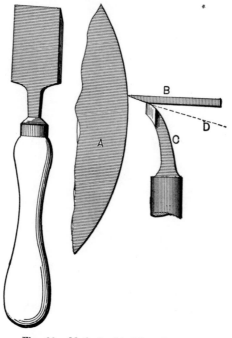

Fig. 66.   Method of holding the tool.

and the position in which it is held, are illustrated in Fig. 66, in which *A* represents a section of a piece of cylindrical work; *B* is the chisel, and *C* is the hand-rest. Some pattern makers prefer to increase the keenness of this tool by holding it so that the plane of its length lies in the direction denoted by the dotted line *D*. This, however, renders it more likely to rip into the work, and the position shown in

Fig. 67.   Another finishing tool.

the engraving is good enough, provided the cutting edge be kept properly sharpened. This chisel is also used on side faces.

Still another tool, sometimes used for finishing plain cylindrical surfaces and side faces, is that shown in Fig. 67 (page 65), the cutting edges being *B* and *C*. It is used in the same manner and relative position as the chisel, shown in Fig. 66.

For finishing hollows which should just be roughed out with the gouge, the form of tool shown in Fig. 68 is used.

Several of these tools, of various sizes, should be kept at hand. They are used in the same position as is the finishing chisel, shown in Fig. 66. The tool *C*, in Fig. 69, is used

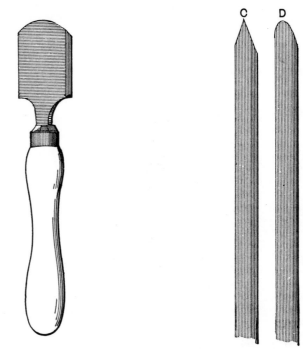

Fig. 68. Tool used for finishing
hollows.

Fig. 69. Two tools used for large
work.

upon large work, and is advantageous because it presents less surface of cutting edge in proportion to the depth of the cut than the gouge, and in consequence it is less liable to jar or shake the work.

It is generally made about two feet long, which enables the operator to hold it very firmly and steadily. It is used with its top face lying horizontally, and should be kept keen. *D*, Fig. 69, represents a similar tool with a round nose. This tool is not made long and may be used in a handle.

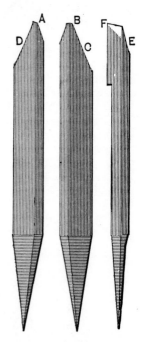

Fig. 70. Three tools for boring and shouldering.

For boring and shouldering purposes the tools *A*, *B*, and *E*, shown in Fig. 70, are employed. *A* and *B* have their cutting edges at *C* and *D*, and are therefore right and left hand tools. When, however, the hole is too small to admit of these tools being used, *E* may be employed, its cutting edge being at *F*. The temper of all these tools should be drawn to a light brown color.—Joshua Rose, M. E.

A Handy Bench to Have.

I herewith describe a very convenient wheelwright's bench with an adjustable wooden vise. Fig. 71 shows the bench complete. It is made from one by four-inch pine, nailed and glued firmly together.

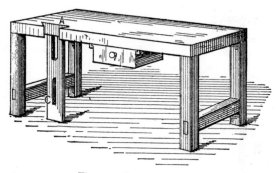

Fig. 71. Bench complete.

Fig. 72. Inside jaw of vise.

A, in Fig. 71, is a dovetail notch, cut to fit the head of Fig. 72, which is put in from the bottom. Fig. 73 is a bolt, with flat head and screw thereon. On the other end is a

hand nut. This bolt is put through hole *B* in Fig. 72 and
slot *C*, Fig. 71. Fig. 74 is a washer that goes on the bolt,
Fig. 73, under the tail-nut. Fig. 75 is the outside jaw of
the vise, and Fig. 76 is a common wooden screw, such as is
in general use for carpenters' and wheelwrights' benches.

It will be seen that by the operation of the bolt, Fig. 73,

Fig. 73. Bolt with hand nut.

Fig. 74. Washer for bolt.

Fig. 75. Outside jaw of vise.

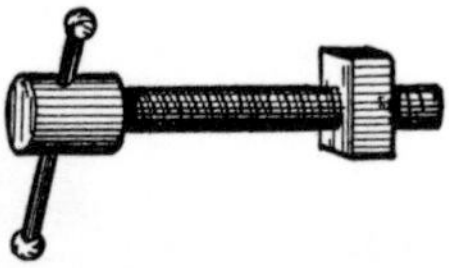

Fig. 76. Wooden screw for vise.

in slot *C*, Fig. 71, the vise can be raised above or let down
even with the top of the bench.

I have found this to be the handiest vise I have ever seen,
not excepting any coachmakers' iron vise. It is just the
thing for carpenters.—*By* G. W. P.

Wheelwrights' Bench.

The bench I am using is a convenient one. I trust a description of it will please wheelwrights. *A*, Figs. 77 and 78, represents a vise which is placed flush with the top of the

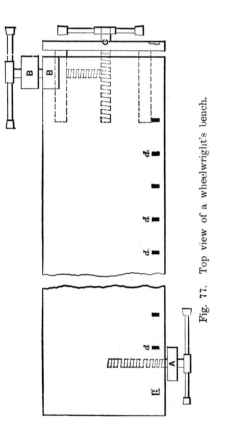

Fig. 77. Top view of a wheelwright's bench.

bench. *B*, at the opposite end, is placed six inches above the bench. The long clamp *C* is placed a quarter of an inch below the top of the bench. All three of the vises have iron screws. The bench is twelve feet long and two feet six inches wide. The top is of ash plank, two and a half inches thick. The holes *d, d, d,* &c., are placed at regular intervals the whole length of the bench, and are to receive the bench stop in planing plank, &c. By this means stuff of various lengths is accommodated. The slide *C* is provided

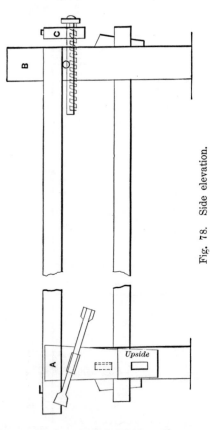

Fig. 78. Side elevation.

with two guides, so placed as to bring the upper edge a half inch above the top of the screw. The vises *A* and *B* each have one guide. The screw *B* is placed immediately below the top of the bench, while *C* is placed just low enough to come under it, as shown. The general construction of the bench is shown in the drawings so as to require no further description.

This is simply a plain bench. If, in addition, a bench is wanted for making wheels, I will describe one I use for that purpose. At right angles to the bench already described, opposite the vise *B*, I have my wheel bench, which is about seven feet long and two feet wide. The top is of three-inch plank. On one end, securely bolted in position on two-inch plank, is placed a tire drill, with a hollow auger. In the center line of the plank one-inch holes are bored at intervals of three inches, thus adapting the bench to wheels of various diameters. To accommodate different sizes of hubs, the wheels are set up from the face of the bench by means of blocks, so as to be in line with the center of the spindle. The bolt for fastening the wheel is fitted into the block. When the wheel is finished, the bolt drops. The tire is then put on, after which the wheel is put back on the bench, so that the necessary holes may be drilled in the tire. The spokes are tenoned with the hollow auger fitted into the tire drill. The spokes are driven, the felloes are put on, and the trimming done, all on one bench. The felloes are trimmed and bored on the vise *B*, which, as mentioned above, is in close proximity to the wheel bench.—*By* J. D. F.

Horse or Bench for Driving Spokes.

A device which I have been using for a number of years, is shown in Fig. 79. I have seen several patent spoke-setting machines, but none of them that I liked as well as this, which has the merit of not being patented.

The bench *A* is nine feet long, made of two-inch stuff, fifteen inches wide. Two legs, *B B*, are placed near one end, while the other end, *C*, rests on the floor. By this construction the bench is placed at an angle which I find facilitates driving the spokes. A man can strike a strong, quick blow when the hub is held in the position shown in the engraving much better than if it were placed vertically in the

center of the bench. The slot *D* is made to suit any size
of hub. The bolt block *E* runs across the bench for the
hubs to rest against. A piece, *F*, eight feet long, two inches
thick by six inches wide, and entirely straight throughout
its length, is arranged as a gauge, all as shown in the sketch.
A slot is cut in the center of this piece, opposite the one in
the bench already described. A second slot is placed near
the end to accommodate the standard *C*, which is mortised
into the end of the bench at *C*. By this construction it may be
placed higher or lower to suit different sizes of hubs. Near
the end of this bar *F*, is placed the gauge *H*, through which
is passed the wheel-rod *J*. A standard, *K*, properly arranged

Fig. 79.   Elkton's spoke-driving device.

to receive the rod *L*, is also fastened into this bar, *L*, and
sustains the movable weight *M*. A cord attached to the end
of *L*, and to the end of the spoke, serves by this construction to hold the spoke against the gauge *H* during the process of driving.

With this description the method of using the device is
readily perceived. The bench *A* and the gauge bar *F* should
be plated with iron on each side of the slots, in order to
protect the wood from wearing. Place the hub on the bench
A, over the slot *D*. Put the gauge bar *F* in position, and
put in the wheel-rod *J*. Allow the hub to rest against the

block E so as to be solid in driving. Fasten in this position by the crank nut on the rod J. Put a bolt through the standard C where it passes through the gauge bar F. Move the spoke gauge H to the point where the rim will be. Run it up or down to suit the dish of the wheel that is to be made. Start the spoke I. Raise the lever L and place the cord N around the spoke, thus holding it against the gauge H.

I may remark in this connection that I do not use this part of the machine except in filling old hubs. It is not necessary in making new wheels. After all has been made ready in this manner, the next operation is driving the spokes. After the first one has been sent home, loosen the crank nut, turn the hub to the next space, and fasten down as already described. In my own practice I employ a four and a half pound hammer with a good face.—*By* ELKTON.

Appliances for Wheelwrights.

Once, while putting on a two and a half inch sprung oak rim, I was called upon by a man who, although a stranger to me, appeared to take more than a passing notice of the work I was doing, and expressed surprise at the ease with which I was able to handle the stubborn piece of oak, which I had almost in place. He informed me that he had followed wheelwrighting for thirty years and had never seen a certain tool I had in use and called a rim clamp. This admission from one many years my senior led me to think that mechanics in general say too little among themselves about the home-made shop appliances, without which they would succeed but poorly in their work, and I am led to believe that a description of this tool will be of service to the profession.

I had a set of eight by fourteen inch locust hubs that had seen forty years' service and were yet sound and as good as ever brought me to be respoked and rimmed. In consequence of the width of the mortises, I had to use two and a half inch spokes with rims to correspond.

For a wheel horse I used a bench made of ash plank twelve

inches wide, four inches thick, and five feet long, secured to
the floor by a three-quarter inch rod, having a hook at the
lower end to fit into an eye bolt screwed into the floor, the
rod coming through the bench far enough to take a fourteen
inch hub and leave room for a hand nut which turned down
on the thread cut on the upper end of the rod and clamped
the hub securely to the bench.

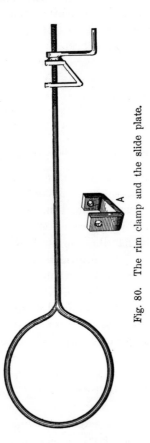

Fig. 80.   The rim clamp and the slide plate.

The old spokes were removed by driving against a clamp
consisting of two plates (Fig. 80) of tire iron two and a half

by three-eighths inch, six inches long, held together at the bottom by two and three-eighths inch carriage bolts, at the top by a nine-sixteenths inch bolt, having a hand nut to get the pressure from, as shown by Fig. 80.

Fig. 81.   The clamp for driving out spokes.

By placing a bit of hard wood against this clamp and driving with a three-pound hand hammer, the most obdurate spoke will come.

The new spokes were then fitted and driven with a three-pound hand hammer. Here was more trouble. These hubs were hand-mortised, and well mortised too, but not so that a truly shouldered spoke would fit. One side would come up while the other was off from one-sixteenth to one-eighth inch, necessitating scribing up. Here the driving clamp again came in play to remove the spoke. The spokes driven were marked, cut off, and tenoned by the use of a common lathe drill, mounted on the bench with a hollow auger fitted thereto, and fed to the work by the hand-wheel, which saves much muscle and does a good job.

The rim marked, gauged, bored, and chamfered, is now put on, which is a faint. term to express that operation, as one must know who has handled a two and a half by two and a quarter inch seasoned oak rim.

The spoke tenons were further apart than the holes in the rim ; but I could not spring them together and hold them without help, so I had a clamp made to pull them together till I could drive the rim on one more tenon, where I held it by the rim clamp, Fig. 81, when I put the spoke clamp,

Fig. 82, on the next pair, drew another spoke up to the hole in the rim, drove on the rim, holding with the rim clamp, and so on.

Fig. 82. ·The clamp plate.

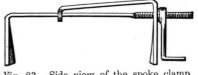

Fig. 83.   Side view of the spoke clamp.

The spoke clamp is made from two bars of one and one-eighth by one-quarter inch tire iron. One has a threaded end of three or four inches, the other end a square bend, say three inches. The other bar has an eye made flat in one end, while the other end has a square bend, four inches long, with a one-half inch hole one inch from the bend on the short side. The bar having the threaded end is passed through the eye on through the hole, and has a hand nut to draw it up, making the bars slide one on the other. This is placed just inside the rim, with the hooks over a pair of spokes; then the hand nut is turned, drawing the spokes together.

This clamp is also useful to draw up joints in the rim that are prone to open. The hooks must be twisted, as shown by

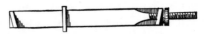

Fig. 84.   The twist given to the hooks of the spoke clamp.

Fig. 84, to conform to the line of the spokes, or the clamp

will slide toward the hub. The rim clamp consists of a rod of seven-sixteenths inch round iron, with a loop or eye long enough to come a little beyond the rim of a four-foot wheel.

A thread is cut on the outer end for a hand nut, inside of which is a plate having two bearings on the rod, and which is crowded to the rim by the hand nut, holding the rim while being wedged or otherwise operated upon.

These devices are easily made by any blacksmith, and will many times repay the outlay by the independence they give a woodworker when once used, obviating the annoying necessity of saying to some one, " Hold on to that a minute while I hold this."

Fig. 80 of the engravings represents the rim clamp, and the slide plate *A* for this clamp is shown also in perspective. Fig. 81 is a view, in elevation, of the clamp used for driving out spokes. Fig. 82 is the clamp plate. Fig. 83 is a view, in elevation, of the spoke clamp. Fig. 84 is a plan view, showing the twist given to the hooks of the spoke clamp to prevent it from sliding toward the hub.—*By* F. C. HALSEY.

A Spoke Tenoning and Boring Machine.

I give herewith a home-made machine, which is a great labor saver as well as an assistant in doing better work than can be done by hand. I will try and explain how it can be made with but little cost.

It is a hand spoke tenoning and boring machine, Fig. 85 (page 78). I find it is very hard work to tenon spokes by hand and have them all true, so that when the rim is driven on all will be perfect. But this machine will do such work easily and well. It is made as follows : First procure a Horizontal Friction Feed Drilling Machine. Then make a horse of plank. Bolt the drill on one end of the horse and cut a slot in the center of the horse from the middle of the end opposite the machine. Have a blacksmith make for you a three quarter inch iron rod, and ten or twelve inches from the top sink on a collar four to six inches in diameter for the wheel to rest on. Take two pieces of flat iron, one-half inch thick, two by four inches, and make nuts of them to work on the three-quarter inch rod below the stationary collar. Run on one of the nuts and slip the rod down through the slot in the horse. Secure the other nut on a board ten

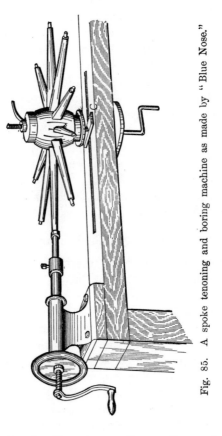

Fig. 85. A spoke tenoning and boring machine as made by " Blue Nose."

or twelve inches in diameter, and run the nut on the rod from the under side until it tightens the rod in a position for the wheel to be operated on. This rod will then be adjustable back and front, up and down, and will hold any

wheel that ever comes to be repaired. Put a crank on the
bottom of the rod to raise and lower the wheel. Take any
ordinary hollow auger, fit into your machine, place the wheel
on the rod, the front down, and raise or lower until the
spoke comes in a line with the auger; adjust the friction feed
to suit the work, light or heavy (I work from seven-eighths
to three-inch spokes on mine), turn the crank, and the auger
will feed up to the work, and as smooth and pretty a tenon
will be made as any wheel machine can turn out. Fit a table
to do your boring also on the same machine.

This machine will not cost you $5 in addition to your own
work. I made mine between jobs. I used it three years
before I had power in my shop, and I still find it handy to
use when steam power is not available.

Another handy little tool to get the length of spokes, that
you put in your old or new work, can be made as follows:
Take two strips of hard wood, fourteen inches long; cut a
slot in one the whole length, except one inch at each end,
and put a thumb screw in the solid one. This makes an
adjustable motion that will suit any wheel and will always be
ready for use, and will be more accurate than a stick or rule.
—*By* "BLUE NOSE."

A Tool for Springing Spokes.

I will describe a tool I use for springing the spoke when
driving on a felloe. It is by no means a new tool, and it
has been used no doubt by some who may read this; but its
use may save other brother workmen a 'swear word' or two.

Fig. 86.   The wooden part.

I take, for instance, a good tough wagon spoke, mortise a
three-eighths by one inch hole, as shown in Fig. 86, about
two-thirds of the distance from the top or small end of the

spoke, and entirely through the same. I then go to the smith and get him to turn a hook on one end of a piece of light stake iron, as shown in Fig. 87, and drill or punch three or four five-eighths inch holes in the straight part. I next bore a five-sixteenths inch hole through the piece (shown in Fig. 88) and the handle, crossing the mortise, and then insert the hook. I use a quarter inch bolt in fastening the two, so

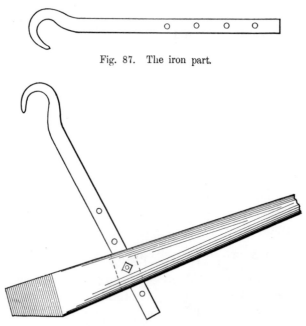

Fig. 87. The iron part.

Fig. 88. The tool completed.

that I can easily remove the bolt from one hole to the other, as the length of spoke to be controlled shall dictate.

The tool is applied to a felloe as follows : I place the lower end of the wooden piece against one spoke and put the hook over the other, and when I pull I spring both spokes instead of one. It will surprise some wheelwrights to see how easily they can handle a wheel with this tool.—*By* F. C.

A Boring Machine for the Wagon Shop.

I have constructed a boring machine that is a very handy thing in a wagon shop. It was made as follows:

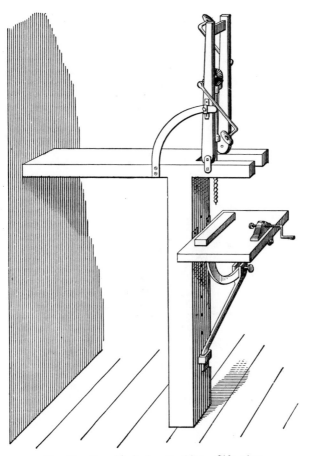

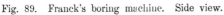
Fig. 89. Franck's boring machine. Side view.

I bought a carpenter's boring machine. I took the seat off, set a post up in the shop, spiked a piece of wood, two by

eight feet, on the top, letting it project over about twelve
inches, and, reversing the machine, bolted it on this piece.
I then made a table that could be tilted, and that had blocks

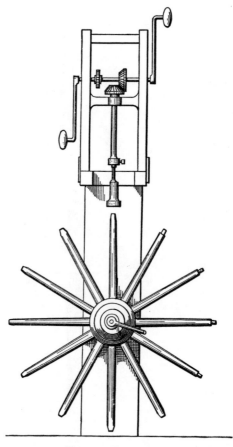

Fig. 90.   Front view.

and screws for holding work. I fitted spoke augers into the
chuck, and held the wheel firmly by means of a rod extending through the hub.

Fig. 89 is a side view of the machine and table. Fig. 90 is a front view, showing the way in which it cuts spoke tenons. Fig. 91 shows a small wooden cone I use to fill the

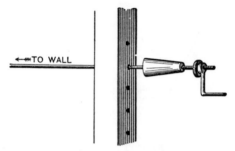

Fig. 91. The cone used in filling the box.

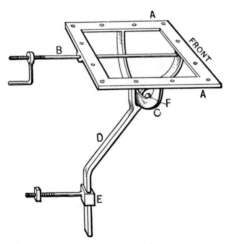

Fig. 92. The iron frame.

box in the hub. Fig. 92 represents the iron frame on which the table is bolted, A being the table, B the rod to secure it, C the circle, D the brace, E the slot for the lower ends of the brace, and F the thrustscrew, which fastens into a piece of iron that is welded to the brace. Fig. 93 represents the top of the table.

The machine should be set high enough to get a strong downward pressure in operating it.—*By* C. FRANCK.

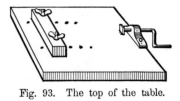

Fig. 93.   The top of the table.

A Handy Tool for a Wheelwright.

In boring holes in the process of wheel making I gauge from the smooth side of the felloe. I bore the holes in sets, drive on, fit up the joints, put in the dowel pins, and then face

Fig. 94.   The piece that rests on the spokes.

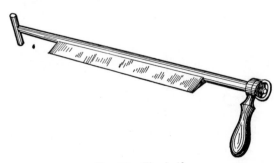

Fig. 95.   The knife.

up the front of the wheel. From this face I gauge for the tread of the wheel—one and a half inch. This leaves all the surplus part of the felloe on the back, which is sometimes five-eighths inch thick; and to remove this surplus I have invented the tool shown in the accompanying illustrations. It is not patented, and any wheelwright can make one for himself. Fig. 94 is the piece that slides down over the spokes. Fig. 95 is the knife, and in Fig. 96 the method of

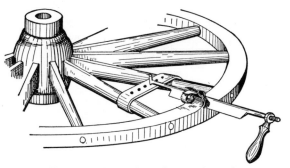

Fig. 96. The method of using the tool.

using the knife is shown. The handle of the knife has ratchet teeth, and can be set instantly at any angle by means of a loop nut.

I cut all the felloes I can in going one way; then reverse the knife and go the other way, finishing in the usual manner.—*By* J. O. H.

Making a Spoke Tenoning Machine.

I have an excellent spoke tenoning machine, which I made as follows: I took a piece of oak one and a half by six inches, and three feet long, and cut in one end a slot two inches wide and six inches long. In the other end I bored holes three inches apart and large enough for a hub to pass through, as shown in Fig. 97. I then made two pieces, as shown in Fig. 98, the dimensions being three and a half by one and a half inch, and made next a piece twelve inches long and three inches square, with a slot four inches long at the top,

as in Fig. 99. I then put a bolt through the pieces shown
in Figs. 98 and 99, and this formed a slide, as in Fig. 99,
by means of which the spoke auger is fed to its work. The

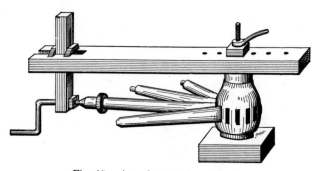

Fig. 97.   A spoke tenoning machine.

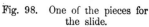

Fig. 98.   One of the pieces for   Fig. 99.   The sliding device
           the slide.   completed.

Fig. 100.   How the spindle is put in.

slot will allow the head to be moved up or down to suit the
length of the hub. With a piece of musket barrel I made a
boxing for the spindle to work in, and the spindle is put in

as shown in Fig. 100. The shank of the spindle is put in just as in an ordinary bit brace.

I place my hub on the bench, drive my spokes, point them, take the tail nut off, and put the tenoner on, as shown in Fig. 97. I adjust to suit the spokes by letting the head up or down. The bolt in the guide, as shown in Figs. 98 and 99, is tightened and the machine is ready to work. I have used it more than a year, and it is satisfactory in every respect. The holes in the end of the board enable me to adjust the machine for wheels of all sizes, and the adjustment to the length of the hub is effected by the slot in the head. —*By* J. B. W.

A Spoke Driving Appliance.

An appliance which I use for driving spokes in a hub is

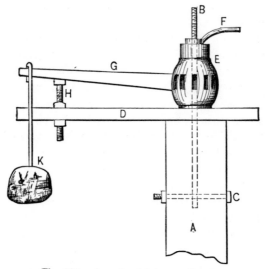

Fig. 101.   A spoke driving appliance.

shown by Fig. 101. I have never seen it in use by any one

but myself, and I think it would be found handy in any wheelwright's shop.

A is a post or box on which the hub is placed while the spokes are being driven in. *B* is a threaded rod, connected with *A* by the bolt *C*, and running through the hub. *D*, on which the hub rests, is a scantling, three feet long, two inches thick and eight inches wide. There are two holes in it, one of which allows the passage of the rod *B*, while the other is occupied by the gauge bolt *H*. The hub is fastened to *D* by means of the tail top *F*. The spoke *G* rests on the flat head bolt *H*. This bolt regulates the dish of the wheel, being lowered or raised, as required, by means of the nuts shown. The weight *K* is hung on the end of the spoke while it is being driven in.—*By* J. W. P.

Making a Wheel Bench.

My way of making a wheel bench is as follows: I get a hollow log about twenty inches in diameter, with two and a half or three inches of solid wood inside of the bark, or, better still, inside of the sap. I cut the log so as to make it eighteen inches long, driving a board across each end to use in setting my compass, and then strike the outside and inside circle on each end. I then dress the log as true as possible, bore a hole in the boards in the end of the hub, put a five-eighths rod through the holes, lay each end on the trestles, and place a block under each end to keep the rod from rolling off the trestle. A board should be placed on the trestle for a rest. I then turn the hub, place a pencil on the rest and mark each end true, marking also mortises. These should be one inch by two and a half inches, and four inches from the top. I make fourteen mortises.

I next make the spokes one and a half by two and a half and leave them square, tenoning them in the usual way. I drive them as I would to make a good solid wheel, and give at least one inch dish.

The rim is made of oak, two and a half inches deep and

two inches on the tread. I next put on an iron tire, two by five-eighths, and then make fourteen grips of oak, the size being one and a half by four inches. They should be made long enough to reach from one inch of the hub to the outer edge of the tire, as shown in Fig. 104 of the accompanying

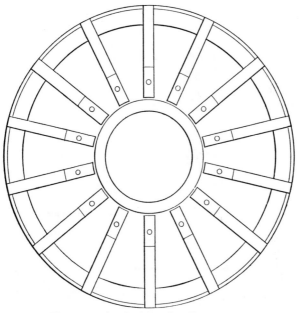

Fig. 102. A wheel bench. Top view.

illustrations. These pieces are bolted on as shown in the engraving. I then plate their tops on top of the spokes, the size of iron used being one and a half by one-eighth. I make them reach from the outer end toward the hub, as shown in Fig. 104.

I then make a cross piece and fit it inside of the hub, fastened in its center, and long enough to reach through the longest hub I may have to set tire on. I make a tail tap for the upper end, as shown in Fig. 103.

When this wheel bench is finished, I give it three or four coats of paint, the paint being ground in oil. If the bench is much exposed to the weather, it should be kept well painted; then it will last a lifetime.

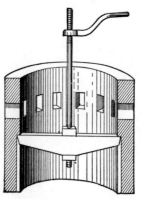

Fig. 103. Sectional view, showing the tail tap.

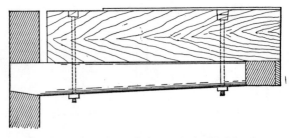

Fig. 104. A spoke and the method of bolting it.

This bench is as true as a wheel and very strong. You can hammer tire on it with a sledge without breaking it. Make it as large as the largest tire you have to set. It is a good idea to turn the bench on edge in a water trough.

If any one in the trade can describe a simpler rig, I would like to hear from him.

Fig. 102 of the illustrations is a top view of the bench,

Fig. 103 is a sectional view, Fig. 104 shows the spokes, grips, and straps, and Fig. 105 represents the hub, which is eighteen inches long and sixteen inches in diameter inside.— *By* W. O. ROBINSON.

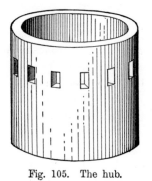

Fig. 105.   The hub.

CHAPTER II.

Making Wheels.—Practical Hints on Repairing.

THE one branch of carriage and wagon making in which the divergences of opinion are the most marked, and in which the laws governing construction are the least arbitrary and least respected, is that of wheel making.

From the oldest to the youngest wheelmaker there is the same contention as to the right and the wrong way, the same difference as to what constitutes the right form of spoke, hub, and felloe.

Those who advocate the old methods claim that the wheels of former days were more durable than those of the present; while the wheelmaker of to-day, who uses the most modern appliances in the way of machinery, asserts that there never was a time when wheel making was conducted so scientifically as at the present, nor when the results were better.

Where the opinions are so varied, it seems but right that no one should assume to possess knowledge of an order so much above that of his neighbor as to attempt to lay down an arbitrary course for all to follow. On the contrary, it is probable that the seeker after knowledge will find it far more satisfactory to study up the writings of practical men, and glean from each hints which may serve as starting points for him who wishes to advance, or advantages for those who are content when they have discovered some practical plan of working out a satisfactory result.

Recognizing the differences of opinion, this chapter is made up from contributions from practical men, giving individual experiences, covering all parts of the country, and all conditions of surroundings. Practice, not theory, predominates, and the reader is asked to treat each as the result of some man's daily study and observation; and no matter how much opinions may differ, it must be remembered that these opinions are based upon conditions which entitle them to credence.

Making Wheels.

To make wheels, three kinds of wood are essential, for hubs, spokes, and rims, all of which should be of good quality and perfectly dry, especially the spokes and rims. It does not matter so much if the hubs are not thoroughly seasoned, as the shrinkage later on will have a tendency to make the spokes tighter. The first thing to do is to attend to the mortises, for I have never yet found a hub that was perfectly mortised. To that end I put a wooden plug in the center of the hub, about five or six inches long, drive it tightly into it until it reaches nearly to the face end, and fasten a gauge, by means of a log screw, and use it just as if I were ready to drive the spokes, with only this difference—in place of a spoke I take a small stick which will easily pass into the mortises, and by pressing the same with the forefinger tight against the front side of the mortise, it will show you at a glance where to trim your mortise to correspond with the dish that you will give your wheel, which is one-sixteenth of an inch for a hind and one-eighth for a front wheel. I consider this a very important point to attend to, for the reason that the spokes, when driven, will rest naturally. Besides it insures easier work and getting a true wheel.

Next comes the trimming of the hubs to fit the spokes into the mortises. Too much care and accuracy cannot be exercised in doing this job. One of the main points is to have the tenons all alike in thickness—not wedge-like; that is, your tenons should not be thicker at the shoulder than at the point. Every part of the same should help to support the spoke. A spoke tenon should fill the mortise on all sides,

A spoke should not be driven too tightly, for if it is, you take a part of the strength from it. Before proceeding to drive your spokes, have two bands put on the hub, within half an inch of the mortises, to prevent splitting while the spoke is being driven. (I am speaking of oak hubs for farm wagons. I have built light buggy wheels with elm hubs, without any bands; but elm wood is not so apt to split.) The back of a spoke tonon should be tapered about three-thirty-seconds of an inch from the shoulder, and the mortise on that part should be one-eighth inch. As to the manner of driving spokes, experience has taught me that gluing them in is the best method; but the glue should not be applied on the tenon, but in the mortise.

After the spokes are driven, the next thing is putting on the rims. For this purpose find out how high you want the wheel, and mark it. Then take a small stick, let it rest against the hub, put a brad awl through at your mark, scratch them off, and saw off what is over your hight.

For boring the tenons, which is next in order, have your spokes pointed. I do this with a draw knife, for I get my tenons always in the center, and have less wood to cut with the hollow auger than I would if they were pointed with the tool called a spoke pointer. The tenon should not run in a straight line with the spoke, but should drop as much as there is dish in the wheel. Your felloe must hang down on the back side, and not incline toward the hub. The size of the tenon for wheels, from the narrowest up to three inch rims, should always be governed by the tread the wheel is to have, making them about one-sixteenth less than one-third of the tread. By following this rule, you will find that you are getting a much stronger wheel than you would with larger holes in the felloes. A felloe, or rim, should be driven pretty snug without splitting the same, to get strength for the wheel, and to do away with wedging-up, which is injurious to any wheel.

In order to try an experiment, I once put on to a set of

new wagon wheels a bent rim, one and three-quarters by two and one-quarter inches, in which I bored the holes in the rim for the spokes only half through, which gave me the other half all solid wood, at the same time adding more strength to the spoke tenons, by having them shortened. That wagon, though used five years, hasn't been sent to a wagon or blacksmith's shop for repairs since, and it looks just as sound as the day it went from my shop.

Having the rims on the wheels, the next thing to do is to trim your felloes on the outside, to receive the tire. This, what I call the face-side of the rim, should be square; that is, when you hold a straight edge across your wheel on the front side, and apply a square across your felloe, it should be square. As to the tread of the rim, when I have my front side planed off straight, I take the gauge and mark off the width, which is one-sixteenth less than the width of the tire, in order to preserve the paint on the rim.

After the wheels are tired, another difficult job is to be done, namely, setting the boxes. Now, a good many may say that there is no difficulty about it, and that any apprentice can do this; but I believe that the run of a wagon or a buggy depends a good deal on the setting of the boxes. They may become loose, after running but a short time, or even the breaking of a box in the wheel is sometimes traced back to faulty setting. I do not wish to be misunderstood. When I speak here of setting boxes, I mean to perform the work with hand tools. With the machines used now in nearly every shop it is not so difficult to do it. The box should be so inserted that the wheel runs true. To accomplish this, drive your box tight at the front end, with a little space on the rear end to give you a chance to true it up by wedging. —*By* C. B.

What I Know about Wheel Making.

I fully believe that a first-class wheel can be produced only by the most judicious exercise of mechanical skill. It is the combination of seemingly simple and trifling things which makes all the difference between a good and a bad wheel. But nevertheless it is a well known fact that many poor wheels are made. I will go further and say that a good wheel cannot be made unless the timber of which it is constructed is first-class. No amount of good workmanship can make amends for the lack of good material. It is no exaggeration to say that there are many more poor wheels than good ones. Most wagon smiths know that all wheelwrights are not masters of their trade. Of what good is a vehicle if its wheels are defective ? There is a well-known and trite saying, "No wheels no wagon."

My idea of what a good wheel should be is this : First, the timber of which the wheel is built must be first-class *and well seasoned*. No other kind would pass muster with me. It is of as much importance that the timber should be well seasoned as that it should be good. No matter how good a workman may be, he *never* can make a good wheel out of unseasoned timber. If the wheels—say a farm wagon—are to be well made, the forward wheels should be straight across the face. What I mean is, that if a straight edge is held across the face of the wheel, it should touch the base of the spokes, and also both sides of the rim. That is what is called a wheel straight on its face, without any dish. For the hind wheels I think barely one-eighth of an inch dish is enough, *before the tire is set*. If the felloes of the wheels set well down on the shoulders of the spokes, and the felloes—if cut ones—are close jointed only between two of them, and only about an eighth of an inch there, the wheel, if the tire is set as it should be, ought to have about one-eighth of an inch dish in the forward wheel and a quarter of an inch in the hind one. I think that is plenty of draft for the first time. Much depends upon the wheels. How much draft must be given, only experience can determine ; but I claim half an inch draft for the forward wheels and three-eighths for hind ones, *when the tire is cold*, is enough. The experienced smith knows how much to allow without cooling the tire. If, when he 'runs' the tire, the weld is at a white heat, he allows less; if at a dull red, then a little more. Before the smith sets the tire, he ought to see that one of the spokes stands above the rim, for if he does not attend to this, he is sure to get more dish in the wheel than he expected. Never put the weld of a tire opposite the open joint of a wheel, but always in the middle of the felloe. I think the notion is quite prevalent among wheelmakers and users of wheels that plenty of dish fills the all-important condition of safety. Now, I think just enough dish to prevent the possibility of the spokes turning back from their angular position to a vertical one, is all that is necessary; and the better the wheel is constructed, the less liability there is of it turning back or inside out. I think some wheels turn back because they were not originally properly constructed.

For my part I think no forward wheel ought to have more than five-eighths of an inch dish, and there should be no more than three-quarters of an inch in the hind wheel. After the wheels get that amount of dish in them, the tire cannot be made tight. You simply pull the spokes over, and as soon as the tension is out of them, the tire will come loose again. And it is also very certain that, after the dish is reached, the tire will dish the wheel very much more than before, for it is a well known fact that when the spokes are once bent or kinked, they never can be made straight again. Undoubtedly many wheels are made too straight; that is to say, they are about the same at the back as they are in front. As a rule you never can put any dish in such wheels, and unless the tire is always kept tight, the wheel will always turn back; and if the vehicle is heavily loaded and the wheels drop into a deep rut, they often break by being turned inside out, or rather inside in. I have seen many such wheels.

Some of our most prominent manufacturers of carriages and wagons practice the system of gouging or cutting out the ends of the spoke tenons below the surface of the rim, in order that the tire, when shrunk on, may draw the rim well up against the shoulder of the spokes, which, if the spokes were not cut out, would tend to kink or bend them. This is not so practical a theory as it may at first seem. It should be borne in mind that because the tire has dished a wheel considerably, it does not follow that the joints and shoulders are well drawn together. Neither does it prove that the tire is on very tight, for as soon as the spokes lose their tension by being drawn over by the tire, the latter may be found very loose on the rim.

In my opinion there is no surer way to dish a wheel than to let the spokes stand above the felloes when the tire is set. I have seen tire set without cutting out the ends of the spokes below a level with the rim, and afterward I could see daylight between the tire and the rim, almost between every two spokes; and the spokes were bent badly.

There are times when it is very difficult to determine how much draft to give a wheel without spoiling it. If the spokes are loose in both the hub and the rim, it is almost impossible to know how much dish you can give the wheel; and I have frequently seen such wheels. It is not possible for me to say how much draft to give a reset tire, for frequently you cannot give the same amount of draft to every tire on a vehicle.

I have not the least doubt that there are more wheels spoiled by ignorant blacksmiths than by wear or tear. There are times when tires come loose from new wheels almost immediately after the vehicle is put to use, and then the blacksmith is always blamed for not doing his work well. It is likely that such things are sometimes owing to one or two of the following reasons: A manufacturer of wagons or carriages may from some circumstance—for instance a larger demand than usual—run out of well seasoned wheel timber. When this happens he has to depend on the timber merchant and take the best he can get. He may be assured the timber is well seasoned; but it may not be true. Suppose he makes up his wheels from this timber, and they shrink; it is clear that the tire will come loose, and nothing the blacksmith can do will prevent it.

Now here is another supposition; I know that such things have been, that wheels are made from the best of timber, well seasoned, and the workmanship without a fault. When the vehicle is first put in use—it may be weeks or months— it is run in mud or slush every day, and in spite of the painting, the felloes of the wheels will absorb moisture; they will swell very much, if they do, and as the tire is rigid, the felloes are pinched. Now let us suppose another case. A very hot and dry spell follows a wet one. It is certain that the felloes will shrink and that the tire will be loose on the wheels.

Whenever these things happen the tires ought to be reset immediately; but in many instances they are not. Instead the owners wait for another wet spell to swell the felloes up again. It is possible that some one may say that a newly painted wheel will not swell in the way I describe; but it must be borne in mind that moisture is always very penetrating, and that there is no paint between the rim and the tire. If any one wishes to see how the swelling of wood may affect a wheel, let him get a new barrel, made out of the best of seasoned wood, and made by the best cooper he can find, and have the barrel hooped with six or eight strong iron bands. Then let him fill the barrel with wine, vinegar, brine, or even water, and let the liquid stay in the barrel for eight or ten weeks; then empty the barrel and let it stand in the sun for two or three weeks. He will then perceive that both heads and all the staves have shrunk. The wood swelled and was then pinched, because the hoops were unyielding. I contend that the principle is the same both in barrel and wheel. It seems to enter the thoughts of but few wheel owners that loose tires do the wheel great harm. When the tire is loose and the vehicle is run in sandy roads, the sand gets between the tire and the rim of the wheels, and grinds the felloes away very quickly, to say nothing of loosening the spokes in the rim.

The consequence often is that, when the wheels can go no longer without the tire being reset, some thoughtless or careless blacksmith sets the tire without cutting down the spokes level with the rim, and so dishes and spoils the wheels. This is done repeatedly. I have often been asked to make the tire very tight; but those who advised this did not know they were asking me to shorten the life of the wheels. Beyond a certain point you cannot tighten the tire; you simply sink the tires into the felloes and bend the spokes.

I believe in having the joints of the rim somewhat higher, but do not believe in a perfect joint there. I have noticed that when a perfect joint has been made, by the time the tire needed resetting, there was a small opening inward, which, in spite of the bolts and felloe clips, got larger, until the rim sagged down at the joints. But by leaving the joints a little open outward, the tendency to sag is corrected. Nothing weakens or disfigures a wheel more than to have it sag at the joints.—*By* W. D. D.

Points for Wheelwrights.

As I had not the opportunity of learning a mechanical trade in my boyhood, having been brought up on a farm, I have found since I took up wheelwrighting as a business— about seven years ago—that many of my ways of doing things differ from those of the trained mechanic. For instance, most wheelwrights first put a rim on a wheel, then plane it, while I always plane to the right size and corner between spokes first, which saves much time and is the easiest and much the most practical way.

I always use the greatest care in mortising a hub in heavy work, so that the spoke at the rim will have only one-eighth inch incline or 'dish,' and I do not use a gauge when driving, because a heavy spoke, properly fitted in a proper mortise, cannot be moved from the position given by the mortise and tenon. For driving heavy spokes I use a three-pound mallet in preference to a hammer, as less liable to split the spoke, and I believe it drives firmer. I always warm my spokes, and use good glue. I think a hub moderately dry is as good and even better than a thoroughly dry one. I saw off the spokes when the rim is tight on the shoulder, so that the tire will rest on the ends of the spokes, and make the spoke tenon one-eighth larger in diameter than one-third the width of the tire.

In making a tongue, I straighten and dress the proper size with a hand ax, then corner from the hounds to the end before planing, thereby saving much labor.

I have had to gain my knowledge of the art by close application and the study of old work brought to my shop for repairs, and my conclusions are : That a heavy wheel needs but one-half to three-quarters dish, when the tire is on, when new. That bent rims are better than sawed, having fewer joints. That dowel pins should never be used, as when the joints get loose, the pins invariably split the felloe. That felloe plates are much better than dowel pins. That tires should always be bolted on, as bolts are better than nails and are easier removed. That a good chilled pipe box is better than the best short box, however well it is fitted up. That a long bearing makes a wagon run steadier and wears longer. That a heavy axle, which does not spring or vibrate, is much better and runs easier than a lighter one. That good quality wheels and axles are of much more importance than ornamental painting (but good paint helps to sell a wagon, and as a buyer, as a rule, looks more to paint than to the quality of the material used, there is a temptation to builders to slight in all but the painting). That one-quarter to three-eighths gather, for four feet and four feet six-inch wheels respectively, is enough to make the wheel 'hug' close to the shoulder without unnecessary friction. That two and a half inches swing for front wheels and three inches for hind ones, with the amount of dish and sizes as I have given herein, are just what is required to make a farm wagon run right. That the greatest care should be taken to get hounds and tongue square with the axle, so that the wagon will follow true.— *By* T. P.

Wagon Wheels.

I will try to describe my way of making wagon wheels, and also making wagons run well.

For a two-horse wagon with a thimble skein three by ten inches, the hub ought to be of good oak, eight and one-half inches in diameter by eleven inches long. The mortises in a factory-made hub are generally about one and three-quarters inches long. I cut them out to two and a half inches by three-quarter inch. I next put all the bands on the hub,

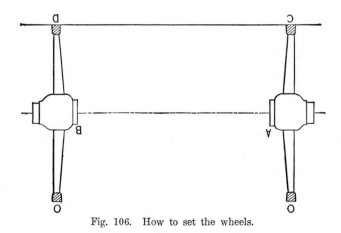

Fig. 106.   How to set the wheels.

and then fit and wedge in the boxes. I am obliged to wedge them in because I do not use a machine in my shop.

I then get out the spokes. I cannot find factory-made spokes to suit me, because they are either too broad at the point or too narrow at the hub. I cut the tenons one-eighth inch wider than the mortise in the hub is long, and about one-thirty-second of an inch thicker than the mortise is wide. I finish my spokes, making them one and three-eighths inch wide at the point, as I am going to use one and one-half by one-half or five-eighths inch tire.

I then boil my hub in water about an hour, or until it is

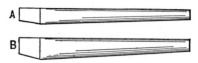

Fig. 107.   The straight-edge.

hot all through. Then put a block of wood in each end of the box. I have a lot of blocks turned on a mandrel, with one-inch holes in them to fit various sizes of boxes. The turning is done perfectly true, so that when the blocks are

Fig. 108.   The factory and the hand-made spokes.

driven into the hub, the holes will be in the center. I next place the hub in the frame used for driving spokes, putting it on the one-inch rod in the frame and passing the rod through the blocks in the center of the hub, and then set

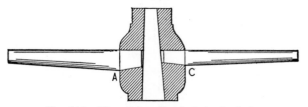

Fig. 109.   How the spokes look in the hub.

my gauges so as to drive the spoke so that it will be straight in front; that is, have no dish. I saw off the tenons of my spokes so that they cannot be driven against the box by one-quarter of an inch, and then I drive them with a heavy wooden mallet. I next take a gauge with an inch hole on one end, slip it on the iron rod, measuring from the center

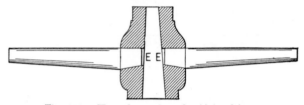

Fig. 110. How the spokes should be driven.

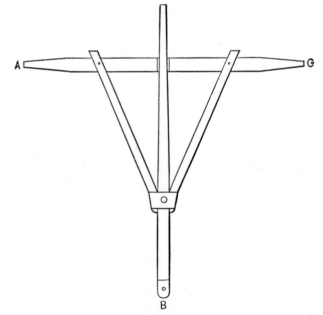

Fig. 111. How to measure to get the axle square with the reach.

of the hole, and set the marker at the other end, just half the diameter of the wheel, and mark each spoke for the sawing off, also marking back from the point of the spoke the depth of felloe to cut the tenons on the point of the spokes to receive the felloes. I then saw off and cut the tenons, taking care to cut them so that when the felloes are driven on—after being bored through in the center—the straight-edge, when laid across the wheel on the front or outside, will touch both sides of every felloe. The tenons should fit tightly in the felloes, without wedging. I drive

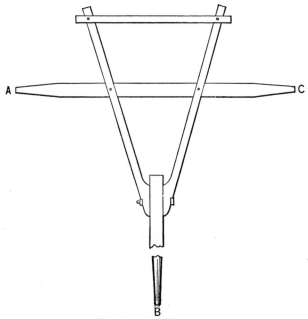

Fig. 112. The first part.

on the felloes, rubbing the saw between them to make the joint between them fit, and then put in the dowel pins and check off the face and back. I next place the gauge again on the iron rod in the center, set the marker to mark the outside of the diameter of the wheel for the tire, cut this off to the line, and square to the face of the wheel. I then have a wheel straight in front and without dish.

I put the tire on this wheel, allowing for drawing, in order to close up all joints one-quarter of an inch; that is, the distance around the inside of the tire is one-quarter of an inch less than the distance around the outside of the wheel. For lighter wagons I allow less for drawing. The ends of the spoke tenons down in the felloes are cut off about one-sixteenth of an inch, so that the felloes will press down on the shoulders of the spokes and the tire will not press on the ends of the spokes.

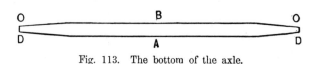

Fig. 113. The bottom of the axle.

Next comes the axle. Set the wheels up plumb; that is, as wide apart at the top as at the bottom; and the distance apart that you want them to be when on the tread is, say five feet from outside to outside of the tire on the ground. Then take a straight-edge and measure the distance from box to box; that is, the length of the axle between the shoulders. Next cut as much off below as above the point of the axle, and your wheel will be plumb, and you will also have a

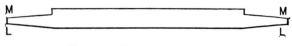

Fig. 114. Side view of the axle.

plumb spoke; that is, the outside of the spoke will be plumb, as the tire will not draw dish if put on the wheel as it ought to be. For the gather, cut about one-sixteenth of an inch more off each spindle behind than before. When the wheels are set on the axle, they should not be more than half an inch closer in front than they are behind. In making such a wagon as I am now describing, I would rather have a quarter inch gather than a half inch.

Make the hounds and coupling pole or reach, lay them on the axle where they are to be fastened, and measure carefully from the point of the spindle to the hole in the coupling pole or reach. The point of each spindle must be exactly the same distance from the center of the hole, to make the wagon run well. If either spindle is too far back, one wheel will press on the nut, and the other on the shoulder. The same care must be taken in measuring the tongue, for

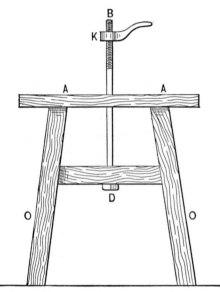

Fig. 115. The wheel bench.

if it is too far to the right, the wheels will run to the left; and if too far to the left, the wheels will run in the opposite direction.

A wagon made in accordance with the foregoing description will run in the mud or out of it, and will carry as heavy a load as one of its size should carry. The wheels will be round and true to the center of the box, and will run straight

forward without pressing on either nut or shoulder. The
tire will run flat on the ground, and not on one edge as most
tires do, wearing away one side faster than the other.

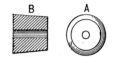

Fig. 116.   The blocks used in the hubs.

Of course it is always understood that a good wagon cannot be made without good, well-seasoned timber.

Fig. 106 (page 102) shows how to set up the wheels to get
the proper length for the axle between the shoulders. The
distance from a A to B is the length between the boxes;

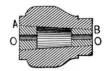

Fig. 117.   How the blocks are placed in the box.

the distance from C to D is the width of the tread on the
ground; the distance from O to O should be the same. If
the wheels have dish, the distance from O to O will be greater
than from G to D.

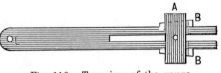

Fig. 118.   Top view of the gauge.

Fig. 107 (page 103) represents the straight-edge used to
get the length for the axle, and also to get the taper for the
axle in dished wheels.

Fig. 108 (page 103) represents the common factory spokes and the good hand-made, *A* being the factory, *B* the hand-made spoke.

Fig. 109 (page 103) shows how the spokes look in the hub. The spoke at *A* is back about a half an inch further than the one at *C*, the front of each being the same distance from the point of the hub, and consequently the wheel is braced as much as the spoke *C* would brace it if it had half an inch dish.

Fig. 119. Side view of the gauge.

Fig. 110 (page 104) shows how the spokes should be driven so as not to touch the box. *E E* is a vacancy of about one-quarter of an inch between the box and the spoke.

Fig. 111 (page 104) shows how to measure to get the axle square with the coupling pole or reach. The distance from *A* to *B* must be the same as from *C* to *B*.

Fig. 112 (page 105) represents the front part, which is measured in the same way as is illustrated in Fig. 111, the distance from *A* to *B* at the point of the tongue being the same as from *C* to *B*.

Fig. 120. The principal part of the gauge.

Fig. 113 (page 106) represents the bottom of the axle, *A* being the back part and *B* the front. At *D D* cut one-sixteenth of an inch more off than at *O O*.

Fig. 114 (page 106) represents a side. Cut as much off at
L L as at *M M* for a straight wheel. For a dished wheel
cut off more at *M M* than at *L L*. The more dish the more
must be cut off at *M M* and the less at *L L*.

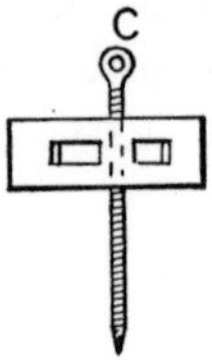

Fig. 121.   Side view of the block **A**.

Fig. 115 (page 107) represents the wheel bench, *A A* de-
noting the top of the bench, *O O* legs, *B D* an iron rod

Fig. 122.   The key used to fasten the block **A**.

one inch in diameter in the center of the bench, with a
thread cut on it at *B* and a head at *D*. It must extend far

Fig. 123.   The marker.

enough above the top of the bench to reach through the
largest hubs. It has a nut on the upper end at *K*. The
rod is square to the top of the bench.

Fig. 116 (page 108) represents the blocks used in the hubs,

A being an end view and *B* a side view. They have a one-inch hole through the center to fit over the rod in the bench at *B*, Fig. 115. They are made by first turning a mandrel one inch in diameter in a lathe, and then boring an inch hole in a block, driving the mandrel in the hole, and turning the block on the mandrel. They are of various sizes, so as to fit the different sizes of boxes. One is used in the

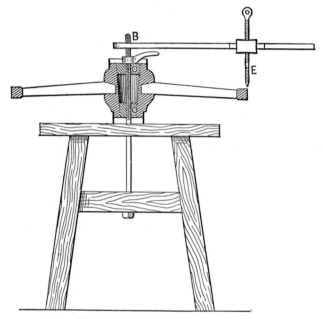

Fig. 124. The wheel on the bench.

point and one in the back end of each box, as at *B* and *B* in Fig. 117, which represents a box with the wooden blocks in it at *A* and *B*. *O O* denote the inch-hole in the blocks.

Fig. 118 (page 108) is a top view of a gauge, *A* being the head and *B* the keys.

Fig. 119 (page 109) is a side view of the gauge.

Fig. 120 (page 109) represents the principal part of the

gauge. It is made of a piece of wood, three feet long and three inches wide by three-quarters of an inch thick. The two prongs are for the block shown in Fig. 121 to slide on.

Fig. 121 (page 110) is a side view of the block *A* in Fig. 118, with the marker *C C* running through it. The two mortises in it slide over the prongs shown in Fig. 120.

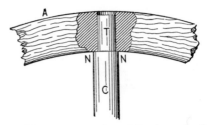

Fig. 125. The proper position of the tenon in the felloe.

Fig. 122 (page 110) is the key used at B B in Fig. 118, to fasten the block, Fig. 121, as at B B in Fig. 118.

Fig. 123 (page 110) is the marker used in the block shown in Fig. 121, and in Fig. 119. It is about twelve inches long and is made of half-inch round iron, threaded the whole length, except the loop at the upper end and the sharp point at the lower end.

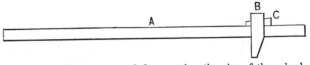

Fig. 126. The gauge used for squaring the rim of the wheel.

Fig. 124 represents a wheel on the bench, with blocks in the box, the rod *B D* passing through the hub, and the gauge on the rod at *B*. The marker *E* set to mark around outside of the felloe in order to make it perfectly round. It will be readily seen from the illustration that if the blocks are true, fit tightly in the box and on the rod, and the rod is straight and the gauge fits on the rod at *B*, and if the marker *e* does not give or spring, that by moving the point around on the felloe, a perfect circle will be made, and that if the spokes are driven true to the center of the hub, the wheel is sure to run true and to be round.

In Fig. 125 *A A* represent a felloe, *C* a spoke, and *T* the tenon, lacking one-sixteenth of an inch of coming through to the outside of the felloe. When the tire, with one-fourth of an inch draw, comes on this felloe, it will draw it down tightly on the shoulder of the spoke at *N N*, and will not spring the spoke as it would if the tenon extended through the felloe so that the tire would press on it.

Fig. 126 is a gauge for squaring the rim of the wheel. The part *A* is five feet long, one and a half by two inches, straight. *B* is a movable block, with a mortise through it, so that it will slide on *A*. *C* is a key to fasten *B* on *A*. *B* at *O* should be set square to *A*.

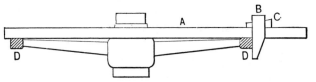

Fig. 127. The method of using the gauge shown in Fig. 126.

Fig. 127 shows the manner of using the gauge illustrated in Fig. 126. The piece *A* rests on the felloes at *D D*, and lies on one side of the hub close to it. The block *B* shows when the felloe is square.—*By* OLD FOGY.

To Make a Good Wheel.

In regard to making wheels, I think driving spokes in with a sledge or with a nail hammer will not result in a durable wheel. The spoke may be driven so tight as to injure the hub. To make a good wheel the timber should be seasoned properly, and then the spokes must be fitted to the mortise with the callipers, the same at the bottom of the mortise as at the surface of the hub; and a wooden mallet is the best tool to use in driving in spokes. I cut the corners of the mortise with a chisel, so the wood will not draw down, as is the case with many wheels. In repairing wheels I have often found that the tenons in the felloes are too large. When the hole is bored, the felloes are cut off once in every ten inches, and consequently the wheel is spoiled. In most of the wheels used now the hub is too small and has too many spokes in it. If the hub were made larger and with two spokes less, the wheel would be much more durable.

Look at the wheels that were made thirty years ago, with a hub as big as a nail keg, and see how much longer the wagons lasted than they do now. Yet wheelwrights are as competent now as they ever were; but they have spoiled the wheels in making them so light in order to be fashionable; and the rest of the wagon is made to correspond. The hub should be about four and three-quarters or five inches and have no more than twelve or fourteen spokes.

Another mistake of our wheelwrights is building the wheel too high. Again, I do not think the blacksmith should be expected to bring up bad joints or make the dish of a wheel correct. The tire should stiffen the wheel, but if it increases the dish the wheel is spoiled.—*By* J. A. G.

Points in Wheel Making.

I am very young in the art of wagon and carriage making. I have had but very little experience—only six years in the service. Three years of that time I was an apprentice, and during the other three I have been carrying on business for myself. But I have been thinking over the many things in wagon building that are worthy of notice, and have selected that most important part, the wheel, as the subject of my few remarks.

What I wish to call attention to most particularly is the preparation of the hub for heavy work. I boil all heavy hubs previous to driving. I select them and number them 1, 2, 3, and 4. Then I take No. 1 and mortise it out ready for driving. By this time I manage to have the water as near a boil as possible. A wash boiler makes a very suitable vessel for the purpose. I then put No. 1 into the water, and proceed with No. 2 in the same way, and so on until I have them all in the boil. A wash boiler will easily hold four hubs. Then I am ready for driving and need not wait a minute. I take out No. 1 and place it in the wheel pit, ready for driving, and when it has been driven I proceed in the same manner with No. 2, and so on until the entire set of wheels is finished. You will find by this mode of preparing the hub that you will be able to drive a much larger tenon in the same mortise and without bruising or crushing the wood. You will be able to do a better and more satisfactory job and with half the labor. I suggest that all who have not tried this plan should try it with at least one set of heavy wheels.

There is still one other thing in wheel building I wish to call attention to. It is rimming a wheel. This, I think, is a very important point to consider in making a good substantial wheel. For my part I prefer a sawed rim; I think it is much better than a bent rim. First, because it holds the tire much better on account of the pressure being against the grain of the wood; and, second, it is not so liable as a bent rim to crush beneath its load and leave the wheel rim bound.

I have still another point I wish to speak about. I wedge up every spoke until the rim fits tightly down on the shoulder and make the spoke come out flush with the outside of the rim. By this means the support of the tire comes directly on the spoke and rim, thus preventing the rim from being crushed down over the shoulder of the spoke until the end of the tenon strikes the tire, a thing which causes the wheel to become rim-bound in a very short time.—*By* D. A. R.

Wheelmaking in Country Shops.

Good sense and judgment, together with a perfect knowledge of material and requirements, are necessary to enable a workman to make a good wheel, one which will be strong and lasting. Nowadays wheelmaking in the wagon shop is confined mostly to repairs; but here is where a man can show his skill.

Finished materials for wheels and wagons can be found in almost every town, at such prices that it would be foolish to make hubs, spokes, and felloes at the shop; but sometimes it will happen that, for a certain job, a suitable article cannot be found; and in such a case a man must work out his own spokes and felloes. It is therefore desirable to have perfectly seasoned timber on hand, for under no circumstances should green or imperfectly seasoned timber be used in a wheel or wagon. It will destroy both the vehicle and the reputation of the workman.

Hickory, white oak, and ash trees furnish the wood for wheels, &c. All three of these can be used for rims or felloes—oak and hickory for spokes only.

The only proper time for cutting down trees for wagon timber is the month of February, because trees are then out of sap. Care must be taken not to wait too long, as in certain seasons the sap will rise early. In the months of November, December, and January the trees are wet and sometimes sap-frozen; but in February milder weather sets in, and the sweeping winds will dry out the timber. Some want the trees cut down in August; but this is, I believe, a mistake, for the following reasons: In January, about St. John's Day, there is for some days a standstill in the growth of trees and plants. The shoots do not grow longer, but ripen, which can be seen by cutting off a twig from a tree near to and looking at the buds just above the leaf-stem. The lowest up to about the middle are an equal distance apart, but then come a few buds which are closer together, and just out of the upper one grows the second-growth shoot. The sap has set in. Trees cut·down in this time are full of sap, and the pores and cells are also opened. But in February they are out of sap, with pores and cells closed; therefore the timber is more compact and will be lasting.

In cutting down trees only a cross-cut saw should be used, which saves a great deal of wasting timber. But cut trees should not lie for months on the ground, as dry rot will destroy the timber. If no saw mill is in the neighborhood, saw into suitable lengths for felloes and spokes, after which set them up, take off sap-stuff, mark out the heart, quarter off, and split in pieces to suit. Timber obtained in this way is by many preferred to sawed stuff, but I have never seen much difference in the quality.

If a shed cannot be used for seasoning timber, it should be done by putting a few heart-pieces on a dry, high piece of ground, and thereon piling timber crossways, giving a little space between for air to pass. The most suitable spot is on the north side of a building, so as to prevent the sun from shining directly on the timber. After being exposed to the action of the air for at least nine months, the timber will be much improved by putting some in a blacksmith shop, around the chimney and close under the roof, to be smoked, which makes timber very hard and lasting.

Most workmen in the country are so situated that they cannot afford to put a good round sum into the purchase of machinery. All their work has to be done by hand or with such appliances as will do their work well, answer for different purposes, and moreover be cheap. I give in the accompanying engravings some sketches of tools used by me, which answer very well. Every wheelmaker can afford to buy what must be bought, and the balance he can make for himself by attending to the following instructions:

I will begin with Fig. 128 (page 118), which is an oaken bar two by six, of any length to suit for hoe handles, hammer handles, double and singletrees, and spokes. One end has a headstock, fastened with two bolts to the bar. The piece above the bar is about five inches. One inch from the top, and just in the center line, is a steel center, pointed. *b* is a front view of this headstock. The tailstock is movable, and fastened with bolts in holes through the bar. There must be, as on the headstock, a steel center, moved by a screw and handle.

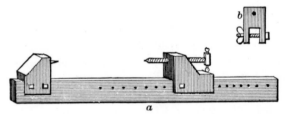

Fig. 128.   The bar, with head and tailstocks.   *a*, the bar.   *b*, front view of the headstock.

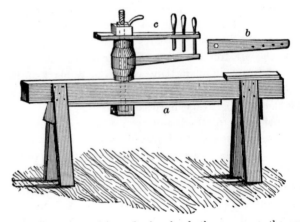

Fig. 129.   The wheel bench.   *a*, the bench.   *b*, the gauge.   *c*, the gauge in position.

Fig. 129 is a wheel bench, of ash or oak plank, six or seven feet long, fifteen or sixteen inches wide, three inches thick, with four legs, fastened and fitted securely. On one end is bolted on top (and true square) a piece of plank two inches thick, on which is screwed, through the base, a horizontal fire drill. The two-inch plank is to bring the center of the drill-spindle high enough to suit hubs eleven by fifteen, twelve by sixteen. To the drill-spindle can be fitted an improved hollow auger (which is the best I have used), or one which is furnished with a stand to bolt to wheel bench. I have not used or seen one of them, therefore cannot tell about its merits. In the center line of the plank bore holes, measured from the mouth of the hollow auger,

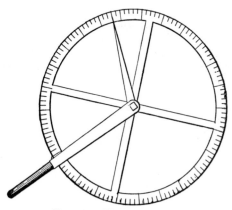

Fig. 130.   The measuring wheel.

with the spindle screwed back half the distance of the hight of the wheels, or twenty-two, twenty-five, twenty-eight, thirty, and thirty-three inches, to suit a bolt three-quarters of an inch in diameter and about twenty-six or twenty-seven inches long. The square head of this bolt is to be fitted into a hard wood block, which block catches against a lath, nailed on the underside of the bench. A gauge, *b*, for dishing wheels, is also shown in this cut. It is an oaken bar, about three feet six inches long, two by two inches at one end, and two by four or five inches on the other end. Six inches from the end, wide apart, bore a hole to suit the bolt, from which hole measure twenty-two, twenty-five, twenty-eight, thirty, and thirty-three inches on the center line. Bore one-half inch holes, to receive round pins of various lengths, to touch the top of the spokes. Plate the part above the hub with iron.

Fig. 130 is the measuring wheel, which should be of about eight inches diameter, so that the periphery will measure exactly twenty-five inches. The periphery must be marked in inches—half and quarter inches.

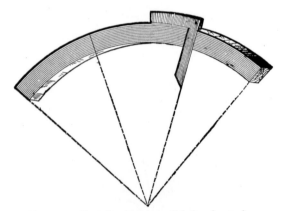

Fig. 131. Tool for marking off holes for spokes.

Fig. 131 is a tool which was once in common use in wheel-wrights' shop, but is not so much in vogue at present. It is intended to aid in marking off the holes for spokes in the felloes. The way in which it is used for this purpose is shown with sufficient clearness in the engraving. But in the best shops this tool is not regarded with much favor. It has a serious fault in the fact that its tendency is to make the spokes correspond with the holes, whereas the better plan is to make the holes to suit the spokes. If this latter mode is not followed, it will be found in practical work that, after the holes have been made and the spokes are ready to be inserted in them, it will sometimes be impossible to do this without bending the spoke slightly one way or the other. The result of bending the spoke is of course an increased strain upon it, and a consequent greater liability to break.

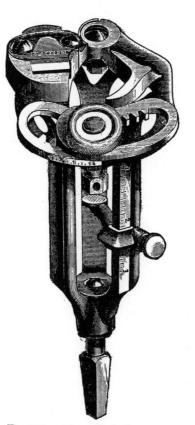

Fig. 132.   Adjustable hollow auger.

Fig. 132 is an adjustable hollow auger. It will be observed that this machine is also provided with a graduated scale or rule, by which the size of the tenon can be regulated.

Fig. 133 represents a spoke pointer. In this machine the knife is held by two screws, and cuts a much longer taper than the old-style pointer. The adjustable shank should be set at a figure on its scale corresponding to the required size of the tenon. It will then leave the spoke the exact size required to receive the hollow auger.

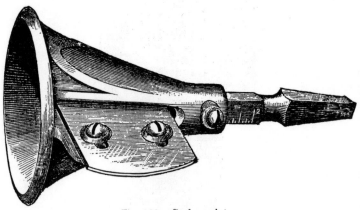

Fig. 133.   Spoke pointer.

I omit just now any further description of tools or machines, but shall take occasion to refer now and then, in the course of this article, to a number of other exceedingly meritorious machines, wherever my text may make such reference desirable.

My purpose at present is to describe the manufacture of hubs and tires. I first measure carefully inside the tire, having thoroughly cleaned it. I next measure the diameter of the hub by means of the calipers, and also take the depth, hight, and width of the mortise in the hub.

I take notes of these measurements as follows: For example, the tire may measure one hundred and eighty-eight and a half; then add one-half for draw and note one hundred and eighty-nine. The hub may measure ten inches in diameter, the mortise three inches, hight two and a half inches, width one and a quarter inches. Measure the hight of the felloes (two and a half inches as wide as the tire.) To find the length of the spokes from hub to felloes, first find the exact diameter of the wheel by dividing the periphery by twenty-two and multiplying the result with seven. Example : One hundred and eighty-nine, divided by twenty-two, multiplied by seven, equals sixty and three-twenty-seconds, or one-eighth as the nearest convenient fraction. Deduct from this total the diameter of the hub and double the hight of the felloes, thus ten, add two multiplied by two and a half, equals fifteen, equals forty-five and one eighth ; divide by two equals twenty-two and nine-sixteenths ; add one-sixteenth for draw, and say twenty-two and five-eighths inches for the length of the spokes from hub to felloes (inside). For the tenon in the hub, add two and three-quarter inches, depth three, less one-quarter inch. For the tenon in the felloes, add two and three-quarter inches. (This is the hight of the felloes—two and a half inches, plus one-quarter inch.) The whole length of the spokes should be twenty-eight and one-eighth.

To find the distance of spoke tenons in felloes from each other, deduct from the periphery of the wheel (one hundred and eighty-nine) twice the hight of felloes, multiplied by three and one-seventh. Thus, two multiplied by two and a half equals five multiplied by three and one-seventh—fifteen and five-sevenths ; and one hundred and eighty-nine, less fifteen and five-sevenths, equals one hundred and seventy-three and two-sevenths. Now divide this sum by the number of mortises in the hub, fourteen, equals twelve and three-eighths.

Having found all necessary measures, put the hub over the bolt ; push up the bolt, slip the dish gauge over the bolt, and screw it down tight. Take a straight edge, insert it in a mortise in the hub and keep it in place by a small wedge. Measure the distance from straight edge to the dish gauge. Take off one-half or three-quarters of an inch, or as much as you want to give dish, and drive out a one-half inch pin, corresponding with length of spoke to measure by. Take a pencil and mark outside of and very close to the hub on the straight edge, which bevel transfer to a bevel gauge. Remove the straight edge and prepare every spoke ready for driving. The lower tenon should measure one-quarter of an inch less than the depth. To the hight of the tenon add one-sixteenth of an inch, and the width exact measure. With the calipers find the measure inside of the mortise, close to the box. Before driving mix dry red lead and varnish; smear some on every tenon, and drive with rather a heavy hammer, with steady, well-aimed strokes, taking care to push the pin in the gauge from time to time over the spoke, to find in which direction it will go. Diversions from the right direction can be remedied by inserting a stout lever under or over the spoke, and using the next spoke as a fulcrum, to pry the spoke so it can be driven in the right direction.

All spokes being up to the shoulder and in line, take off the dish gauge and screw tight again. Then take the straight edge, on which is marked the inner and outer length of the spokes, and transfer these marks to the spokes. Saw off where necessary, and set the spoke pointer to the size of the tenon; put in the bit brace and point off every spoke, keeping the tool always in the same direction, till the shank grinds on the spoke.

Generally I take one-sixteenth of an inch less to give the spoke more point, and allow easier entrance to the hollow auger, which is set over the auger bit, to insure exact size, and fastened with a set-screw in the spindle of the drill. Bring one spoke in front of the hollow auger and force the screw over the spoke, after which turn the handle with the right and feed up with the left hand. Every tenon on the spoke will then be in line with others, and the shoulders will all be square and even, which cannot be done so accurately with the hollow auger used in bit-brace.

Now the felloes can be taken in hand, for which set one compass at twelve and three-eighths inches, distance of the center of the spokes at the shoulder, and one compass at a little more than half the distance, say six and one-quarter inches; lay one felloe on two spokes, inside of the felloe, touching the shoulder of the spokes; put the straight edge on one spoke, over the center line, touching the hub on one end and resting on the felloe; mark the direction of the center line of the spoke along the straight edge on the felloe, and transfer this bevel to the felloe gauge. Bevel obtained in this way suits almost every other wheel, as I have found by practice. Mark one end of the felloe with the bevel, and square across inside; measure with small compass from the crossmark the next hole for the tenon, from which mark with the large compass the other hole for the tenor ; mark square across and bevel on the face side ; also, with marking gauge, mark the exact center of the felloe. Holes can be bored for tenons, the bevel on the face side giving direction for the auger bit. Saw off the left end of the felloe ; cross, and bevel mark to give direction for the saw, and drive on two spokes, touching the shoulders. Proceed to the next felloe, using the same bevel and compass measures, and so on. Before driving the next felloe, put it on the spokes, exactly above the tenons, and mark where the left end of felloe No. 2. touches the right end of No. 1; add a little, say one-eighth to the length of felloe No. 1, and saw off over bevel and crossmark. Go on in this way all around, and if the felloes don't come up to the shoulder, saw out the joints till no more pressure is exerted on the saw at any joint, always driving up felloes against the shoulders of the spokes. If there is now a good, tight fit all around and in the joints, insert a wedge in one joint and saw out the opposite joint till the wedge shall enter about three-quarters of an inch, according to the size of the wheel. Mark every felloe and spoke with numbers, drive out felloes, mark and bore dowel holes, round off the felloes according to your taste, and drive them back, inserting dowel pins between the joints as you proceed.

Now the felloes are in place, doweled. Next prepare some wedges. Open a split in the spokes and wedge every spoke tight in the hole, after which saw off the surplus length of the spokes just outside and even with the felloes. The wheel is now ready for the tire. To put this on, place the wheel on a stout platform which has a hole in the center to admit the hub; heat the tire, but do not make it too hot, for burning the wood will result in the tire becoming loose. Quench evenly around with water, taking particular care to drive the tire flush with the face of the wheel. Then let it cool and dry off, after which bolts can be put on. Should it be necessary to drill new bolt holes, put the wheel back on the bench, punch the centers of the holes midway between the two spokes and drill; then countersink and put in bolts.

Boxing wheels is a job very seldom necessary in country shops; therefore a boxing machine would be an expensive and almost superfluous tool. Under these circumstances it is best to do the boxing by hand with tools suited to the work, such as gauges, chisels, &c. If the tire is perfectly straight, and the spokes are all driven true to gauge, the wheel will be tolerably straight. . The exact center of the hub being found, mark it with one compass circle for the box, on the large and small end, and with the other compass circle for the collar and cup; drive out the blocks and use the gauge for removing the wood inside the circles, first taking the size of the first circle for the box proper, and then for the collar and cups. The size of the circle for the box ought to be one-sixteenth of an inch less than the size of the box, butt, and front. Near the spokes it should be a little larger than the box.

I have already alluded to the matter of boring dowel holes, and, to make this point still clearer, would call attention to Fig. 134 of the two accompanying engravings, showing a fel-

home with a hammer of medium weight, inserting a smooth hard wood block between the box and hammer. Wheels boxed in this way need no wedging, and the box will be tight.

Having now finished the practical part of my remarks, I will devote a few words to the theory of wheelmaking.

Wheels are a certain number of levers, all inserted in a common center, the ground being the fulcrum and the axle the power to move the lever, as boys use a stick for jumping. The rim of the wheel is for holding the spokes or levers in the hub or common center and at an equal distance apart. Now, look at a boy jumping on a stick. If he inserts the stick in the ground in a slanting direction and jumps, the stick will throw him sideways; but if it is put on the ground in a plumb line, when he jumps he will be thrown a greater distance and in a straight line. It therefore follows that a wheel should stand on a plumb spoke, on the face or front, because if taken plumb from the back, the spokes would be standing in a little slant, on account of the taper in them. The axle pulls or pushes in the wheel from one direction— from behind—and therefore spokes should be braced against this strain of pull or push. In a wheelbarrow wheel the spokes taper from both sides, because the strain comes from both; but in a wagon wheel the strain comes from one side only. The spokes are therefore tapered on one side and braced against this taper by dishing the wheel on the front.

In carriage wheels this bracing is effected partially by stepping out every other spoke; and such wheels require less dish. In order that the wheels shall be thrown forward by every spoke with the same leverage and for the same distance, the spokes should be all of the same length and same distance apart in the hub and rim.

To make a dished wheel stand on plumb spoke, the arms of the axles are made tapering, and the under side at the taper is thrown a little on a point below the level. This is done by setting the axles to provide for the taper in the box. By this means every spoke touching ground will be plumb, and the other spokes will slant by degrees to the rim. The proper amount of set in axles and dish in wheels depends on the taper and length of the axle arm and spokes.

A few rules for measuring wheels will not be amiss here, as I have often found workmen who were not acquainted with them.

A circle is, around the periphery, related to its diameter as twenty-two to seven. This assumption will at any rate suit all practical purposes. Therefore, if we know the diameter of a circle we can find its periphery or circumference by multiplying the former by twenty-two and dividing the result by seven, or multiplying the diameter by three and one-seventh; or we can find the diameter by dividing the periphery by twenty-two and multiplying the product by seven, or by dividing the periphery by three and one-seventh.

I have already alluded to the matter of boring dowel holes, and, to make this point still clearer, would call attention to

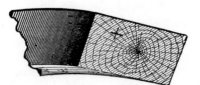

Fig. 134.   The felloe marked for the dowel hole.

Fig. 134, showing a felloe with a cross marked on the proper spot for boring the dowel hole. It is, I suppose, unnecessary for me to explain even to the youngest apprentice that the hole is made where it is shown in the engraving, in order to best meet the peculiar strain to which the rim is subject.

Fig. 135 of the engravings represents the Little Giant Hub Borer, a machine so well known to the trade that I need not expend further words upon it.

Now to proceed with the job of putting the tire on the wheel. To do this accurately, measure with the measuring wheel around the felloes before you bore the dowel pin holes. If the felloes are all of the same thickness and true to the circle, and all joints are tight except one, the wheel should measure one hundred and eighty-nine inches, inclusive of the open joint. In using a measuring wheel the periphery of which is exactly twenty-five inches, it will travel around its own center seven times and fourteen inches more. Of

Fig. 135.   Little Giant hub borer.

course wheels and tires can be measured with a wheel on which the inches are not marked, by making pencil or chalk marks where needed; but for calculating the diameter of a wheel, and, having found this, getting the proper length for spokes between the hub and felloes, a measuring wheel divided into inches, halves and quarters, is far preferable to any other, because every measure can then be taken on geometrical principles. Measures taken from old spokes and felloes lead often to mistakes, and in some cases only the hub and tire are at hand. If the wheel measures more than one hundred and eighty-nine inches, say an inch and a half, divide the surplus by six, and with the hollow auger take off from each spoke a quarter of an inch, leaving a hairbreadth on the mark. This reduces the hight of the wheel, and consequently the periphery. Then fit the felloes at the joints. But by being careful to take the exact measure of the tire, calculating from this, measuring the diameter of the wheel, and therefrom the proper length for the spokes, every wheel can be made to fit a tire perfectly.

To get the diameter of a wheel from a given tire, to the measure of a wheel around the felloes (or periphery) a half or three-quarters of an inch should always be added for 'draw.' From this sum calculate the diameter of the wheel, deducting the size of the hub and double the depth of the felloes, in order to get the length for spokes between the hub and felloes. To this sum add the full depth of the mortise in the hub, less a quarter of an inch, and the depth of the felloe, plus a quarter of an inch.

Example 1: A wheel is forty-four inches in diameter. To find the measure of the tire, forty-four multiplied by twenty-two equals nine hundred and sixty-eight; divided by seven equals one hundred and thirty-eight and two-sevenths. Take off one-quarter or three-eighths—for small carriage wheels require less dish—and take one hundred and thirty-eight inches for the measure of the tire. If the tire is made smaller it will draw more on the wheel, and spokes will become crooked.

Example 2: To find the diameter of a wheel from a given tire. Tires are often not a true circle, and will give different measures, if measured across the center for the diameter. Therefore it is always better to find the exact diameter by measuring the periphery and calculating from this. Suppose a tire measures one hundred and fifty-seven and one-eighth inches. Add a quarter of an inch for draw, and say one hundred and fifty-seven and three-eighths. This, divided by twenty-two and multiplied by seven, gives fifty and an eighth inches as the diameter of the wheel. From this sum deduct the size of the hub and double the size of the rim, and we have got the length for the spokes between the hub and rim. For example, fifty and an eighth, less five, add two, equals forty-three and one-eighth; divided by two, equals twenty-two and nine-sixteenths. Now add one-sixteenth for pressure exerted by driving, we have twenty-two and five-eighths inches.

To find the proper distance of spokes from each other in the rim of a wheel of forty-four and fifty inches diameter : Take off double the size of the rim, multiply the remainder by twenty-two and divide the result by seven; then divide the sum by fourteen or sixteen, according to the number of spokes in the hubs. Example : Forty-two multiplied by three and one-seventh equals one hundred and thirty-two; divided by fourteen equals nine and three-sevenths, or nine and three-eighths inches; or forty-eight multiplied by three and one-seventh equals one hundred and fifty-one; divided by sixteen equals nine and seven-sixteenths, or nine and three-eighths inches.

In conclusion let me say that these remarks of mine are not put forward as a perfect treatise on wheelmaking, and in some respects my views may be open to criticism. At the same time my critics must remember my object has been simply to describe the methods of work best adapted to the average country shop. I have not attempted to lay down rules for large establishments in which machinery of every kind is at the service of the operator.

Wheels for Farm Wagons.

For hubs, spokes, and rims the wheelwright needs, first of all, good, well-seasoned timber, for if the timber is bad or not dry enough, the best wheelmaker cannot make a good wheel.

For general farm wagons I use hubs eight by ten inches, and two and a quarter inch spokes. The front side of the spoke is driven perfectly straight, or one-sixteenth of an inch backward rather than forward, for a blacksmith who understands his trade can set a tire tightly on a straight wheel, and draw it to just the dish he wants; but if the spokes are driven with too much dish, the tire cannot be set on tightly without giving the wheel a great deal more dish than it ought to have. Then the wheel is in bad shape, and is much less durable than a straight one.

If I use staggering or set mortised hubs, I dish the front spokes nearly half of the stagger backward, and the hind ones forward. When the smith sets the tire tight he draws it enough to get the front spokes straight. I have never known a staggering spoke wheel to be dished backward by any cause if it once was forward. But they are liable to be dished too much forward if not made in proper shape at first. A good wheel should not have more than one-eighth or three-sixteenths of an inch dish after the tire is put on tightly.

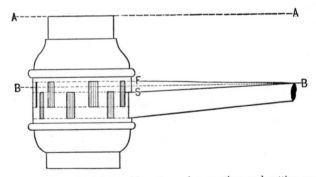

Fig. 136. E. S.'s method for making staggering mortises and setting spokes.

Fig. 136 shows what I mean by a staggering mortise, and how the spokes are set. *A* denotes the gauge line, *B* the center line of the stagger, *F* the front side of the front spoke, and *S* the front side of the set spoke.—*By* E. S.

Driving Wagon Spokes.

For a three and a quarter inch skein I use an eight and a quarter inch hub. I mortise holes for a two and a quarter inch spoke, making the mortise two and a quarter inches deep, two and one-sixteenth inches at the top or face of the hub, and one and eleven-sixteenths inch at the bottom, and so place it that the face of the mortise is square with the face or front end of the hub. Next I band the hubs, driving the bands on snugly and within three-quarters of an inch of the mortises. Then I fit the spokes by first facing them with a jointer. Next I cut the tenon off two and a quarter inches long. Then measuring from the face of the spoke, make it two and a quarter inches at the shoulder. Measuring at the end of the tenon from the face, I make it two and one-sixteenth inches, which gives three-sixteenths inch edgeways. Then I give it one-twelfth inch sideways by chamfering. I edge it well off at the point. This completed, the spokes are ready for driving. I have my glue ready for use; I put the hubs in a kettle of water, and place it over the fire, allowing them to boil for twenty minutes. Then I take them out and drive as fast as possible,

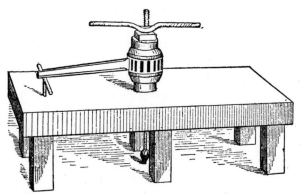

Fig. 137.   J. A. B.'s bench for driving wagon spokes.

with a helper, using the glue on the spokes. Fig. 137 represents the bench which I employ in the driving. It is six feet long, ten inches wide, and five inches thick. It is furnished with six legs, made of two by four stuff, mortised in three inches deep to make it stand firm. A strong staple is placed in the floor immediately below the center of the bench. I have a rod of seven-eighths inch iron, with one end threaded to receive a nut, and the other end finished with an eye to hook into the staple, which I pass through a hole provided in the center of the bench for the purpose. I have a mandrel which will fit in the small end of the hub, and which has a hole sufficient to let the rod through. I drive this mandrel in snug, and then taking another one which fits the butt end of the hub in the same manner, drive it home also. I prefer driving from the back, as the hole is tapering. I next place the hub on the bench, face end down, letting the rod run through the mandrel just described. Then I place a block of wood which has a hole through it, on the hub, and with a handle nut, shown in the sketch, draw the parts all snug together. The mortise I wish to use first is turned toward one end of the bench. With my square and try square I next ascertain the hight of the face from the top of the bench. If I desire to drive the spokes with one-eighth of an inch dish, I set the foot gauge shown under the spoke in Fig. 137 so as to get it. For example, if the measurement of the hub shows the face of the mortise to be five inches from the top of the bench, I set the gauge four and seven-eighths inches from the face of the bench to the top of the foot gauge. In driving I set my foot on the spoke over the gauge, and with a heavy woodmaul drive with both hands.—*By* J. A. B.

Making Shoulders for Spokes and Mortising Hubs.

I for one am of the opinion that spokes are better without shoulders than with. My reasons for this belief are as follows :

I find in mortising a set of lumber hubs, and driving the

spokes into them, there are always a few spokes in the bundle that are one-sixteenth inch smaller than the rest. And as the mortise is not made for each particular spoke, there will be, if not properly fitted, when the job is finished, a few spokes that are uot driven as tight as the rest. And these few are the first that wear out.

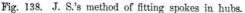

Fig. 138. J. S.'s method of fitting spokes in hubs.

Again, in repairing wheels with shouldered spokes I find that nine out of ten are broken off directly under the shoulder, the square jog making the starting point, and the tenon being the weakest part. Now then if the shoulders are removed from the spokes as they come from the factory, as shown in Fig. 138, they will not be so liable to check. Of course each shoulder must be taken off in the same way. In

driving spokes the smaller ones must be driven a little further than the others, by which means the bearings become
alike on each spoke, and all are tight. A spoke without
shoulders will stand a much greater strain without breaking,
as there is no starting point for the break.

In mortising the hub it will be necessary to make it a
little different from the old way. Take the chisel and cut off
a small shaving, as shown in Fig. 138. This makes a bearing for the bevel of the spoke. Then the hub will not be

Fig. 139. Ordinary method of making the shoulder and mortising the hub.

so liable to check. Fig. 139 shows the ordinary style of
making the shoulder and mortising the hub.

As regards the taper of the spoke, give it as little as possible and drive it tight, say one-sixteenth of an inch on two

and a quarter, and the spoke will not get loose as quickly as it would if it is given more taper. The principle is the same as a wedge. A slim wedge drives tight and remains tight longer than a blunt one.—*By* J. S.

Putting the Rims on Wagon Wheels.

There are many ways of putting rims on wheels, but we poor fellows in country shops, surrounded by factories of all kinds, where prices are cut to their lowest point, have always to try to get the best and quickest way of doing anything in order to keep up with prices and make an honest living. The good old-fashioned way of putting on sawed or pieced rims is just as good as any; but it takes too much time, and as everybody knows, time is money.

Why not have a correct pattern of the rim, the ends sawed off correctly and the holes for the spokes marked at their right place? Lay this pattern on the rim, mark the ends and holes for spokes, saw off the rim to the mark, bore the holes for spokes and dowel, round off the inside of the rims and put them on. My advice is to leave one piece a little longer than the rest, so that if any of the joints should not fit correctly, one can run a saw through without getting what is called too much open wood. In this way I get all spokes an equal distance apart. I have seen wheels where some spokes were three-quarters of an inch and more further apart at the rims than others. Saw off and bore all the rims at the same time, and no matter how many sets there are, they will fit on any wheel of the same size.

I suppose everybody can make a pattern, but if any cannot, I am willing to show him how to do it. I don't use sawed rims except for repair work, for in my part of the country most all farm wagons are put up with three or three and a half inch tire.

First turn the tenons on the spokes and then get the correct length of the half rim, by laying one end on the center of a tenon on the spoke; and lay the rim tight up to the shoulder where it should go. Then make a mark on the rim, on the center of the opposite spoke, lay the other end on that spoke, and lay the rim around the other half of the wheel. If the mark strikes the center of the first spoke, it is all right, and if there is any difference, divide it, and that gives the correct half of the rim. Then take the dividers and divide the half rim into twelve equal parts for six spokes or fourteen parts for seven; mark off for the spokes, bore the holes around the rims and drive on. After the dividers have been set once, as many may be marked off as is desired.—*By* MICHIGAN WOODWORKER.

Driving Heavy Oak Spokes.

When the spokes are ready for driving, I place the hub end close to a stove in which there is a hot fire, and put a dish of boiling water on the top of the stove. When they have been heated as much as they can be without scorching them, I dip one in the hot water, place it in the hub, and drive it as rapidly as possible. It must not be soaked in the water, but simply dipped.

The object of heating is to shrink the wood, and the dipping in hot water is intended to moisten the outside so that the spoke will not rebound in driving. If it is desired to repair an old wheel with a greasy hub, plunge the spoke into ashes after dipping it in the water.

Wheels repaired by me in this way have lasted through twenty years of constant use, and the spokes are as firm now as on the day they were driven.—*By* A. M. T.

Something about Spokes.

I prefer wheelmaking to anything else in the line of carriage and wagon manufacturing, and I have made all sorts of wheels, from the best to the cheapest. The mortises should have one-eighth inch squeeze, or be one-eighth inch smaller at the bottom than at the top. I make my spokes fit tightly sidewise, and then face them up with a plane; that is, I dress the front side straight at the tenons. I then set my dividers to correspond with the side of the mortises at the outsides and cut the tenons to the length desired. I then apply my dividers to the face and prick the back, as shown

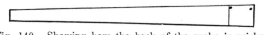

Fig. 140. Showing how the back of the spoke is pricked.

by the dots in Fig. 140. I make the spoke as large at the point as at the shoulder, so that when it is driven it will be tight at the bottom, and when tight there it will not work loose. A spoke should be just tight enough at the shoulder to fill the mortise well. If it is any tighter, the grain of the wood in the spoke will break, and this will of course weaken and tend to loosen the spoke.—*By* A. L.

Putting Rims on Wagon Wheels.

I will describe how I put the rims on the wheels. I first cut my pattern from three-quarters to one inch larger than the wheel is to be. This will cause the ends of the felloes to stand out a little at the joints, but when the tire is put on all will be right and your rim will not settle at the joint. I next lay my felloe on the spoke tenons the way it is to go on, take a straight edge and lay on the spoke at the hub and on the felloe directly over the center of the spoke, and then mark across the felloe. This will serve as a guide in boring the hole for the spoke tenons. Mark the end of the felloe also to saw off, and then with a thumb gauge mark the inside of the felloe for boring. Then saw off the ends, set your gauge to half the width of the tire gauge from the face of the felloe and the back, and bore for the dowel pin. Then round off the corners between the spoke and drive the felloe on. When the second one is driven on the joint must be sawed, and before this is done the opposite end of the felloe should be driven out, so that when the work is done

the outer post of the joint will be open. This will keep
the rims from opening at the joints inside. When the rim
is on and the joints are sawed, drive the felloes back, put in
the dowel pins, drive up and wedge. Cut the spoke ends off
just a little below the rims, because this will keep your spokes
from kinking and your wheel from dishing so much as it
would if the spoke end were left out flush with the rim.

As there are several ways of doweling rims, I will try to
explain the one I think is best. It is to have the holes straight
in the end of the felloe. This is not the easiest or shortest
way, but I believe it is the best. Some dowel by boring in
the joint, but this is apt to cause the end of the felloe to
split while its tire is being set. Others bore diagonally across
the joint, but this is not a good plan, for it may weaken
the felloe and so cause it to split off on the inside.—*By*
JAMES B. WOOD.

The Dishing of Wheels.

To decide upon the best form for any part of a vehicle, it
is first necessary to become familiar with the actual work
that part is expected to perform. Let us then, in the first
place, inquire what the real work of the wheels in a common
cart or wagon is. They are required first to support the
weight of the cart and its contents. To fulfill the duty in
the best manner, leaving out of consideration all other questions for the moment, it is self-evident that the opening
through the hub in which the axle rests should be horizontal. The spoke directly under the hub should be vertical,
and a cross section through the felloe and tire should show
that the latter is horizontal in its bearing upon the road.

Fig. 141 illustrates the several requirements above enu-
merated. Another requirement of wheels is that they ro-
tate in the best possible position to allow of an even on-
ward motion. To accomplish this all that I have just named
is essential, with the addition that the axle arm be parallel.
A third duty which wheels have to perform is to resist the

horizontal strains due to uneven roads, and in some instances, as in light carriages, to turn corners at high speed. It is this last duty required of wheels that brings us face to face with the subject of dishing.

Let us examine into the action of horizontal strains upon

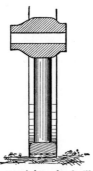

Fig. 141. Section through a straight wheel, illustrating the best form for supporting weight, irrespective of other considerations.

Fig. 142. A straight wheel supported upon a fixed vertical axle arm, sustaining a weight, illustrating the action of horizontal strains.

wheels. For this purpose the sketches Figs. 142, 143, and 144 have been prepared. Each of these illustrations represents a wheel placed upon a vertical fixed axle arm, with a weight upon the rim. In Fig. 142 is shown what is termed an upright or straight wheel. It has only the stiffness of the spokes, the excellency of the tenons and mortises in the hub and felloes, and the strength added by the tire, to support the weight. This wheel has nothing essentially bad in its design, nor has it anything good. While it does not actually violate any principle of construction, it does not take advantage of any by which its strength may be increased. It

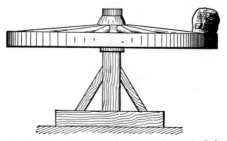

Fig. 143. A wheel with reversed dish, presenting a bad form for resisting horizontal strains.

Fig. 144. A wheel properly dished, and presenting the very best form for resisting the horizontal strains to which it is subjected in actual use.

therefore occupies middle ground. It is neither the worst nor the best. It represents such a wheel as would be made without any consideration of scientific principles.

Fig. 143 shows a wheel which is bad in design, and which is less advantageous for use than the one just described. The natural leverage of the parts is against stability and not in the direction of strength. The weight upon the outer rim, which is an equivalent of the horizontal strains upon a wheel in actual use, has a tendency to pull the felloes away from the spokes, and the spokes away from the hub. In Fig. 144, on the other hand, is shown a form which makes the best possible use of the mechanical principles involved, and which has such a shape that the heavier the weight on the rim, or, what is the same, the greater the horizontal strain, the more the felloes press against the spokes, and the more the spokes press against the hub. The hub is subjected to the strain it is best able to bear, namely, that of compression, while the tire performs its proper duty, that of binding all the parts together, and resisting the outward thrust of the spokes. The strain which comes upon it is a tensile strain, which by its nature is the kind it is best adapted to. In Fig. 143 the action of the weight diminishes the strain against the tire. Like folding an umbrella the depression of the spokes makes the diameter of the wheel less, producing in the tire a tendency to slip off. The reverse of this is the case in Fig. 144, in which the greater the weight, or what is the same, the greater the horizontal strain, the greater will be the pressure against the tire, and the more firmly will it be held in place.

In practice, wagons are employed upon both smooth and rough roads, and upon level ways and side hills. Figs. 145 and 146 (page 144) illustrate the position of a wagon or cart upon level roads and upon those which incline latterly. If now it can be shown that the strains coming upon a wheel in actual use are the same in character as are illustrated by the weight on the rims of the wheels in Figs. 142, 143, and 144, I have presented quite enough to prove the advantage of dishing wheels, if not to show the practical necessity of so designing them.

When the wagon or cart is upon a level road, as shown by Fig. 145, the weight is equally distributed between the two wheels, and of course no horizontal strain is possible, especially

Fig. 145. Position of a wagon or cart upon a level road. The vertical line drawn through the center of gravity falls midway of the track.

Fig. 146. The position of a wagon or cart upon a side hill road. The vertical line drawn through the center of gravity falls to one side of the track, thus showing that the lower wheel sustains the larger portion of the load.

when only a low rate of speed is maintained. On a side hill, however, provided the surface is rough enough to prevent the wheels from slipping, the strain is taken in its full force by the wheels, as shown in Fig. 146. If the lower wheel, as shown in this figure, is examined, it will be seen that the dished form, with the horizontal strain acting at the center of the convex side of the wheel and the resistance acting at the rim on the concave side, is the strongest form that can be adopted. Or, in other words, having exactly the same conditions that are illustrated and explained in connection with Fig. 144, the form and arrangement of parts is favorable to strength and stability. On examination of the upper wheel in Fig. 146, it will be noticed that exactly opposite conditions prevail. The strain acting at the center of the concave side and the resistance at the rim of the convex side, produces the same relative arrangement of parts as is illustrated in Fig. 143. From this it would appear at first sight that what is best for one wheel is worst for the opposite. This, however, is an erroneous conclusion, for one important factor—the amount of effective horizontal strain upon each wheel—has been overlooked.

What I have termed effective horizontal strain depends on the adhesion of the wheel to the road acting in opposition to such strain. This adhesion is determined by the weight thrown upon the wheel, by the weight of the wheel itself, and by the nature of the road. If, for example, the road was a side hill, and smooth like ice, the horizontal strain, so long as the weight was not sufficient to destroy the surface, would be very small. If, on the other hand, it was rocky or otherwise rough, so the wheels did not slip at all, it would be very great. On a level road, as already stated, the strain would be practically nothing.

Referring again to Fig. 146, it will be seen that a vertical line from the center of gravity in the cart, instead of falling in the middle of the track, as in Fig. 145, falls on the side next the lower wheel. By this it is shown that the weight on the lower wheel is greater than that on the upper wheel. But I have already proved that the lower wheel, by its position and construction, is better adapted to receiving a strain than the upper one. Therefore it is fitting that the greater weight should fall upon it. The upper wheel is subjected to a less amount of horizontal strain, which compensates in a great measure for its defective construction for resisting strains.

Assuming that this explanation will be readily understood, and that it will be deemed by all satisfactory reason for dishing wheels, I will give brief consideration to the amount of dish.

What regulates the amount of dish ? To satisfactorily answer this question several particulars must be considered, the most important one among which is the nature of the material from which the wheel is constructed. It is safe to say in general terms that the amount of dish depends upon the crushing strength of the material of the wheel. The softer this material is, the more dish is necessary. When a wheel is dished, it is impossible for it to assume the upright form without the material crushing. The length of the spoke must be reduced before it can change from its angular position to a vertical one in the wheel. It must force its extra length either into the hub or the felloe. This is clearly indicated in Fig. 147. The dish must at least be just sufficient to prevent the possibility of the spokes assuming the position of the dotted lines.

The dish then may be said to vary according to the hardness or softness of the material, and the amount of the safe margin adopted by designers.

Two other questions may be with propriety considered in this connection. The first of these is, What is the best position of a wagon wheel ? In answer, I would say, for reasons made evident in the foregoing, that the lower spoke should be vertical, so far as carrying the load is concerned, and on no account must it deviate far from this position.

In practice good results are obtained by allowing the lower part to spread a little, thus avoiding the possibility of the wheel taking the opposite position, which would be bad.

The second of the two questions last referred to is, What kind of an axle arm is most suitable for the work to be performed? This question, of course, presumes a dished wheel, but I have already shown that, all other considerations aside, the opening through the hub should be horizontal when the axle rests upon it. Hence it follows that a taper axle is a necessity, for nothing else can be used under the conditions

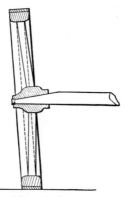

Fig. 147 is a dished and straight wheel compared, showing how material must be crushed in either the hub or felloe in changing the spokes from an angular to a vertical position.

existing. The taper of the arm depends upon the amount of dish, just as the size depends upon the weight to be carried. In practice, the under line of a taper axle should be somewhat lower at the outer end, in order to prevent too much wear on the outer collars. If a wheel is used which has but very little dish, a parallel axle may be employed, and in such cases it is likely to wear longer than a taper axle, because it has a larger surface area to support the weight resting upon it, and therefore sustains less weight per square inch.— WAWAYANDA.

Taking the Dish out of Wagon Wheels.

Being a wheelwright and blacksmith, I will give my practical experience in tightening spokes in the hubs and taking the dish out of wheels. But let me here remind the craft that a wheel being thus worked over is not as good as the newly filled.

First, I have found it impossible to set the tire on a wheel that has become very much dished, and make a good job. My usual method is therefore to place the wheel on my wheel block, and screw it down as though I was going to put in new spokes. I mark all of the felloes and knock them off; then a few light blows with a hammer on the face of the spoke, about one-third of the distance from the hub to the point of the spoke, will usually drive it out, and it will gen-

Fig. 148. The spoke before the trimming.

erally look as in Fig. 148. I then trim off the front of the tenon to make it straight with the face of the spoke, or in line with the shoulder of the felloe, as some of the spokes may be sprung from the strain which caused the wheel to become dished.

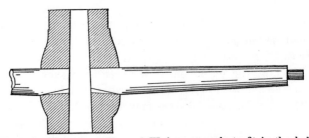

Fig. 149. How the spoke and Wedge are made to fit in the hub.

Fig. 149 shows how the spoke and wedge are made to fit

n the hub. I use hard wood—hickory or oak—to make my wedges, the shape and length of which depends upon how much is taken off on the front of the tenon. If much space is to be filled, I make my wedge the length of the tenon, and lay it in the back side of the mortise; or, if there is but little space to fill, I split the tenon from a quarter to a half inch from the back, and start the wedge, which is driven up by butting against the box. With a piece of hard wood with a hole in it to fit the felloe tenon, and as thick as the tenon is long, I am ready to redrive the spokes, which may be driven to a gauge, as new ones are, and without bruising the tenon. The dotted lines show the shape of the tenon and how the wedge fills. I then mortise and set the spoke to its original position. When the spokes are driven I replace the felloes, and if there is a space at each joint, cut a piece of leather, and put at each joint one or as many as are required to fill the space; or, still better, bore the tenons off enough to let the joints come together; or crack the end of the tenon that comes through the felloe, wedge and drive the felloe up loose, and cut the tenons smooth with the felloe. To avoid having my wheel felloe-bound, I leave about an eighth of an inch space, which is ascertained by driving a wedge in one of the joints, measuring the neat length around the wheel, leaving out this space, and giving the tire from a quarter inch to three-eighths inch draw. I never heat the tire red hot, as it chars the wood and the coals will pulverize dust out and cause the tire to get loose, if it does not do so from any other cause.

Fig. 150.   The spoke after the trimming, and how the wedge is inserted.

Fig. 150 shows the spoke after it has been trimmed, and also shows how the wedge is inserted.

I prefer to oil the felloes thoroughly before the tires are

set, thereby preventing the wood from absorbing moisture, which would cause it to swell; the tire, being unyielding, the wood is compressed, and perhaps the wheel is again dished, and the tire needs setting again. This extra work and expense cannot be incurred for nothing. I mention these facts to my customer, and if he is unwilling to pay the extra charge, he cannot blame me if, after the first good soaking rain, and when dry again, his tires are loose.

The climate in the South is very trying to wagons. It is so dry and hot in the summer that timber shrinks to its smallest dimensions, and then the long continued rains of the winter complete the ruin of a wagon in about five years, if it is not painted and properly cared for.

I would here remark that a set of wheels made of *bois d'arc* timber are proof against any of the contingencies I have mentioned. I reset the tires on a set of wheels of that wood about fifteen years ago, that had never been oiled or painted, and they are as tight to-day as when first set, and have not been loose since. If all wagons were made of this timber, the blacksmith would get only one job of setting tires, for then they are tight indefinitely, and the painter is dispensed with entirely.—*By* D. W. C. H.

Sawing Felloe Joints.

Perhaps my method of using clamps, in sawing up felloe joints may be sufficiently interesting to warrant its publication.

In Fig. 151 the two felloes are shown as they appear on a wheel that is to have new felloes, and the clamps are also shown. By screwing down tight with the thumb nuts, the felloes are held in place so they can be sawed without danger of crimping the saw. By having a straight piece to which the clamp is screwed fast, you can always get a straight wheel without any trouble. In Fig. 152 the clamps are shown on a piece straight on the face and the circle of the wheel. Any blacksmith can make these two clamps. I am a blacksmith, but have been compelled to do wood work, not having any wagonmaker near.—*By* G. W. P.

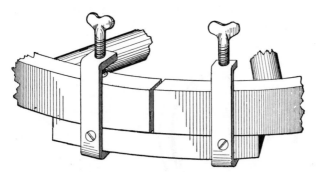

Fig. 151. The felloes on the wheel.

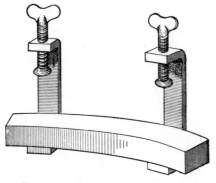

Fig. 152. The clamps on the piece.

Straightening Felloes.

Fig. 153 represents a tool that I have found very useful or straightening bent felloes. I get wagon felloes which are bent too much at the end, and which if put on the wheel in that shape will make a low joint. Heavy rims should be put on with a high joint, and the tire will then draw the joint n true. To make the tool, get the staple *A* half an inch by two inches and bolt it to the floor, as shown in the engraving. The piece *B* is five-eighths inch, with ends bent to catch the pin in the lever *C.* This lever should be five or six feet long. With this device one man can straighten any rim.—*By* J. L. P.

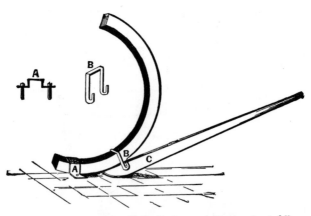

Fig. 153.   Tool used by J. L. P. for straightening bent felloes.

Spoking Old Hubs.

"To make the hubs soft," says one writer, boil them in water for an hour; and to take out the grease, add saleratus to the water."

Now, I have not repaired wheels for thirty years, still I will venture to give my opinion and practice on the subject. Before doing so, I will say that I have no faith in the boiling of hubs as preparatory to the driving of spokes in them, because after the dry spoke tenons are driven they absorb the moisture from the wet hub, and consequently expand to a considerable degree. But when the spokes and hub become perfectly dry, it will be found that the spokes are loose, and so is the band around the hub.

I have seen spokes driven into boiled hubs with the greatest care and firmness, and after an interval of several months the felloes were put on, and then the spokes were found to be loose in the hub. This surely would not have happened if dry spokes had been driven with the same care into a perfectly dry hub.

The use of saleratus to remove grease may be desirable, but I doubt if one hour's boiling would leave the mortises in a condition to make a permanently adhesive glue joint, and the boiling must, of course, be injurious to the painted surface of the hub.

Since time is money, it is desirable to do work quickly, if it can be done as well. It is generally necessary to mend a broken wheel as soon as possible. A clever workman, by using dry material, can finish such a job in a short time. The process of boiling and the mechanical manipulation consume a great deal more time, and an extra charge would have to be made for this as well as for the additional labor.

My practice in spoking old wheels is simply as follows : I examine the condition of the mortises to see what dish they indicate, and if remortising is not absolutely necessary, I fit the spoke tenons, being careful to obtain a light fit sidewise, without any taper from the back to the front, or at least as little as possible.

If the axle box is in the hub, as is usually the case, I saw off the ends so that they will just reach to the box when the shoulders are driven firm upon the hub. Instead of chamfering—the corner of the tenon ends with an edged tool—I knock them blunt with a hammer or mallet. This insures a greater surface contact and less liability to draw out. If the mortises in the hub are greasy, I wipe them out with a rag. I am careful to see that the spoke tenons are perfectly dry, and if convenient I place them in some hot place so that they may contract as much as possible before they are driven in. If in driving them into a greasy hub they should bound back, I do not lose patience and run for the drawshave or chisel and slash off a portion of the tenon, but I direct a blow to meet the resistance. Sprinkling ashes or any other abradant in the mortises will help wonderfully in driving a spoke into a greasy hub.

My experience justifies me in saying that by the method I have here described a substantial and durable wheel may be made without the use of glue.—*By* F. W. S.

To Tighten Boxes.

Axle boxes that have become loose in the hub, can be tightened by heavy paper—old flour sacks are best—as many ply as you think can be forced in with the box, and cut as in

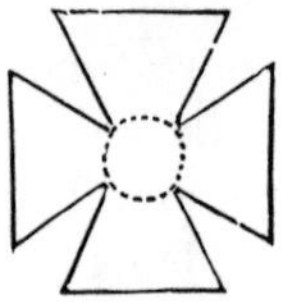

Fig. 154.

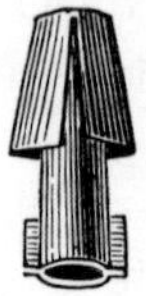

Fig. 155.

Fig. 154.   Double over the box, as in Fig. 155; force into the hub and wedge at the butt.   Never wedge at the point of the hub.   The paper will hold the box if enough of it is used.— *By* P.

Repairing Wheels.

In repair shops it often happens that wheels of family carriages and other valuable light wagons are brought in for repair.   These wheels are good in almost every respect, except that the spokes are slightly loose in the hubs, the cause being the driving of the wagon with the tires loose.   To repair such wheels, and make a good job, remove the tires and rims; then fasten the hub on a wheel top, draw out the spokes, and if any of them are crooked, put them in an oven or some place where you can warm them slowly.   When warmed as hot as they can be without injuring the paint, take them to the vise and straighten them.   When cold they are ready to be driven back in the hubs.   Use good glue, and if any of the spoke tenons seem to be too thin, cut a piece of canvas the width of the tenon, and use as many thicknesses as are needed to fill the mortise. Be sure to allow the wheels to stand undisturbed until the glue is thoroughly hard before driving on the rims. When the rims are on, set the tire in good shape, and the job is completed.—*By* S. A. D.

Removing Old Boxings from Wagon Hubs.

It often becomes necessary to remove the old boxings and replace them with new ones. To do this I procure an old one, heat it red hot, drop it into the one I wish to remove, and let it remain until it heats the other sufficiently to melt the grease about it, for I find there is more or less grease worked in and around these boxings. Then I turn the wheel over and with a hammer and punch drive the boxing out. A few blows will drive them when they are hot, but the old way of driving them out cold requires a great deal of work. —*By* E. W. S.

Setting Boxes in Hubs.

In many small shops, where they make heavy work, such as trucks and carts, they are not apparently aware of the progress that is being made in labor-saving machines, which apply as well to their specialty as they do to the lighter grades of work.

During a recent call at a shop of the class mentioned, I noticed one of the men cutting out the hub of a truck wheel with a gouge and setting the box. I could not state definitely the amount of time wasted, but I know it was fully fifty per cent. more than would have been necessary if the proper tools had been used.

I took the liberty to explain to the boss that for a few dollars he could buy a good hub borer that would do the work in less than one-third the time, and so completely that no wedge would be required beyond the matter of one or two for truing up the box when all was done. I also informed

him that for a few dollars more he could himself construct
an appliance for setting the boxes in the hub without the
use of a sledge, and without danger of breaking the box or
splitting the hub. I explained my way of setting boxes as

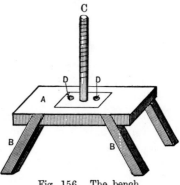

Fig. 156. The bench.

clearly as I could, which is as follows: For setting light
boxes I first make a good stiff bench or trestle, as shown in
Fig. 156, in which *A* is the bench, B B B B are legs, *C* is
a threaded pin (square thread preferred), which is held in

Fig. 157. The lever.

position by bolts passing through at the holes *D D*. Fig.
159 represents the plate which sets on the top of the bench.
Fig. 160 represents the screw pin (*C* of Fig. 156). I insert
the box in the hub, then place the wheel on the bench, with

Fig. 158. The disk.

the butt of the hub down and the screw passing through the box. I then place on the foot of the hub the disk, as shown in Fig. 158, and next put on the lever represented in Fig. 157. *E E* are ends of the lever. *F* is the swell at the cen-

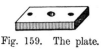

Fig. 159. The plate.

ter, and has a thread to fit the screw pin (*C*, Fig. 156). A few turns will set the box in motion.

For heavier grades of work it becomes necessary to have appliances much larger and stronger. I make a bench as

Fig. 160. The screw pin.

illustrated in Fig. 161, to which I attach legs, or adjust it to two strong trestles. *H H* are two strong bolts fastened to the bench, with bolts and two collars, upon which rest the crosshead, as shown in Fig. 165, through the holes *W W* of

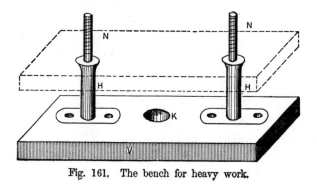

Fig. 161. The bench for heavy work.

which pass the cords of the bolts *N N*, shown in Fig. 161. They are secured with nuts on the upper side. The dotted lines in Fig. 161 represent the crosspiece in Fig. 165, as adjusted.

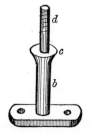

Fig. 162.   The bolt.

Fig. 162 shows the bolt, the bottom of which is secured to the bench. *b* is a stem, *c* is a collar, and *d* a bolt on its threaded end.

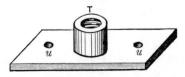

Fig. 163.   Plate which goes under the bench.

Fig. 163 is the plate which goes under the bottom of the bench *V*, and is secured with two log screws run in the holes *U U*. *T* is a barred portion with a thread, which is inserted in the hole *Y*, in Fig. 156, from the under side, the threaded portion of the screw *R*, in Fig. 164, fitting the same.

Fig. 164 is the power screw. *R* is the pin and threaded portion. *P* is an eye or socket for the insertion of the lever, shown by the dotted lines *O O*.

The hole *K*, in Fig. 161, is used when forcing the box out of the hub, and ought to be furnished with an iron plate

three-eighths of an inch thick on the upper and under sides.
To use this device, insert the box as before, remove the
crosshead, and place the wheel on the bench, the face of the
hub down; adjust the crosshead, and place on the back of
the hub a piece of round cover like that shown in Fig. 164.

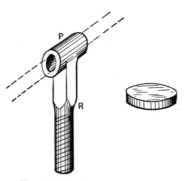

Fig. 164. The power screw.

The iron should be counter sunk on the top so as to admit
of a proper seating of the point of the screw pin; then apply the lever. The job is done much quicker than it can be
described.

To remove boxes, place the wheel on the bench with the

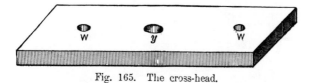

Fig. 165. The cross-head.

butt of the hub down, put pieces of round iron on the box,
and apply the pressure. The box will soon drop through the
hole in the bench, as shown at K in Fig. 161.

These tools are not very expensive, and earn their cost in
half a dozen sets of wheels.—*By* IRON DOCTOR,

Making a Spoke-Tenoning Machine.

A good spoke-tenoning machine can be made as follows:

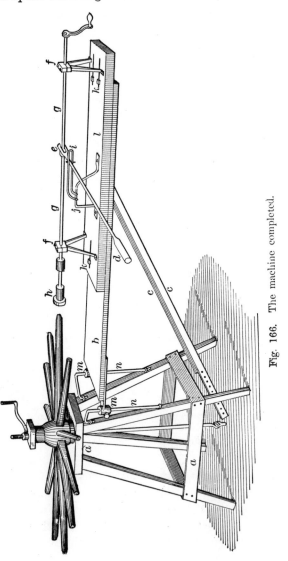

Fig. 166. The machine completed.

Fig. 166 represents the machine completed. Fig. 167 represents the movable joint with set screw, as shown at *m m*, in Fig. 166. This device enables the operator to raise or lower the machine to suit hubs of every length. Fig. 168 is

Fig. 167. The movable joint.

one of the rests with wooden boxes for the shaft, as shown in Fig. 166 at *f f*. This rest should be ten inches high. Fig. 169 is the feed lever, which should be twenty inches long, and have a steel fork at one end to fit over the shaft,

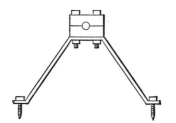

Fig. 168. A rest and box for the shaft.

as shown at *e*, in Fig. 166. The lever should be made from flat iron, one-quarter by one-quarter inch, and have a hole punched in it, as shown in Fig. 169, to connect it to the piece shown in Fig. 171, and also in Fig. 166 at *i*. The

Fig. 169. The feed lever.

springs should be closed at *e*, so that the lever will not drop off the shaft. Figs. 170 and 171 represent pieces which connect the lever with the bench, as shown at *i* and *j*, in Fig.

166. The piece shown in Fig. 171 is connected by means of a rivet with the piece shown in Fig. 170, and the latter is bolted to the bench. Fig. 172 represents the shaft. It has a solid collar where the lever connects with it, and it also

Fig. 170. A piece which connects the lever to the bench.

has a common brace chuck to hold the auger. This shaft should be three-quarters by twenty-four inches long.

In Fig. 166 *a* is the wheel stand, screwed to the floor, and *b* is the bottom platform, two by twenty-one inches by thirty-six inches. *c c* are braces to keep the auger level with the

Fig. 171. Another piece used in connecting the lever with the bench.

bench. *d* is the lever. *e* is the solid collar with the fork in position. *f f* are the rests with the boxes. *g g* is the shaft. *h* is the chuck on the shaft. *i* and *j* are the irons shown in Figs. 170 and 171. *k k·k* are the slotted holes in the top or

Fig. 172. The shaft.

loose table, by which the machine can be moved backward or forward to suit any size of wheel. These slots should be six inches long. *l*, the table, lies on the platform *b*, and bolts and thumb screw taps pass through the slotted holes. This

table should be one inch by twelve inches by eighteen inches.
m m are the pieces shown in Fig. 167.   *n n* are iron attach-
ments to fasten the machine to the wheel bench.   It will be
noticed that they are fastened at both ends with staples, so
that the machine can be lifted off by taking off the two taps
that hold the braces *c c* to the bench legs.   The holes in the
braces *c c* should not be over a half inch apart.

This machine makes tenon boring easy work, and all the
tenons are straight.—*By* H. L. CORDREY.

A Tool for Springing Spokes.

A handy tool for springing spokes (Fig. 173) is made by
taking a piece of wood two feet long, making one hole in it
about an inch from one end, and another hole four inches
from the end.   Then take half-inch round iron, turn a hook

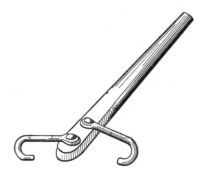

Fig. 173.   A tool for springing spokes.

on one end and punch a hole in the other large enough for
a three-eighths-inch bolt.   When the two hooks are made and
bolted on the tool, as shown in the cut, it is complete.   It
will not slip as will other devices for the same purpose.—*By*
H. T. G.

A Hub Borer.

I have a hub borer which works nicely. This machine is easily made and can be used for cutting out hubs for old-fashioned skeins, also for nuts, or regular thimble skeins.

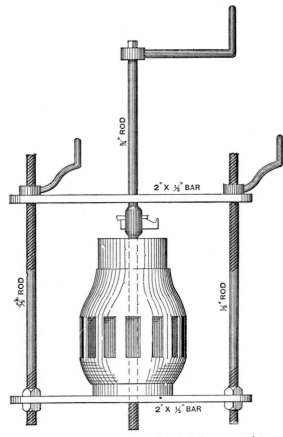

Fig. 174. Showing J. W. C.'s hub borer complete.

Fig. 174 shows the machine complete. Cut threads on half-inch rods. Put one nut above and one below the plate, and screw tight. Cut threads on three-quarter-inch bar at the bottom for the feed. Swell the bar where the knife goes in the punch. Square the hole and fit in the knife. The knife is turned square at the cutting part. Fasten the knife with a slim wedge or a set nut. In using this machine the rods will come between the spokes of the wheel.—*By* J. W. C.

Removing Old Boxes from Hubs and Getting a Plumb Spoke.

The following is my method of removing old boxes from hubs and my rule for placing wheels on a plumb spoke. For the first job, heat an old thimble, put it in the box, and the latter will soon become so loose that it can be easily knocked out.

My way of getting the plumb spoke for a wheel of any dish may be clearly understood by the aid of Fig. 175, which I will suppose to represent a spindle for a three by ten

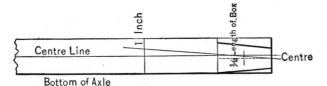

Fig. 175. T. S. M.'s method of getting a plumb spoke.

thimble. The hight of the wheel is four feet eight inches. First strike a line one inch and a half from the bottom; that is, half the diameter of the box; then measure back five inches from the end; that is, half the length of the box; then take half the diameter of the wheel, from the center of the box backward, which is in this case two feet four inches. Make a mark, and next find the dish of the wheel, which is, say one inch. Put that one inch above the "center line;" then strike a line from that, and let it cross the center line five inches from the end, which is the center of the box, and let the end of this line represent the center of the point box. You will see from this that the more dish there is in a wheel the less you take off at the bottom at the point of the spindle. In all cases take half the length of the box— half its diameter and half the diameter of the wheel. I get the gather of the wheel on the same principle.—*By* T. S. M.

An Adjustable Rim Clamp.

A handy rim clamp that I use to set rims to a joint at the shoulders of the spokes, and also for other joints in wood-

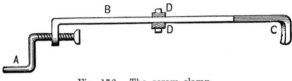

Fig. 176. The screw clamp.

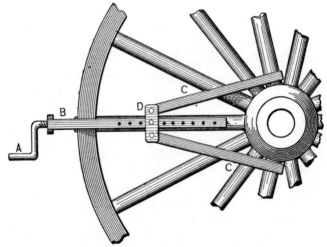

Fig. 177. The method of using the clamp.

working, is shown by Fig. 176. *A* denotes the screw clamp,

B is the body of the clamp, D D are two crossbars riveted on each side of the lugs C, which are shown in Fig. 177. These lugs have the ends hooked to go around spokes. The lugs are made of iron, three-eighths by three-quarter inch by twelve inches. For the body of the clamp take iron three-eighths by three-quarters inch by sixteen inches. The screw clamp is made of half-inch round iron. D D are one-quarter by one inch by three inches.—*By* J. W. S.

Rimming and Tiring of Wheels.

To properly rim wheels it is necessary first to have the tools that will do the work, one of the most important of which is the spoke auger to cut the tenons and the ends of spokes. To make a durable wheel these tenons must be cut true with the face of the wheel, and their shoulders square with the tenon. This is the first and one of the most important parts in rimming.

Next in importance is thoroughly dry material for rims, well bent to the proper hight. The rim should be a perfect semi-circle, and not twisted sideways. By casting the eye over the edge of the rim any variation in this degree can be seen. Each piece should be carefully faced up out of wind, and the inside squared with the face.

The wheel being firmly fastened to the wheel-clamp or bench, each spoke should be marked on the rim, so that the exact position may be maintained when the rim is bored and driven on.

Boring the holes in rims is another vital part in rimming. These holes should be on an exact angle with the spoke on which they are to rest. Any deviation from this line will cause the spoke to spring under the draft of the tires In gauging for the holes, they should be one-half the width of the tire back from the face, so that the tenon will be in the center of the tread. After boring, the rim can be rounded. This can be done more expeditiously in the vise than on the wheel, especially with what is taken off with the drawing knife. The filing can be done after the rim is driven on the wheel.

In driving on the rim don't use a light hammer; use a heavy hammer or hand ax, and set them down on the shoulder solid. No wedges should be necessary to keep it in place; but occasionally they may be needed. The tread of the rim should be square and true with the face of the wheel.

Now we are ready for setting the tire, and it is important that it be well done, in order that our job of rimming may be satisfactory.

If one is going to put on a new tire, lay the bars on the floor, take the wheels one by one, and roll each of them on the bars, allowing three times the thickness of the tire over the circumference of the wheel for bending. A wheel with spokes tight, and nearly or quite straight, will stand more draft than when they are loose and badly dished.—*By* "OLD ZIP."

Does the Mortise in an Unseasoned Hub Shrink or Enlarge?

It is claimed by some that it does not matter much if the hubs are not seasoned, as the shrinkage later on will have a tendency to make the spokes tighter. A man who can make such a statement as this must be, to say the least, peculiar. I am no mechanic, but common sense says the mortise in an unseasoned hub does shrink, and consequently loosens the spokes.

I am a blacksmith, and have been in business for forty years, much of the time working on wheels, and this I will say, never work up any unseasoned timber into a wheel. No first-class wheel can be made out of unseasoned or poor timber.

The question is, Does the mortise in an unseasoned hub shrink or enlarge? All that I have heard or seen tends to make me believe that the mortise does shrink with the hub. This much I do know, if the hub is not thoroughly seasoned the bands will come loose, and more than once I have put the bands on a hub three times over before they would stay. Now, as the hub shrinks smaller and all around, is it not reasonable to suppose that the mortise shrinks with it?

There is, however, one phase of the question which I think has never been taken into account. Let us suppose a wheelmaker runs short of any particular kind of hubs—more than once I have seen such a case—but has plenty of dry spokes and felloes. He procures some hubs, and he knows they are not thoroughly seasoned; but the work will not wait, and he must do the best he can. He makes his mortises in the hubs and drives in his dry spokes. Now the question is, Do the spokes absorb some of the moisture of the hubs, and are they pinched to that extent? If so, most assuredly when all the moisture has dried out from both the hubs and spokes, the latter will become loose.—*By* M. D. D.

Locust for Carriage Parts and Wheels.

The difficulty experienced in procuring first quality hickory causes much extra expense to the builders of really first-class light carriages. White ash has been substituted in some cases with good results; but prime white ash is really more difficult to obtain than hickory, so that the evil is not remedied by the use of ash. The only timber possessing the requisite qualities which grows in quantities sufficiently great to afford real relief is locust. This is found in the North, but it is lacking in the one quality—elasticity; but the locust of the South, notably that growing in Tennessee and in the sections of the States which join on Tennessee, is remarkable for its elasticity up to a certain point. It will not retain it to the same extreme point that hickory will, but it is more active when the deflection is slight. It is also a wonderfully durable timber, takes paint well, and retains its form. In the latter respect it is equal to the best white ash and superior to hickory. Light wagons in which locust is used for axle beds, spring bars, side bars, and shafts, have been built which have proven by actual test to be equal in every respect to those built of hickory. Locust has long been approved as a good hub timber, use having proven that it is more durable than elm, the only objection to it for light hubs being its solidity, or rather hardness, which does not permit the spokes being driven as tight as they can be in elm. Light wheels having locust spokes as well as hubs have been made, and the spokes have stood the test to the satisfaction of those who have used them. This being the case, it seems but politic that locust should be put on the market in quantities that will enable carriage builders to procure enough to make good the deficiency in hickory.

What to do with Wheels that are Dished Back.

One evening a two-wheeled road cart, drawn by a spirited bay horse, came down Woodward avenue. At Michigan avenue a coupé drove across the street directly in front of the rig, causing the driver of the latter to suddenly sheer off. As he did so the tire of his wheel caught on a paving block, and the wheel was dished back. The horse was caught by passers-by and held, as the owner looked ruefully at his wheel, which was a new one.

Policeman Wagpole, of the Broadway squad, came up and calling on two or three onlookers to assist him, succeeded in pulling the rim into place and setting the wheel up as it had been before. The owner, after thanking him, got in and drove off.

"This is something that more buggy owners ought to know. If a wheel is dished back without breaking the spokes off, it can easily be sprung into shape if three men will tackle it, and, catching hold of the tire at various points, give it two or three good strong pulls. That makes five wheels that I have straightened in the same way on this very corner," said the policeman.

How to Make a Wheel for a Wheelbarrow.

I will describe my way of making a wheelbarrow. I make the wheel of iron, all except the hub, which I make of locust or mulberry, four inches in diameter and twelve inches

Fig. 178. Shape of the spoke.

Fig. 179. The wheel ready for the axle.

long, with an inch hole through the center from end to end for the axle, and put two strong bands one inch apart in the center, lay off and bore eight seven-eighths-inch holes with an ordinary brace bit or auger for the spokes between the bands. I then cut my spokes from rod iron, seven-eighths-inch diameter, nine inches long, and shape them as in Fig. 178. I make the tire of one and a half by three-eighths-inch iron, and drill eight three-eighths-inch holes for the spokes. I then put it together as in Fig. 179, and cut my axle six-

Fig. 180.   Shape of the axle ready to drive through the hub.

teen inches long and one inch in diameter, and sharpen one end like a pencil, as in Fig. 180, and drive it through the hub, which forces the spokes out through the tire. Brad them on the outside in a counter-sunk hole. Saw off the sharp end of the axle, and the wheel is complete.—*By* J. M. W.

To Find Length of Fifth-Wheel Before Bending.

Some people have a practice of making a bushel of preparation to arrive at one gill of product. I have noticed a

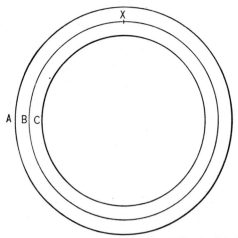

Fig. 181.   Showing how to find the length of fifth-wheel before bending.

number of times how some blacksmiths go to work to find out how much iron it takes to turn a fifth wheel of a certain diameter. Long problems in figures have been shown, all of which would require more time to decipher than to cut the piece from the bar, and turn and weld and fit the wheel. It is an easy thing to do if one goes at it right. First, with a compass, strike the outside diameter of the circle, as per circle *A* of the illustration. Then strike the inside diameter of the circle, as per circle *C*. Next strike a circle midway between the two, as per circle *B*. Take a thin piece of band iron, lead, or harness leather and start at *X* and end at *X*, by following circle *B*, and you get the exact length at which to cut off the piece, allowing enough for lapping and welding. The outer part of the iron elongates and the inner circle contracts in bending, but no change occurs at the center line. The whole business of laying out the circle and getting the measurement usually occupies from three to five minutes, and I never make a mistake.—*By* IRON DOCTOR.

Taking the Dish out of Wagon Wheels.

Before describing my method of taking the dish out of wheels, I will relate how some blacksmiths who think they "know it all," do the work.

Farmer Jones got his wagon tires set last year, and the other day the tires became loose again. Jones wants to try another smith, and so he goes to Mr. Know it All's blacksmith shop and tells him that the wheels got dished last year, and that the tires are loose again. He wants them set, but he does not want to have the wheels dish any more. Now, Mr. Know it All sees a new customer and says: "Yes, yes. I can set them better." And he goes to work. Removing the tires, he sees that the spokes are loose in the hub, and that he must give the tires a good three-quarter inch draw each; so the spokes get tied, and he forgets to fit the pins of the spoke even with the felloe on the face. He calls the job done.

Mr. Jones gets the wheels, and the first thing he notices

is that they have got another inch of dish and that the tires rest on the pins of the spokes, or as shown in Fig. 182. He can also see an open space between the tire and felloe. The joints of the felloe are not tied to the shoulders on the spokes. He tells the smith of it. "No, no, no; that job is all right, and the tires are tied," is Mr. Know it All's

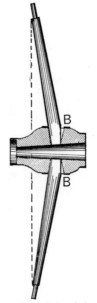

Fig. 182. The dish of the wheel.

reply. But in three months the tires come off, and all the joints work so badly that the wheel must be repaired again.

Now, Mr. Brown brings me a set of wheels in the same condition as those which Mr. Know it All tried to repair. Mr. Brown tells me to set the tires and get the dish out of the wheels, and to set the spokes down into the hubs. I say: "Yes, yes," as Mr. Know it All did, but I take a somewhat different way. I take the tires off, and cut the ends of the spoke pins off with a round chisel at *C C,* in Fig. 183. In Fig. 182 is shown the dish of the wheel as it is when I begin to work. The tire and the hard strain pull the spokes from the hind shoulder of the hub and on the back of the spokes.

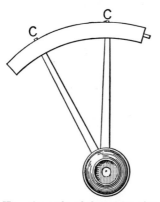

Fig. 183. How the ends of the spoke pins are cut off.

In Fig. 182 will be noticed a small open space, *B B,* large enough to let a knife blade enter half an inch or more. I have a tire stone with a hole in the center large enough to let the hub in. I put the wheel on the stone, face down, and with a three-quarter-inch rod, with a tail screw on top, I begin to screw the wheel down, as shown in Fig. 184.

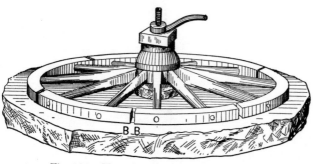

Fig. 184. How the wheel is screwed down.

In Fig. 185 is shown a wooden hammer twelve inches in length and four by four inches, with a long handle. This hammer is placed on the backs of the spokes, when the wheel

Fig. 185.   The hammer.

is on the tire stone, the helper gives the hammer a good blow with another hammer, and in this way I go round the wheel and give every spoke at the hub a good blow. I then

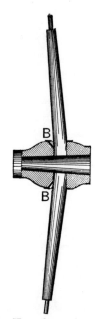

Fig. 186.   How the wedges are applied.

turn the tail screw again, go round the wheel once more or oftener with the wooden hammer, and so keep on until the dish is out and the wheel is straight on the face. While the wheel is kept down with the tail screw I measure from B to B, as in Fig. 184, and give the tire five-eighths inch.

The tire must be almost red hot, because there is an allowance of one inch, and the tires get five-eighths inch. I put water on, and with a sledge hammer walk around the wheel, giving a heavy blow on each spoke, and blow after blow on the tire opposite the spoke. When it is cold, I have driven the spoke into the hub, and the opening into the rim is closed. The wheel is now ready to come out. Fig. 186 shows the dish in the wheel.

When done, this time the spokes are in their places, as shown in Fig. 186 at B B. I make wedges of good hard wood, fasten them with fish glue in the openings B B, Fig. 186, and cut them off even with the hub. I drive up the hub band so that the wedges cannot come out; then the job is done.

The dish is out of Mr. Brown's wheels, the spokes are fast in the hub, and I am not afraid that the tires will come off in three months.—*By* E. K. WEHRY.

Dish of Wheels.

Improperly or insufficiently seasoned timber all through will cause a general shrinkage of the wheel after the tire is on, which means that the wheel will lose its dish. A wheel with the spokes driven without dodging is more likely to change its dish than one with the spokes dodged. The greatest influence exerted on the wheel after it is contracted and tired is by the rim. Its shrinking or swelling will reduce or increase the dish just as often as such changes occur with the rim, as it takes up or throws off the humidity or moisture of the atmosphere. Use a thoroughly seasoned rim. Try and have the spokes of each wheel of equal caliber and weight, and as soon as the rims are finished, give them two or more coats (tread also) of metallic paint (good white lead is the best)—never mind the new-fangled fillers with fancy names—and while you will not wholly overcome the trouble, you will reduce it to the lowest possible minimum.—Bot. Any.

Repairing Wheels, with Criticisms and Suggestions.

The one troublesome part of the carriage is the wheel. It is difficult to make, and when made is subjected to innumerable conditions which impair its durability, and when broken it must be repaired by putting new wood to old in a manner that will insure solidity, and at the same time not weaken the old part by unduly strengthening the portion where the break occurred.

The prevailing idea is that the great point in building a wheel is to insure strength at the hub, as it is popularly supposed that the most breaks occur at that point. This is a mistake. Close observation, extending over a period of several years, resulted in establishing the fact that the breakage of wheels at the hubs and at the rims was as five at the hubs to seven at the rims. The breakage at the hub was due in most cases to the hub being damaged by grease, or rather the hold of the spokes in the hub was loosened by the grease. The breakage at the rim, on the other hand, was due almost entirely to the rotting of the tenon at the rim. The difficulty of repairing, so as to make a good job, is much more marked at the hub than at the rim, because of the grease, which prevents the spoke tenon getting a grip. The first step to be taken therefore by the repairer is to remove as much of the grease from the mortise as possible if a new spoke is to be inserted, and from the mortise and tenon if the old spoke is to be put in. This can be done by strong acids, such as vinegar or beer. These will eat the grease without doing any harm to the fiber of the wood. Alkalies will cut the grease to a saponaceous substance equally injurious as the grease. After as much of the grease has been absorbed as possible, the timber should be allowed to dry before the spoke is driven into the hub. If the old

spoke is to be returned, the chances are that the mortise and
tenon will both be bruised a little. In that case glue a strip
on the back edge of the tenon, leaving enough of the new
wood to fill the mortise, but not to the same extent as if
the hub and spoke were new.

It seldom happens that the sides are bruised to an extent
that will render it necessary to enlarge the tenon on the
sides. But when this is the case, it is .best to use a new
spoke even if the old one is good. But in using the new
spoke it must not be larger than the old, even if the tenon
has to be enlarged both ways. One way of fitting the old
tenon into the old hub is to surround it with wet canvas and
then drive the spoke as tightly as possible. This is a botch
job, one that no man claiming to be a mechanic should allow. It fills the mortise, it is true, but it also helps to bat-
ter the tenon and the edges of the mortise, and as it is a
substance that can be compressed, it works away quickly, and
the second condition is worse than the first.

Old spokes have been wedged in by removing the axle box
and inserting an iron that fills the hole in the hub. The
tenon is then split midway between the face and back, and a
thin, slender wedge is inserted. The spoke and mortise are
then thoroughly coated with white lead, as thick as it will
work. As the spoke is driven in, the wedge comes in contact with the iron case, and as the spoke is driven home, it is
forced up, and the lower end of the tenon is expanded. This
insures a firm hold, but I doubt if the advantage is not
more than counterbalanced by the disadvantage arising from
removing the box. I prefer working entirely from the top,
and where the space must be filled to make the spoke hold,
to fill it with wood, and when driving the spoke, to use as
much pure white lead as I can get into the opening without
interfering with the driving. The white lead will soon harden,
and it will hold all parts better than any other material. It
will also resist water longer.

Where new spokes are required because of the breaking of

the spoke at the felloe or elsewhere, without injury to the hub mortise, care must be taken to clean out the mortise, but not to enlarge it. Fit the spoke snugly and drive in glue the same as with a new wheel.

"It is good enough for repairing," is a common expression when condemning spokes for new wheels. To a certain extent this may be correct, but not to the extent it is too often carried. A straight grained spoke of second or third quality as to timber, will often be the article wanted for repairing an old wheel. But if the wheel is comparatively new, the spoke used for repairs should be as near in quality as possible to the one removed. If the wheel is weakened throughout by wear, a second or third grade spoke should be used, as a first grade will be so much firmer and more rigid than the old spokes as to contribute to their destruction by not yielding in common with the others.

Spokes that have become crooked from any cause are unfit for use, no matter how prime their quality. They can be straightened so as to appear all right, but they will go back to the original bend in a short time, and except for the filling of a gap, they might as well be out of the wheel. The springing of a spoke, unless by pressure, is due to the contraction of the grain on the concave side. If straightened, this grain is simply relaxed and weakened, while the grain on the convex side is as rigid as ever, and it will in a short time assume its former bend.

It is sometimes necessary to replace a broken spoke without removing the tire—a bad practice, but one that is excusable under certain circumstances. To do this, mortise out the broken tenon in the hub to the depth of half an inch, and about the same in the felloe tenon. In both cases the tenons on the spoke should bear upon the old tenon, otherwise the shoulders will crush in and the spoke will loosen. Fit the spoke carefully between the shoulders, and insert the felloe tenon. Protect the hub by a piece of thin band iron. Set the wheel upright and secure it in position with the face o the wall, or, what is better, in a position where one work-man can work on each side of the wheel.   Construct a lever with an opening in the end to admit the spoke, and round the op a little, so that the lever will not bruise the felloe. Nick he underside of the lever, and make the fulcrum with a top nd slightly wedge-shape, and the bottom end hollowed out, o bear upon the hub at the front band.

For carriage wheels the purchase need not be severe, but or heavy wheels a long lever is necessary. In all cases set he fulcrum nearly upright. When the weight is applied to he lever, the tire should be struck with a heavy hammer on ach side, covering a space of two or three feet. This will ssist in equalizing the strain, and will enable the workman o get one-half to three-quarters of an inch spring over the poke. This amount of spring will admit the spoke, which he workman should enter from the back without bruising he hub. As soon as the spoke is in its place, release the ever, and set down the rim by quick, sharp but light blows pon the tire, over the entire half of the wheel where the ew spoke was inserted. I do not favor this springing in of pokes, but it is much better to do this as a temporary ex-edient when the tire is firm and where the facilities for etting a tire properly are lacking, than to cut the tire and ave it reset badly.—*By* W. N. F.

Shrinkage of Hub Mortises.

The general impression among wheelmakers is that, because hub shrinks so as to loosen the hub bands, the mortise in hub naturally shrinks and tightens the spoke. This is a mistake. The shrinkage at the most is but a trifle, but such s it is, is in a direction—when the spoke is in the hub—ot to affect the mortise except in depth, or in the line of he diameter of the hub, as shown by Fig. 187 (page 182).

The shrinkage that takes place in a mortised hub before he spokes are driven, is an entirely different operation. It s a well established fact that timber shrinks, no matter how

well it may have been seasoned, whenever a new surface i
exposed, and that the shrinkage is greatest edgewise of th
rings.   It naturally follows therefore that when a hub i
mortised numerous fresh surfaces are exposed extending t
the center of the hub.   The mortises, as shown by Fig

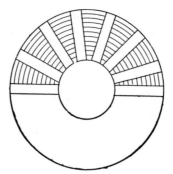

Fig. 187.   Shrinkage of hub mortises.

187, represent about one-half the substance of the hub, and
the cutting is in the direction to expose that part which is
most susceptible to the action of the atmosphere.   The effect
therefore upon the mortises is to·give the sides the form in-

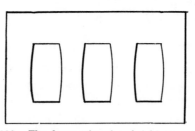

Fig. 188.   The forms taken by shrinking mortises.

dicated (Fig. 188).   In large mortises—one and a half to
two inches—this concaving will increase the width at the center from one-thirty-second to one-sixteenth of an inch.   The
fiber at the front and back being held by the solid wood, yields

but little, and in order to give a correct surface to the sides of the mortise, it must be cut away; otherwise the tenon cannot get the grip necessary to hold it firmly in the mortise. This being the case, it is evidently disadvantageous to mortise the hubs any great while before driving the spokes, for shrink they will, even if they have been seasoned for years; but if the spokes are driven immediately after the mortises are made, the surfaces which would be affected by the atmosphere are covered, and no shrinkage can occur.

If, after the wheel is finished, the hub shrinks, it will be in the same direction as if the mortises had not been made, and as that decreases the diameter, whatever change takes place is in a direction that will tend to tighten rather than loosen the spoke. But any hub that is at all fit for use, is too dry to shrink to a perceptible degree after the spokes are in.

CHAPTER III.

Forms of Mortises and Laps.

As EVERY workman knows, timber shrinks very much
more transversely than in the direction of its length. But
the contraction of a board or plank is not always in the
same direction. It is regulated by the part of the tree from
which it is taken. I have not space here to give the laws,

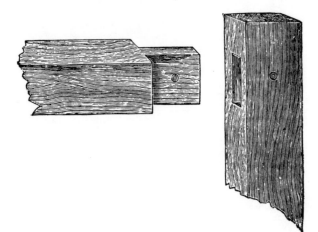

Fig. 189. The tenon and mortise joint.

for there are fixed laws in this as in other branches of science. I will content myself with stating as concisely as I
can their result.

In conversion, a tree always shrinks or contracts in the

direction of its circumference; that is, the wood shrinks more on the outside than at the heart. Thus, if one cuts from the middle of the tree a plank having the heart in the center, and leaves it to dry, there will be but little decrease in thickness at the middle of such a plank; but toward the edge the reduction in thickness will be considerable.

It will also be noticed that this plank does not bend or warp to any great extent. The planks or boards taken from

Fig. 190. The stump tenon and mortise.

that part of the tree next adjoining the heart, will also retain their thickness to a great extent in the middle, and will also evince the same tendency to shrink at the edges; but it will be observed that they are inclined to bend or curve outward from the heart. The planks from the outside will lose little of their thickness, but will show signs of bending still more from the heart; consequently they decrease considerably in width while seasoning.

Thus, if the bodymaker takes the trouble to acquaint himself with this highly interesting subject, he may, by simply examining the end grain of the wood to ascertain from what part of the tree it has been cut, be able to choose and apportion his timber in such a manner that his work will not afterward fail by reason of shrinkage and bending.

A subject that might with very considerable advantage re-

Fig. 191. Tenon and mortise, with beveled or circular shoulder.

ceive greater attention at the hand of those responsible for the conduct of our technical classes is the science of carpentry or joinery, which may be defined as the art of framing timber for the purposes of structures in which any considerable weight or pressure is to be supported.

A brief instruction in the principles of this science, and particularly in that branch which treats of joints, enables a

workman to connect his framing with a due regard to the
nature of the strains the various pieces are intended to resist.

In coach bodymaking there are several complicated joints
adopted that are never seen in ordinary joinery; but again

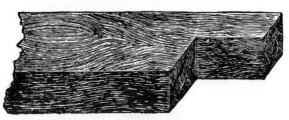

Fig. 192.   Bare-shouldered tenon.

there are other joints in this art that never occur in bodymaking.

Those used in a carriage body are known as framing joints,
the most general being those on the principle of a tenon and
a mortise.

Fig. 193.   A half-lap joint.

Such useful rules as the following are worth remembering:
No joint can be made so good as by its own stiffness or
resistance to motion to add anything to a framing.

The strength of a wooden framework should depend not on the stiffness of joints, but chiefly on the arrangement of the timbers.

No joint should be used in which shrinkage or expansion can tend to tear the timbers. Tenons are best made a third of the thickness of the timber they are cut from.

When tenons have not only to resist lateral displacement, but a strain tending to draw from the mortises, they must be pinned or wedged.

Fig. 194.   Another half-lap joint.

Pinning is the general practice of the coach bodymaker, who drives a wooden draw-pin through both the tenon and the sides of the mortises. He is also careful to see that the grain of the wood at the tenon is not twisted, and that two pins are not driven in the same line.

The accompanying diagrams show examples of the commonest joints used in carriage bodies of various kinds.

The rough sketches are made more with a view to depict the formation of the joint than to represent any part of a carriage framing.

Fig. 189 (page 184) is a fair example of the tenon and mortise, the neatest of all joints.

Fig. 190 (page 185) is a joint in which the tenon is very short, and is known as a stump tenon. It is sometimes used at the foot of a gig pillar.

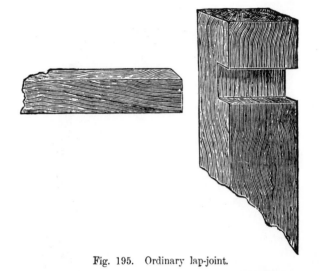

Fig. 195.   Ordinary lap-joint.

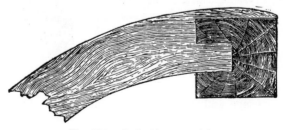

Fig. 196.   A double tenon joint.

Fig. 191 (page 186) is another variety of the same joint, and may have a beveled or circular shoulder, as in the seat rail and pillar of a gig or Stanhope phaeton.

Fig. 192 (page 187) is another variety of tenon, and has only one haunch or shoulder. It is called the bare shouldered tenon.

Figs. 193 and 194 (pages 187, 188) show what is known as the half-lap, now very largely used in cheap work instead of the mortise and tenon.

Fig. 197.   An ordinary miter joint.

Fig. 198.   A rabbet joint.

Fig. 195 (page 189) is an ordinary lap-joint used in inserting battens, &c.

Fig. 196 (page 189) is a double tenon joint, sometimes used in framing the elbows into the corner pillars of such carriages as landaus.

Fig. 197 is an ordinary miter joint, such as is used at the top quarter panel of a brougham to conceal the end grain of the wood.   The adjoining edges are cut at an angle of forty-

Fig. 199.   A groove.

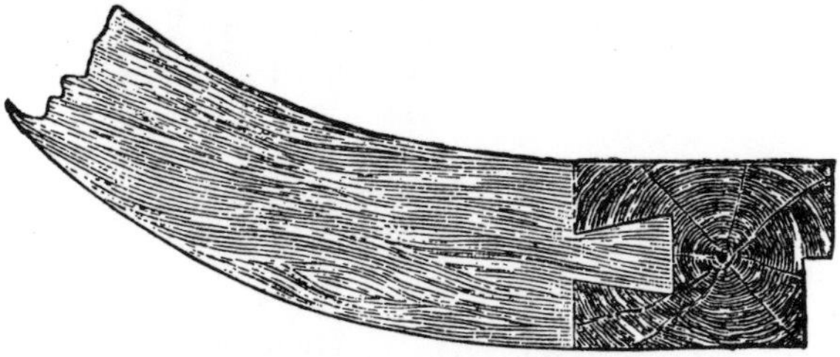

Fig. 200.   A dove-tail joint.

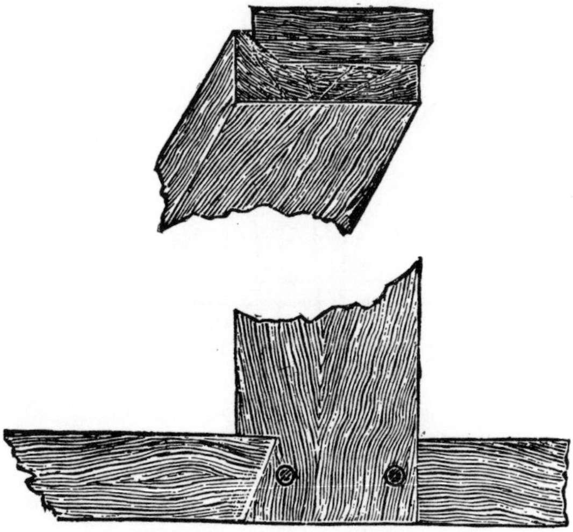

Fig. 201.   Another dove-tail joint.

five degrees.   Fig. 198 is a rabbet joint, a ledge for bottom boards and similar purposes. Fig. 199 is a groove. This is necessary for the insertion of panels, &c.

Figs. 200 and 201 are joints that are used in some instances—the first for fixing a circular front to brougham pillars, and the second in framing the boot cross-bar.—*By* JOHN PHILIPSON.

Carriage Parts.

That part of the carriage called the carriage part, Fig. 202, might with equal propriety be called the plebeian part, for it is that part which does the hard and dirty work, while

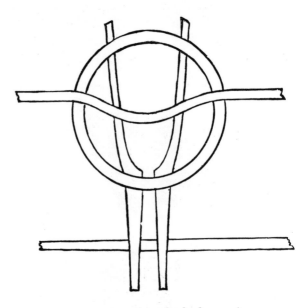

Fig. 202. Plan view of a landau gearing.

the aristocratic body rides upon its willing shoulders. Like all plebeians, its first great need is strength—strength to bear the burdens and endure hardships; and this brings us at once to the consideration of the materials of which it is or should be composed—wood and iron. And allow me to say right here, in regard to wood, that the timber does not grow and never will grow too good for the running part of any vehicle, whether it is for business or pleasure, whether it has wheels or runners.

I include in the carriage part all the gearing which is back of, under, or in front of the body. Especially is good wood needed in whiffletrees, shafts, and poles.

Timber which is good in one part of a carriage may not be good in another. Poplar, or white wood, as it is called, makes good panels, but it would be good for nothing in the carriage part. There are certain qualities imperatively needed in the carriage part, namely, strength, stiffness, and durability. These are primary considerations. Timber must be found that is hard, that is stiff, that is strong. These terms are not interchangeable—they are not synonymous. Wood may be stiff, and yet be brittle and soft. This is the case with forest ash. It is stiff enough for the purpose, but it lacks hardness and strength. The best second growth ash and hickory, all things considered, is superior for this purpose, and it will not do to trust to the name alone. Hickory may be good or may be poor; it may have the qualities which are needed, or it may lack them entirely.

There is nothing which equals American hickory for spokes, light felloes, whiffletrees, and neck yokes.

The finest quality, when under great pressure, can be bent as shown by Fig. 203 (page 194), and even when cold will not break off.

When I said that all wood found under and in front of the body, I meant in all kinds of carriages, light and heavy. And certainly there is nothing, in my opinion, which equals our best hickory for light buggies. Ash will not take its place. Ash is excellent timber and has excellent qualities; but for light spokes, rims, perches, and axle beds we must have hickory.

For side bars I prefer other wood for the reason, or main

reason, that while hickory is the hardest and the strongest,

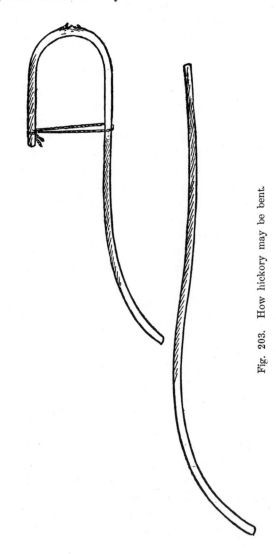

Fig. 203. How hickory may be bent.

it is not the toughest. It has not that spring, that elasticity, that ash or locust or iron wood has. Iron wood seems to be very popular as timber for side bars, and I think justly so.

Soft wood will not do for a carriage part, no matter how stiff it may be. It will yield under the pressure of the bolt head and the clip. If it is a coach bar, and things are loose and shaky, it must be hard in order to hold the iron and the bolts. It must be stiff in order to keep its place, and it must be strong to sustain the strain that is placed upon it.

Twenty years ago hickory was almost exclusively used for side bars. The trouble with them was, not that they lacked toughness and strength, but that they would settle in hot weather.

I think the reason that they settled in hot weather was because they were used mostly in hot weather. Hot summer weather is very damp, and that dampness will affect wood, whether painted or not. I cannot really understand how it penetrates the paint; but it will. In the summer season we have a damp atmosphere, and it also affects the wood, making it more pliable or limber, the same as steam.

When you can find fine grained hickory of equal weight with coarse grain, it is better; and yet as a rule the coarser grained will be the heavier.

I would not recommend coarse grained hickory for spokes if the finer grained could be had. I should not reject a wood because it was coarser grained. If I was going to select the best piece that I possibly could get for exhibition, I should not take the coarse grained. I should take fine grained of good weight. I would, however, only be governed in part by weight. I would take the finer grained first for any purpose about a carriage.

It has been stated that some hickory, grown, for example, in New Hampshire, was so hard that it would check at the spoke when used for rims.

I do not know that hickory will check on account of its being hard. My experience is the harder the hickory the more difficult to split. I would not say that no good hickory grows except in Connecticut; but I do believe that the best specimens in the world grow upon the seashore of Connecticut.

The question of a northern or southern exposure is one I have thought a great deal on. Farmers will come in to us and say:

"We have some excellent hickory. It grew upon the top of the hill where the winds could blow it and toughen it up."

Another one will say he has the very best hickory. It grew down in the valley where the soil was moist and could get plenty of water to nourish it. He has consequently the best hickory in the world. Now, my observation leads me to believe that exposure has very little to do with it. The best and the poorest grow together, even of the same varieties. You may take what we call the shagbark, growing side by side, apparently under the same circumstances and same conditions, and yet the timber will appear to be hardly related at all; so that it doesn't seem to be locality so much as it is individuality of the tree itself. It is something I cannot explain.

As to the best month in which to cut hickory, is a subject I have been considering for many years, and I have watched the timber after it has been cut the different seasons. I have cut for myself in August, September, October, November, December, January, and February, and I can see but very little difference in the hickory cut in those months. I believe any month, after the leaves are matured—after the sap has stopped rising, as you may say, to nourish the growth of the leaves and the new wood—I believe any time after the leaves fall, and before the buds swell, will do.

The main reason why white oak is not the best wood for beds and other carriage parts is that it lacks the element of stiffness. It is strong and hard, yet it never seems to season and become stiff. In bending it is very liable to check afterward, so that it is not advisable to use it in any place about a carriage where it has to be bent. White oak is hard enough and strong enough, and it will resist decay better than ash or hickory. We all know, or those who have been carriage makers do, that oxide of iron is the most destructive thing to timber that comes in contact with it. Oxide of iron and water destroy the life of timber very rapidly. But white oak will resist it better than ash or hickory.

The draftsman in many carriage shops has too little to do with the carriage part. He leaves that to the carriage part maker. The latter has his own ideas, and he is apt to follow them without regard to what the body is; but there should be harmony between the two. Now this is a very important point. If the body was of a light, airy, gaunt appearance, the carriage part should be the same; it should be light, and apparently gaunt and airy. In that respect there is harmony between the two.

Sometimes it is necessary to make the carriage part appear light, and at the same time be really strong and heavy. To do that we must make wider irons, putting on more iron and less wood; but the carriage part should always be in harmony with the body. It is a very important matter, for I care not how well the carriage is made, how artistic the carriage part may be, how stylish the body, how well it may be painted or elegantly trimmed, if there is no harmony between the different parts there will be no beauty in the whole. This is the reason, or one reason, why people sometimes dislike some particular carriage, and yet cannot point any special fault in it. Each part by itself may be excellent, but as a whole they don't like it. Now the chances are it is because it is badly proportioned—the wheel and the carriage part are not in harmony with the body.

In making a carriage there should be one master mind from the beginning to the end. In too many of our shops each department has its own boss, who has full charge of it, and designs his part to suit himself.

We often see a very crooked body on a carriage that is straight. That throws the carriage out of proportion, giving too much wheel in front of the bed and too little back of it. Then we often see the futchells spread so far apart that the carriage is not in harmony with itself.

If I wanted to have my carriage a little different from a hackman's, I would put on a stiff bar and worry the horses. But the experience of men who have been much among coachmen is that our colored brother, who wants very little trouble in driving, favors a swivel bar, but that the best coachman wants a stiff bar, because his eyes are never off his horses, and he keeps them always together. But if in a pair of horses one differs from the other in spirit, it requires constant attention to keep them together. But the lazy man wants to sit at leisure, with slack reins, and let the horses drive themselves.

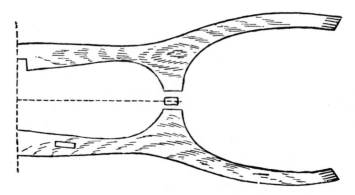

Fig. 204.   Front view of a landau gearing.

We all know that it takes but a small blemish to spoil a very fine picture. It is the same with a carriage.

In the sweep of the sides the most important and difficult part lies between the fifth wheel and the spring on the bottom bed (Figs. 204 and 205). The top and bottom sweeps

at this point incline to conflict with each other and make
the bed small and weak between the bearing of the fifth
wheel and the spring, a point that is called upon to bear

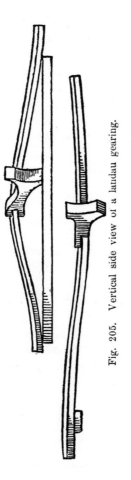

Fig. 205. Vertical side view of a landau gearing.

more strain, according to its ability to bear it, than any other
part of the two beds; and care should be taken to give it
all the strength possible, by giving the bed a good taper

from the fifth wheel to the spring. The center of this bed is supported by the top one, but out beyond the fifth wheel it stands unsupported, with the exception of the stays, and is subjected to the twist that comes when the carriage wheel strikes an obstruction; so we may very often find that right there the carriage part gives out. Carriage part makers, or some at least, do not seem to understand this, and in sweeping the carriage they make the weakest part between those two bearings when it should be the strongest.

Another thing. The carriage part maker will taper his bottom bed on the side and make it smaller or narrower at the point than it is at the center. This is a mistake, for the very reason, as I said before, that this is the weakest point and needs more strength than any other part of the bottom bed.

In sweeping the carriage part and laying out the design it needs to be wide on the bottom. In fact, it should be laid out very much as the Dutchman out West built his fence. He lived in Iowa, where they have those blizzards and tornadoes, where the wind blows like a politician running for office. He was troubled with his fence blowing down, and he conceived the idea of making it wider than it was high, so that when it blew over it should be higher than it was when standing up. Now this bottom bed should be built about the same way. It should be wider than it is high. Then when the iron is put on you will find it higher than it is wide and in good proportion. The carriage part maker should also remember and make his carriage look lank and lean, and remember that the iron is to go on there and fill out what looks like a deficiency. It is very important to get a Rockaway body as low as possible, and that does not give you much room for the carriage part. If the beds are made perfectly straight, it will take about four and a half inches between the body and spring for the carriage part. But if the bottom bed is dropped or sweeped down, the space is increased.

Speaking of this common fault of a carriage part, the bottom bed, in the weakest point, is cut the smallest. In the center there is a great bunch where the king bolt goes through. There is no call for it at all. One point of beauty is to make the work without bunches. The top must be in harmony with the bottom. Those who are desirous of studying this part of the carriage can certainly learn as much from the faults of a badly made carriage part as they can from a well made carriage. They will learn what to avoid, and when that is learned, they have gone a great way toward learning what to do.—*By* W. G. SHEPARD.

Swept Front Beds.

As to why the front beds of some jobs are swept while others are made straight.

To go into a full explanation would require much time and space. I will try to get along without full detail, and think I will be understood. When called upon to construct a vehicle to order, make a sketch or rough drawing of the craft to be built. Next make all calculations as to hight of wheels and springs, length of or track of axles; length, hight, width, and cant of body, and make a scale drawing; and then, to assure yourself that you are right, put a full-sized drawing on the black board to see how it looks, and to again satisfy yourself that there are no errors. Next place the working drawing on the draft board, and go on with the work, satisfied that when completed there will be no faulty construction.

Having learned while making the draft that if you are to

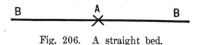

Fig. 206. A straight bed.

make a straight bed, the same as Fig. 206, in which *A* is the kingbolt and *B B* is where the body rests, that with a

narrow front track the wheels would clear the cut under, but
with a much wider track the wheels would strike the cut

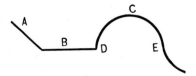

Fig. 207.   The positions of the wheels with a wide or narrow track.

under *E* (Fig. 207), instead of at *C*, which would bring the
front wheel in too close contact with the body.   The bed
could be moved well to the front of the boot *B*, and yet not
clear, and would have to go even beyond and get under the
bracket *A*.

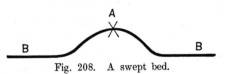

Fig. 208.   A swept bed.

To overcome that make a swept bed, as Fig. 208—*A* kingbolt, *B B* body rests—which, with the wide track, would
bring the wheel at *C*, Fig. 207, center of cut under; while
if you were to use the same bed with a narrow track, you
would bring your wheels at *D*.   As the width of the track is
increased, so must the pivot or kingbolt be set ahead; and
as the track is diminished, so is the pivot brought back by
lessening the sweep in the front.—IRON DOCTOR.

Shortening of Bent Beds.

The propensity of a bent piece of wood to shorten the
cord of the arc is a peculiarity observed by bodymakers in
using bent bottom sides; also by carriage part makers in
working out bent bottom and top beds.   No information,

however, has been given as to what extent bent pieces are thus changed, and therefore data relating to the subject may prove to be of interest to others, as it was to me.

A carriage part maker a few days since brought to me a finished bed that he had worked out a day or two previously, and it had shortened in the way to which I allude. The bed was of ash, coarse, stright grain, and the form fibers of the average for good timber. The bed originally was five inches deep, being of the usual thickness—about two inches. It had been made to finish the full depth of the bed. The two ends were dressed horizontally on the dotted line B, as

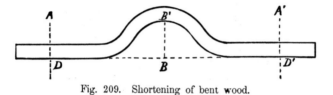

Fig. 209.   Shortening of bent wood.

shown by Fig. 209, with the distance from B to B four and a half inches. The distance from A to A was thirty-seven inches. When brought to me the distance A A measured thirty-six and five-eighths inches, showing that the bed had shortened three-eighths inch, and the distance B and B had increased from four and a half inches to four and eleven-sixteenths inches. The horizontal line B of the bed had not changed materially. One end was perfectly straight, while the other had changed slightly. Let D be supposed to be the end that had changed. By placing a straightedge against this face, it was found that it failed to touch the face D′ by about one-eighth inch. Owing to the fact that but one end had changed from the horizontal, the inference was drawn that the change was due more than anything else to the natural inclination of timber to spring.—By JEFF POTTER.

Cutting the Bevel on Express Shafts.

One job that has given me some trouble to get right is cutting the bevel for express wagon shafts, and especially double bend shafts. My way now is to clamp the top sides of the shafts together, as shown by Fig. 210, and then with a straightedge mark across the ends of both of them, which will give a square mark to work from. Then I cut the top

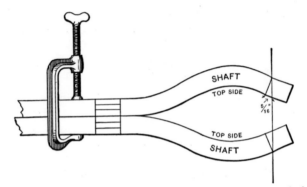

Fig. 210.   Stewart's method of cutting the bevel on express shafts.

side five-sixteenths of an inch shorter than the straightedge mark. That will be right for any ordinary job, and both shafts will hang alike at the fronts.

Some have a form to mark by, but that takes up room in the shop, and the less of such things any one has around the shop and in the way the better.—*By* J. D. STEWART.

Flaring Seat Corners.

Dress up boards for back and ends. Joint the edge that is to be used for the bottom. Gauge the outside for beveling, but do not bevel it until after the joints are laid out and cut. When two different bevels are to be used, as, for example, when the back is to be of the bevel indicated by line 1 in Fig. 211, and that of the ends is to be as shown

by line 1, Fig. 212, two bevels should be used, each being
set to its own proper angle at the outset, and not changed.
Place the stock of the bevel for the back against the edge of
the drafting board A, so that the blade lies against the point

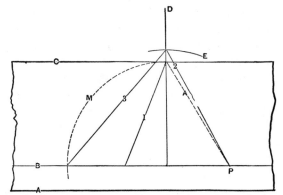

Fig. 211.   Laying off the width of board and obtaining the lines of bevel
for the back.

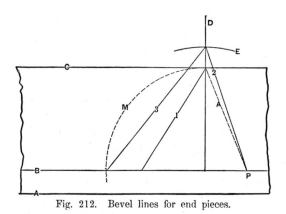

Fig. 212.   Bevel lines for end pieces.

of intersection between the perpendicular D and the line C,
and draw line 1, prolonging it until it meets the line B, all
as indicated in Fig. 211.   This will give the width of board
necessary to use in order to give the seat a straight hight

equal to the space between B and *C*. Set the dividers with
one foot at the intersection between lines 1 and B, and the
other at the point of intersection between lines 1 and *C* and
D. With the dividers thus set for radius, from the point of
intersection between *D* and B as center, describe a short arc,
cutting *D* as shown by *E*. This operation will give the required width of board upon the perpendicular line *D*. Since
the upper edge must project as much as the ends, bevel off
at the same hight, place the stock of the bevel set for the
ends against the edge of drafting board *A*, so that the blade
lies against the point of intersection between lines *D* and *C*,
as shown by the dotted line *A*. Mark the intersection of the
dotted line *A* with B, as shown at *P*, and draw line 2, extending from *P* to the point of intersection between the
short arc *E* and the perpendicular *D*. This gives the bevel
for the fore-projection an actual width. Set the dividers with
one foot at the intersection of lines D and B, and the other
foot at the intersection of lines D, *C*, and from the former
point or center describe the arc *M*. From the point at which
the arc *M* meets the line B draw the line 3 to the point of
intersection between the short arc E and the perpendicular
line D. This will be the bevel for a square miter. All the
lines by which to set the bevels for cutting the joints on the
ends of the back are now obtained. Next lay out Fig. 212
by which to cut joints on the ends in the same general manner.
The only difference to be observed is to substitute one bevel for
the other; that is to say, where the bevel for the back was
used, as above described, use the bevel for the end, and *vice
versa*.

After this has been accomplished, the next work requiring
attention is the shape of the blocks for bracing the corners.
The bevels required in these parts are illustrated in Fig.
213. Use lines B, *C*, and D, as already described. Place the
bevel as set for the back against the drafting board, so that
the tongue shall lie against the point at which *C* and *D* intersect, and draw line 1. Next place one point of dividers

at the intersection of lines *B* and *D*, and the other point at the intersection of lines *B* and 1, and from the former, as a center, describe the arc *T* in the figure. Place the bevel set for ends on the drafting board so that the tongue rests against the joint where the curve line *T* and the line *D* intersect; mark the point *S* and form dotted line *A*. Then take the

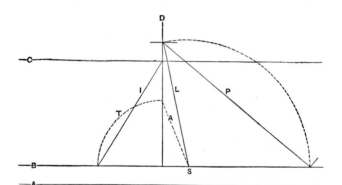

Fig. 213.   Bevels for the blocks to brace the corners for the construction shown in Fig. 214.

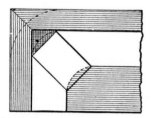

Fig. 214.   One form of constructing the corner braces.

length of line 1, and lay off from the *B* on *D*, and draw the line *L* from the point of *S*, so as to intersect with *D* at the point on *D*, the exact length of the line 1.

The next step is to lay out a draft of the work, which may be done as follows:

Set the bevel by line 2, Fig. 211, and place the stock

against the bottom edge of the board; for the back, mark across the side of the board. Then set the second bevel by line 3 of Fig. 211, and placing the tongue or blade on the side, make a mark across the edge. Next take the first bevel, place it on the mark on the edge, and mark the opposite side. Measure the length from outside to outside required at the bottom on the gauge mark, which was made for build-

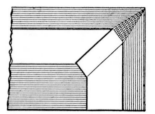

Fig. 215.   Another method of constructing the corners.

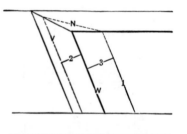

Fig. 216.   Measurements for laying out the form of corner block shown in
Fig. 215.

ing the bottom edge, and lay out the same as the first end. Proceed in the same manner for the ends, using the bevels set by lines 2 and 3 of Fig. 212. After the work has thus been laid out and the joints cut, bevel off the bottom edge a little scant, so that the parts will stand in, say a quarter of an inch in the width. The effect of this is to hold the joints close when the work is put together.

To get out the blocks for the corners, set the bevel by line *L* of Fig. 213. For the cut on the bottom ends, set one bevel by line 2, Fig. 211, and the other by line 2, Fig. 212. This operation will form a corner, as shown in Fig. 214. To make a corner as shown in Fig. 215, when laying out the back and end, make a mark on the inside of the bevel, as line 1, Fig. 216. After the miter is cut, gauge the dotted line *V*. Take the corner as drafted in Fig. 213, and place the line *P* on the line *B*, as shown in Fig. 217. Other lines of the first corner, same as corresponding letters, show position.

Next make line 2 of Fig. 216 at right angles with the gauge line to the corner *W*. Take the length of line 2 and

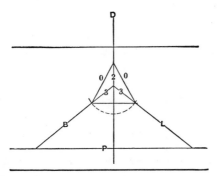

Fig. 217. Bevels for laying out the corner block shown in Fig. .215.

add on to line *D* of Fig. 217, as shown above the first corner. Next make line 3, Fig. 216, at right angles to corner of miter marked *W*. Take the length of line 3, and mark down on lines *B* and *L* of Fig. 217 the same distance. Strike lines from the points thus obtained upon *B* and *L*, to mark of hight raised on line *D*. Next cut the second bevel off from the ends from lines *V* to 1, as shown by the dotted line *N* in Fig. 216. To make the corner block set the bevel by either line. As already explained, this operation forms the corner shown in Fig. 215.   * * *

Laying off Corner Seats.

The best way to cut corners for flaring seats is to miter them. Now, a flaring miter may seem hard to cut. On the contrary, it is easy to cut if you only know how.

In the first place, determine the required flare. Get that bevel on a piece of board and cut to the line. Square from

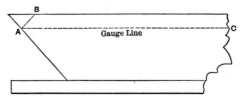

Fig. 218. "Steel Square's" method of getting the corners for flaring seats.

that cut down to one corner (the long corner), and cut it off from the thickness of the stuff on the corner that is cut. Get a regular miter and saw up through by the first cut. Then gauge it to straighten the corner that is cut off. By this means one end of the shape required will be obtained.

Referring to Fig. 218, square off the corner as shown at *A B*, and then cut a common miter.—STEEL SQUARE.

An Arrangement for a Bakery Wagon.

A customer of mine had a fine bakery wagon with curtains at the sides, but he thought that doors with a glass window would be better. He wanted me to make them so that he could open them from the inner or outer side. The doors were made of hickory, one and a quarter by three and a half, and the windows were at the top as shown in Fig. 219. B, Fig. 220, represents the lower track on which run the wheels. It was of iron and attached to the bottom of the bed. The dimensions were one by one-quarter inch by five feet eight inches, and there were five angle irons welded on it. *A* in Fig. 220 represents the upper track. It was one by a quarter inch by five feet eight inches, and had five loops welded

on it so as to bring the bolt holes above the guides in the
door at the top.   The guides at the bottom also were run on

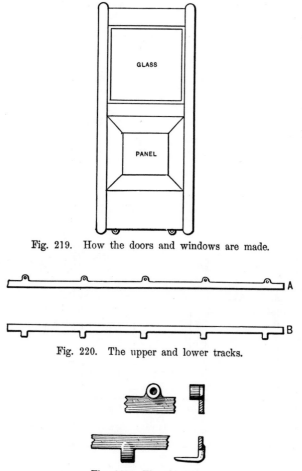

Fig. 219.   How the doors and windows are made.

Fig. 220.   The upper and lower tracks.

Fig. 221.   The thimbles.

each side of the lower track.   The upper track was held out
from the top by means of five thimbles five-eighths-inch long,

as shown in Fig. 221. A quarter-inch bolt ran through the track and thimbles and into the lower rail of the top.

The rub lock was on the outside, as indicated in Fig. 222, and I had to move it out of the way of the drawers *B*. I

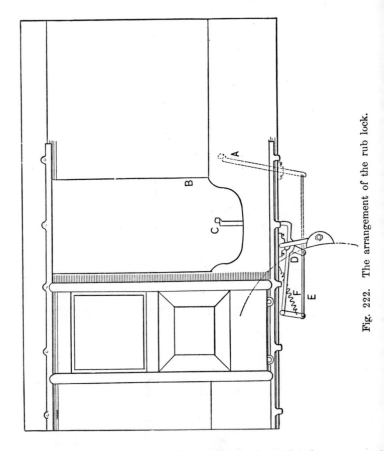

Fig. 222. The arrangement of the rub lock.

made a back-action rub lock, so that when the foot was put on the loop *C*, that would move down. The loop ran under the block rod at *D*, and was attached to the bed back of it, and connected with it by the rod *E*, so that by bearing down it C, the rod E was pulled back. The block on the wheels F, is a spring to throw the lock off the wheels.

I think that this arrangement would be a good one for makers of bakery wagons to adopt. It is useful in cold weather, and allows the driver to get in and out quickly.— *By* G. W. P.

How to Make a Wooden Axle.

A great many wheelwrights who make wooden axles do not know how to shape them so that the wagon will run light. Out of sympathy for man's best friend, the horse, I will attempt to show how to make an axle so that it will make a wagon run easily.

I will suppose that the axle is for a box of four-inch butt and two and a half inch point. Such an axle should not be used for a hub of less than twelve inches. First set the butts of the hubs together and measure from the outside of the spokes. I will say, for convenience, that they measure fourteen inches. You want your wagon to track five feet two inches to the outside of the felloes, the latter being two inches wide.

The stick you use to make the axle of should be five by four and a quarter inches square. You must allow for length of hub the measure of fifty inches from shoulder to shoulder. The most important part is the setting. The wood being straight on the under side, you must measure one-fourth of

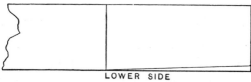

LOWER SIDE

Fig. 223. How the bottom is cut.

an inch from the bottom, as in Fig. 223, and cut away.

Then measure four inches from the under side to the top and two and a half inches from the point up, as in Fig. 224

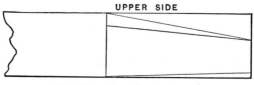

Fig. 224. How the top is cut.

Then cut. Then you have the top and bottom sides of your axle.

The next step is to get the sides. Your wood should be four inches wide. Cut one-third off the front side and two-

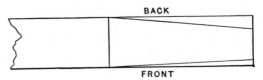

Fig. 225. How the sides are cut.

thirds off the back side, as in Fig. 225; or, as it is four inches, cut one-half from the point and one inch from the back. That leaves two and a half inches point, the size of the box. Now round up to fit the skein, and with this axle you will have a light running wagon.—*By* A. B. C.

Putting in Axles and Getting a Plumb Spoke.

A trestle that may be useful to some of my fellow-workmen is represented by Fig. 226. It often happens that we have to put axles on old wagons that are broken or worn so badly that it is difficult to get the exact length without fitting up and measuring, which is the "fit and try rule," as some would call it.

By the use of this trestle all we have to do to get the length is to hang the wheels on the spindles *C,* lay the track stick *D* across the top of the wheels and measure on *A* from box to box in wheels, which will give the length of axle on the bottom from shoulder to shoulder.

To make the trestle, take a piece of wood three by four feet, plane the top straight and level, and taper the bottom up so that it will not bear on the box. Then let in and

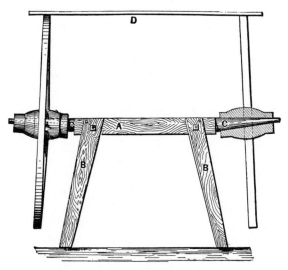

Fig. 226.   Trestle designed by J. L. P.

bolt or mortise four legs long enough to raise the highest wheel you use off the floor.

If you wish to work to a plumb spoke, make two long thin wedges of hard wood and slip them in on the top of *A.*   If the wheels are badly dished, you will need the wedges at the point of the hub; if straight, at the back of the wheel. The bottom of the axle will be "out of straight" in proportion to the thickness of the wedges where they touch the box.— *By* J. L. P.

Putting in Wooden Axletrees.

I have a good rule for putting in wooden axletrees. It is as follows :

Take the dish of the wheels from the rear end of the hub box to the face of the felloes, and deduct the amount from five feet two inches. Stand your wheels up, so that they will stand on a balance that will give the swing of wheels. Add half of this swing to the balance of the five feet two inches, and that will give the length of the axletree between the arms. Then take a straightedge with a hole in it; get the length of the hub from one end and measure from that half the hight of the wheels. Put a nail in the hole in the straightedge and down in the bench, and move the straightedge up from there a quarter of the swing of the wheels. Then measure to see how much it has moved at the other or hub end of the straightedge; measure that down on the axletree from the center of the large box for the center of the small box. That will give the crook of the arms, which will make the wheels stand on a balance so as to run very easily.

To make this method perfectly plain, I will repeat the foregoing directions in a slightly different way.

In doing this job the first thing to know is how wide you want your wagon to track. I make my wagons to track five feet two inches from out to out. The next thing is to take the dish of the wheels from the back end of the hub box (not the band) to the face of the felloes. Put a straightedge up against the felloes and on the face. Measure from the back of the box to the straightedge; also measure both wheels. Add these measures together. Ordinary wheels measure about eight and a half inches. Twice that makes seventeen inches. Take that amount from five feet two inches and that will leave three feet nine inches. Then stand your wheels up against the bench to get the swing of the wheel. Ordinary wheels swing about six inches. Now add half the swing of the wheels, which will be three inches, to three feet nine inches, and that will make four feet between the shoulders of the axletree.

The accompanying illustrations will be of great assistance in understanding my plan. Fig. 227 shows how the straight-edge is used, and Fig. 228 shows how to fix the length of the axletree between the arms.

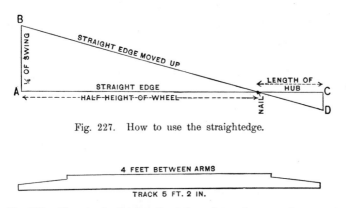

Fig. 227. How to use the straightedge.

Fig. 228. How to fix the length of the axletree between the arms.

To get the gather of the wheels, set your compasses one-eighth of an inch nearer the front side of the axletree from the center of the large box to the center of the small box. This is for the rear wheels. For the front wheels set your compasses for one-eighth and one-sixteenth.—*By* W. L.

Making a Wagon Run Well.

I claim that, except in width, the rim has nothing to do with the mortises, and the center of the box for a wheel with one and a half inch tire should be three-quarters of an inch back of the front of the mortises, or half the width of the tire. This will always throw the center of the box over the center of the rim, no matter how much dish the wheel may have, provided it is set properly on the spindle. I think a wheel standing plumb will have a tendency to run in a circle or slip on the ground, for the wheels are propelled by the axle, and the axle tapers from the shoulder to the point both on the front and bottom. The draft forward tends to crowd the wheels against the nuts. As to throwing mud on a muddy road, if built with three-quarters of an inch dish and set plumb, supposing the wheel to sink to the hub (allowing one and a half inch for width of tire, three-quarters for dish and three-quarters for taper in spokes), it would cut a rut at the top three inches wide. And this is not the worst feature of such a wheel, for the spokes stand on a pry, each wheel crowding the opposite one; and for this reason the skein will wear on the point at the bottom and front, and at the shoulder on the top and back.

A great many seem to have an erroneous idea of what a wheel is given gather for, and believe it will slip on the ground in proportion to the gather given. Such is not the case. I admit that a wheel may be given too much gather, and in that case would slip on the ground the same as one set without any gather. I build all wheels with three-eighths of an inch dish, set them on a plumb spoke (not a plumb wheel), and give them one-quarter to three-eighths of an inch gather, according to the dish they have.—*By* H. L. CORDREY.

INDEX.

PRACTICAL

CARRIAGE BUILDING.

Containing information regarding Axles, Plumbing of Spokes,
Gather of Wheels, Making Yokes and Whiffletrees, Laying off
a Fore Carriage, Special Tools, Making Ovals, Blocking
Corners, Making and Laying Off of Patterns, Draw
ing Tools, Complete Instructions regarding the
Laying Off and Framing of Carriage Bodies,
Construction of Carriage Parts and
Wheels, Light and Heavy Sleighs.

COMPILED BY M. T. RICHARDSON,

Editor of " The Blacksmith and Wheelwright," "Practical Blacksmithing,"
" Practical Horseshoer," etc.

PROFUSELY ILLUSTRATED.

VOLUME II.

NEW YORK:

M. T. RICHARDSON COMPANY, Publishers.

1892.

CONTENTS.

CHAPTER I.

CHAPTER II.

CHAPTER III.

CHAPTER IV.

CHAPTER V.

CHAPTER VI.

CHAPTER VII.

CHAPTER VIII.

CHAPTER IX.

CHAPTER X.

PREFACE.

In preparing the second volume of Practical Carriage Building, the Publisher has kept in view the importance of placing all matters in a clear, simple light, stripping descriptions of working of all doubtful or blind meaning, and condensing each specific article into the smallest space possible without robbing it of the points necessary to make it understood.

The opening chapters are given up to a series of articles by practical workmen upon pertinent subjects, illustrating such points as will aid to make their meaning understood by the most unskillful mechanic. Following up this latter idea, the balance of the book—complete in text and profusely illustrated—is devoted to special instruction in connection with the woodshop.

The day of the "cut and try" rule has passed, and the man who hopes to become a good workman must have some information regarding drafting, and also a general knowledge of working from the scale up to the full size drawing. It is not possible for all workmen to learn the French or geometrical rule for drafting and laying off patterns, &c., but all may obtain information as to the leading points, and by studying their application to each class of work, they can master many jobs which otherwise would be entirely out of their reach. To meet this condition, and to aid any workman who may be willing to devote a few hours to study, the entire field has been traversed, beginning with the simplest instruction regarding the selection of drafting tools, making draftboards, laying off and arranging patterns, and placing the full size drawing upon the draftboard.

To make the subject clear, the simplest vehicle receives the same attention as the most complex, and the names of all pieces are plainly printed on the respective parts, thus avoiding the necessity for referring back to numbers or index letters. All the minor details of working are described in the simplest language, especial care having been taken to avoid technical terms. This is best for all.

Attention has also been devoted to the peculiarities of the timbers used and their value for each part of the vehicle, particularly the combinations of woods used in bodies.

To make the book the more valuable to the small factory, space has been devoted to carriage parts and their construction, points regarding wheels, and a very complete line of sleighs.

The aim has been to make the work one of great value to the younger workman, but it is believed that it can be studied with profit by the trade generally. In short, the book affords much useful information, and hereafter there will be less excuse for a lack of knowledge on the subject of carriage building.

                                        THE PUBLISHER.

NEW YORK, June, 1892.

PRACTICAL CARRIAGE BUILDING.

CHAPTER I.

Thimble Skeins.—Plumb Spokes.—The Gather of Wheels, &c.

To Lay out a Thimble Skein Axle.

PLAN ONE.

As THE width of track varies in different localities, I will present a rule applicable in all cases Take the distance from center to center of track, and from it subtract the length of one hub. The remainder will be the distance from shoulder to shoulder. After the stick is ready to lay out, strike lines across it where the shoulders are to come. Mark the diameter of the inside of the thimble at the shoulder on these lines, measuring from the bottom upward. Find the center of the diameter, as shown by A in Fig. 1 (page 8) and through this point strike a line parallel with the bottom of the axle. Measure back from the shoulder on this line fully one half of the diameter of the wheel. You thus obtain the point B. Place a straightedge on the wheel, as shown by dotted line C. Measure from the straightedge to the center of the spoke at the hub and at the rim. Use the front spoke when the spokes are dodged. Take the difference between the two measurements, and set off a like distance from B upward, as shown by $B D$. Then strike a line through D to A, continuing it to the end of the stick. The point at which it cuts the end of the stick E will be the center of the arm at the front.

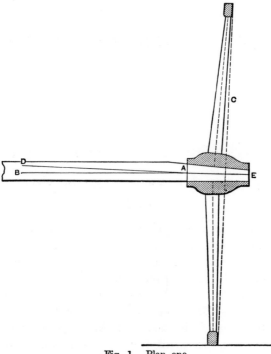

Fig. 1.   Plan one.

Fig. 2 shows an arm laid out for a thimble skein that has so much taper as to make it necessary to take off something

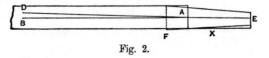

Fig. 2.

from the bottom of the stick at the front. If, however, we take off the wedge shape from the front back to the shoulder at *A*, the skein will not be filled back of the shoulder on the bottom. So we must measure forward of the shoulder the same distance as shown by *X*. This point *X* is so located that the skein will reach back of the shoulder, and raise up the arm center line the same distance that the bottom line is above the bottom of the stick at *X*. By this means the taper to take off from front back the full length of skein is determined.—*By* D.

PLAN TWO.

My way of laying out the work in question is as follows: Take two pieces of thin board about four and a half feet long and five inches wide. Fit them into the skein, thereby getting the shape of the same. Lay off the track on the floor. Drive the pieces snugly into the skein and put on the wheels. Set them to the track, bringing the patterns together and fastening them with a clamp. This accomplished, try the wheels to see if they stand on a plumb spoke and are square with each other. If they are not correct, change by loosening the clamp and raising or lowering one of the other patterns. Mark the patterns at the shoulder. Screw them together firmly and remove the skeins. Lay the pattern on the stick for axles, to mark, to cut off and mark for shoulder. Dress the bottom of the axle, getting the shoulders out of wind. Lay on pattern in proper position and scribe around it. Work the bottom to mark. Find the centers of the shoulders, and make a straightedge from end to end. By means of a try square mark across ends from the center mark. Set the compasses to size of inside of skein at point, setting centers a little more than a sixteenth of an inch in front of the mark at end. If the axle is larger at shoulder than will fit the arm, work down equally on each side of the center. This may appear like a long description, but it shows the quickest way of laying out an axle I have ever seen.—*By* HAME.

PLAN THREE.

My plan for laying out an axle is to strike a center line through the butt boxes from one end of the axle stick to the other. Then I measure back from each butt box or shoulder of axle half of the diameter of the wheel. I set off from the bottom of the axle stick on the center line at the half diameter, the dish of the wheel, a half inch, a three-quarter inch, or one inch, as the case may be. Then, with a straightedge, put on dish mark, and run across the center line at the shoulder on to the point, I scribe a line which becomes the center line from which to work. With the compasses, set to half of the diameter of each box. I lay off the

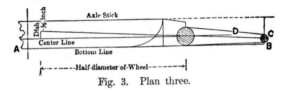

Fig. 3.   Plan three.

spindle on this line, all as illustrated by Fig. 3. This throws the wheel on a plumb spoke, or, in other words, the spoke stands vertically or at right angles with the bottom of the axle.—*By* YOUNG MECHANIC.

Making a Wagon Run Well.

What I understand by a perfectly running wagon is one that enables all the power of the team to be exerted in moving the load forward, none being called for to overcome unnecessary friction. In order to make such a wagon, the first thing necessary is to properly determine the width of tire and dish. Suppose we have a three-quarter inch dish and a tire one and a half inch wide; then we must next find a suitable hub—that is, a hub with the mortises in the right place. This is a very important point, because if the mortises are not properly placed, it will be impossible to construct a perfect wheel. In the case now being considered, the front part of the mortises must be in the center of the box—that is, where the center will be when the box is put in; so that when the wheel is finished and set up plumb on the edge, a line drawn from the center of the tire on top will pass through the center of the box to the center of the tire at the bottom where the wheel rests on the ground.

The wheels should all be plumb—that is, the same distance apart at top as at bottom. I am not taking the matter of plumb spoke in consideration just here at all, but am referring simply to the position of the center of the rim or tire in respect to the center of the box. This wheel will not need any gather. I take the same off the bottom and top, and also the same amount off the front that I do from the back of the axle. The wheel should set in this position—that is, plumb, for various reasons, among others—

1st. It will not have a tendency to run out in a circle, as some seem to think it would, for there is no weight outside of the center to draw or pull it around in a circle.

2d. This wheel will not slip on the ground, as all wheels do that have gather. If each wheel is given a three-eighths inch gather, allowing nothing for play on the spindle—supposing the wheel to be sixteen feet in circumference—the shoulder will have to push the wheel out; or, in other words, will cause the wheel to slip three-eighths inch sideways every four feet that the wagon moves, and consequently calling for much more force to move the load. Then the outside of the back part of the tire would throw mud on a muddy road in proportion to the depth of the mud. If the mud was up to the center of the wheel, it would throw out three-eighths of an inch of mud, and would cut a track in the mud three-eighths of an inch wider than a wheel with no gather, because a straight wheel would run without throwing any mud. The back would come out where the front went in.

3d. The tire sets flat on the ground, as all know a tire

should; and it is impossible to set the tire flat on the ground if the wheel is not set plumb.   I say the wheel—not the spokes. You never see a tire set at a right angle or square with the spokes, except in a wheel that has no dish.

One will claim that the wheel should have enough gather to make the revolving wheel run against the shoulder in front.   This is an error, because it causes too much friction on the ground and shoulder.   The wheel must play back and forth from the shoulder to the nut continually, to run perfectly.

Another thinks that the least gather a wheel or axle has, without dispensing with it entirely, the better the result, and suggests one-eighth of an inch for buggy wheels.   I am inclined to think that is about correct, because there are but few buggy wheels which have more than one-eighth of an inch play, and practically this would be no gather, as the wheel would naturally run straight forward.   I am aware that most wheels are not properly constructed, and a great many are so badly made that no man can make an axle so that they will run properly.

This is the principal cause of the different opinions as to the amount of gather.   A man will put an axle into an imperfectly constructed wheel, setting the under spoke plumb, perhaps throwing the top of the wheel out two or three inches, and the bottom of the wheel perhaps two inches too far out or too far in; and in order to remedy this, he gives more or less gather.   The mistake is in supposing that if an axle is properly constructed, any kind of a wheel will run on it.

I learned my trade with an "old fogy," who had a certain rule for all wheels and axles.   His wheels had about one and a half inch dish.   A line passing from the center of the tire, from one side to the other, would miss the center of the box some two inches.   His axles were all straight on the bottom, and he always took off a half inch more on the back of the spindle than on the front for gather, and the consequence was he had a strong wagon. It would take about one horse to pull the wagon over an ordinary road, and the mud would be turned out as if a turning plow were at work. Of course these were wooden axles.

A line or a straightedge, placed against the back part of the hind wheel, even with the hub and on the front part of the fore wheel, ought to touch the front of the hind wheel, and the back of the fore wheel. As to the 'Plumb Spoke' matter, we all know that practically there is no such thing, because our roads all throw the wagon higher at one side than the other. The spokes on the lower side would be under too much, and those on the upper side would be out too much.—*By* M. J. S. N.

How to Get a Plumb Spoke.

The device shown by Fig. 4 represents one that I have used for a number of years, and have found it to work well in all cases. In making it I select a stick suitable for an axle; plane the front and bottom sides perfectly true from end to end. Then I find the center of the stick endwise, and mark it on the top and bottom sides. I then insert an arm in the center, and secure it firmly by a brace. Next I measure up from this arm four and a half inches. Then again twenty-one inches, and a third time twenty-three inches. I then bore holes at each of the three places, fit and drive in pins, *D D D*, about twelve inches long. I next measure and saw off the pins, leaving them seven inches, in the clear, from the post, making sure that the ends of the pins stand at a right angle with the arm. I then place the wheel on the arm, with the face of it toward the post, press its face against the pins, and shove a wedge in at the opening on top of the arm at the outside, until the space is filled, but no more. The wedge should be rounded on top to fit the box. When the wedge is in, and I am sure the face rests against the pins, and that the front of the box rests on the arm, I then mark the wedge with a pencil against the box, take the wedge

out and get the size of it at the mark with the calipers. I
then know what should come off the bottom at that point.
I next take a skein and place it in the wheel with the bottom side up, take a large pair of calipers, open them wide,

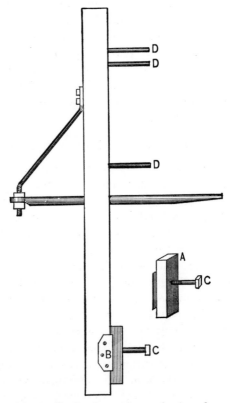

Fig. 4.   Device for getting a plumb spoke.

place one prong on the end of the box at the bottom, pass
the other prong between the spokes, close the calipers on the
front side of a spoke, close to the hub, and screw them up
tight. I next place the axle in the vise, with the bottom side

up, measure from the mark previously made in the center, twenty-eight inches for a narrow track, and make a mark; then take the calipers as they stood with the last measurement, place one prong on the last mark made twenty-eight inches from the center, let the other prong strike the axle toward the center, and mark by driving the scratch awl well into the wood. I then take a square and mark the axle on the four sides even with the last mark, and drive the scratch awl into the wood on each of the other three sides, for this is where the skein must come to, and a pencil mark would be cut out in rounding up. I next measure the length of the skein inside on the bottom, measure the same distance out from the scratch awl, mark on the bottom of the axle, and saw the axle off. I then have the neat length of one-half of the axle.

To get the gather, bore holes in the post twenty-four inches and twenty-six inches from the arm below, and place pins in them loosely, so that they can be taken out. To give a one-quarter inch gather, make the lower pins a quarter inch shorter than those above. Place the wheel on the arm, as before, with the face in, press it against the top and bottom pins, and fit the wedge in the opening over the arm as before. Now, if it is a ten-inch box, measure ten inches from the place marked on the axle for the shoulder, toward the end of the axle, and by using a straightedge, cut the axle down on the front side from the shoulder to the point, until the wedge will pass under the straightedge, or between the straightedge and axle, ten inches from the shoulder. If the box is longer or shorter than the one just referred to, always measure the length of the box from where the shoulder will be, and cut down until the wedge will pass between the axle and straightedge, and you have the gather. Instead of pins, I use below the arm a movable block, as shown at A, Fig. 4. This block is four by four inches by six inches long, and works in the flanges shown at B. The small holes at B receive pins which hold the block at any desired hight.

The bolt at *C* is a common skein bolt, which can be screwed in or out to give any desired gather. The pins, *D D D*, can be stationary, but must be at a right angle with the arm— that is, a square placed with the short end on the arm should touch the faces of all the pins. By placing a straightedge against the pins *D*, and letting it extend past the arm to *B*,

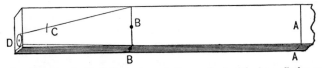

Fig. 5.   Showing half of the axle and the method of laying off the end.

the skein screw can be set for any desired gather. In Fig. 5 *A* is the center of the axle; *B B* is where the shoulder comes, or the places punched by the scratch awl; *C* is the mark ten inches from the shoulder, where the wedge must be fitted to give the gather.

After the front and bottom are tapered to give the gather and pitch, set the compasses on half the size of the skein at the point inside, and lay off the end of the axle, as shown at *D*. Now round up and fit the skein, but be careful not to take any off the front and bottom, except to round. To make it smaller, take something off the back and top. All the wheels should be measured in the same way, as the dish may vary.

For a wheel with a quarter inch dish and one and a half inch tire, the center of the box should be set half an inch back of the front of the mortise. If the boxes are set properly, the variation will be but little. As each wheel is measured it should be marked, so that after the work is painted the mark may be found and the wheel placed where it belongs.

Large wagon factories generally use patterns for all work. It is more convenient for them to do so, and they can get the work almost perfect, because most of it is done by machinery, and consequently every piece is made in accordance with the standard measurements of the factory in which it is manufactured.—*By* H. L. C.

Getting a Plumb Spoke.

My apparatus for getting a plumb spoke is shown by Fig. 6.

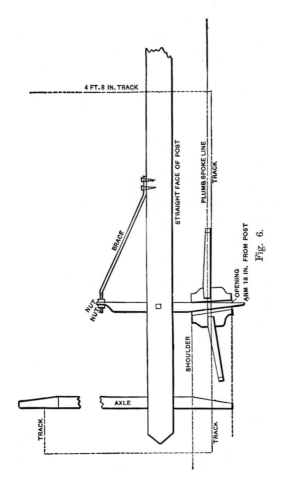

Fig. 6.

It consists of a post with a straightedge face, an iron bar put through it, with the top edge at a right angle with the face of the post, and at the back end of the bar, a brace passing through it, with nuts to regulate it and keep it at the proper angle with the face of the post. The front end of the bar is drawn out small enough to allow a light buggy wheel to hang upon it.

Now to get a plumb spoke, hang on a wheel, heavy or light, with much or little dish, tip it either way until you get a plumb line through the center of the spoke and *parallel* with the face of the post. The *opening* made on the bar at either end of the hub by plumbing the spoke, gives the pitch for the axle arm. From this we get the rack, the length of axle, length of arm, and all that is required to make an axle.—*By* S. W. K.

Plumb Spoke.

Some wheelwrights seem to think that when a spoke is plumb, the wheel must be the same width at the top as at the bottom or tread. My idea of plumb spoke is different, and I will try to explain it with the aid of Fig. 7.

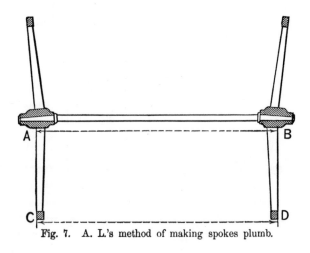

Fig. 7.   A. L.'s method of making spokes plumb.

I don't think it makes any difference where the spoke sets in the hub. It may be in the center or not. Neither does it matter whether the front of the spoke is in the center of the box or not. I think the face of the spoke should stand plumb from the hub to the felloe. The distance from face to face of the spokes should be the same at *A B* as that from outside to outside of the felloes at *C D*. The gather should be half the width of the tire; that is, if the tire is one and a half inch, the gather should be three-quarters. I mean by this that the wheel should be three-quarters of an inch nearer together in front than they are at the back.

This is the proper rule to follow, and it makes no difference how much or little dish the wheels have.—*By* A. L.

Plumb Spoke.

I don't think the plumbness of a spoke has much to do with the matter, because all really depends on the box and rim. In a wheel properly constructed, a line from the center of the tire on one side to the center on the other would pass through the center of the box (Fig. 8, page 20), which represents a straight wheel. If designed for a tire one and a half inches wide, the front of the mortises in the hub should be three-quarters of an inch nearer to the point than to the center of the box. This throws the center of the tire and center of the box in a line, as shown by the dotted lines.

In Fig. 9 the front parts of the mortises in the hub are in the center of the box. This gives three-quarters of an inch dish for one and a half inch tire.

Fig. 10 represents a heavily dished wheel, in which the fronts of the mortises are back of the center of the box, but the center of the tire is in line with the center of the box. Now set the fronts of these wheels plumb, that is, as wide apart at the top as at the bottom, and the same distance apart in front as at back, that is, with no gather, and I defy any man to tell the difference in the run of the

wheels. They will all run equally well on the same axle, but
of course will require different length of axles to give the
right tread. The idea that the gather of a wheel is governed
by the dish, I cannot understand. I cannot see any reason
for it.

A wheel and axle constructed on this plan will run without that slipping on the ground sideways, common with all
wheels that do not run straight forward, and the tire will
run flat on the ground, not on one edge, and will not have a
tendency to run in a circle. In the illustrations *A B* represents the spokes. *C* is the center of the box from the point
to the back, and the dotted lines in each figure show the
center of the tire and the box.—*By* **M. J. S. N.**

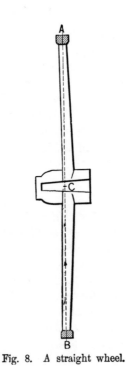

Fig. 8. A straight wheel.

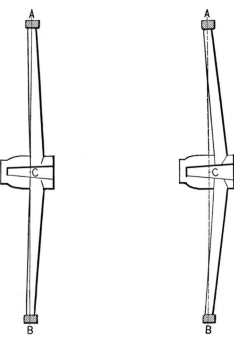

Fig. 9. A wheel in which the front part of the mortises are in the center of the box.

Fig. 10. A wheel in which the front part of the mortises are back of the center of the box.

What Constitutes a Plumb Spoke.

There appears to be a marked difference in opinions as to what a plumb spoke really is. I have my theory, which I will try to make plain.

In Fig. 11 the spoke is shown on a plumb line from its center. The spoke is on a plumb line from its center. The wheel is a four foot one; the spoke is one inch at the shoulder, and the rim is seven-eighths of an inch. Now an examination of this cut shows that the square touches the spoke at B, two and a half inches below the hub. A one-inch, properly tapered spoke at the point shown at B, on

the top end of the square, will be found to be about seven-
eighths of an inch.   Now the rim is seven-eighths of an inch
wide, and where the square touches at *B* the spoke is seven-
eighths of an inch wide.   Now place the wheel on a level
place and set the square against the rim and spoke, as in

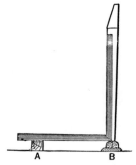

Fig. 11.   The T edge of the square on a line with the center line of the spoke.

Fig. 11.   When the bottom of the square touches the rim
and floor, and the top of the square is against the spoke at

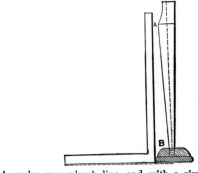

Fig. 12.   A spoke on a plumb line, and with a rim much wider than the
spoke.

a place the width of the rim, as in Fig. 12, then a plumb
spoke is obtained.

My starting point in testing axles and getting a plumb spoke is the center line of the under spoke. This is fully explained by the illustrations herewith.

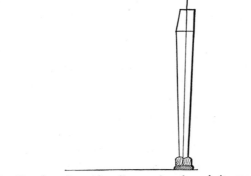

Fig. 13. A spoke with a line passing through its center.

In Fig. 13 I show a spoke with a line drawn at right angles, the line passing through the center of the spoke. Now this spoke stands on what I would call a plumb spoke.

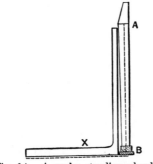

Fig. 14. A spoke standing plumb.

In Fig. 14 is seen another spoke standing plumb at *A*. This spoke is one inch at *B*, the rim or felloe is seven-eighths of an inch wide. The tire measures seven-eighths of an inch between the round edges, or one inch with the round edges from out to out. Now the square touches the tire at B and the spoke at A. The dotted lines passing through the center of the spoke show the plumb line from the middle of the spoke. This cut proves that the tapered end of the spoke has nothing to do with the getting of the plumb line.

In Fig. 12 is shown a spoke on a plumb line, and the rim is represented as much wider than the spoke. In getting a plumb line in such a case, I generally draw a line through the center of the line with a pencil, as shown by the dotted lines; then I measure from the outer line to the edge of the square, and when the distance from the center line on the spoke and the line of the square is the same between A and B, then I have a plumb spoke. Another way to get it when the rim is wider than the spoke, is to draw a line through the center of the spoke, as shown in Fig. 12; place on the floor a block of the same diameter as the felloe, put the square on this block, and let the T edge of the square come on a line with the center line of the spoke, as shown in Fig. 11.

There are many things to be taken into consideration in setting axles, but I think I have now said enough to make myself fully understood on the subject of getting a plumb spoke.—*By* H. R. H.

The Gather of Wheels—Plumb Spoke.

I have experimented on thimble skein setting for the last twenty years, and among other things have learned to throw the point of the skein so far forward that when both wheels are placed on the axletrees they will measure across the front side three-quarters of an inch less than on the back side—in other words, three-eighths of an inch to each wheel. To get an exact measurement, the wheels should be perfectly true. I believe this plan is the best, because by adopting it the shoulder and nut will wear alike.

I prefer having the wheels set under a quarter of an inch from plumb spoke for the reason that the first time the tires are reset the wheels stand out, and then the wagon does not run as well as before.   Besides, when a wagon is set on plumb spoke, and is then loaded heavily and run over a rough road, the axles must spring a little, and then it does not run well. —*By* C. B.

Plumb Spoke and the Gather for Wheels.

I think there is no universal rule for plumbing a spoke. Some wheels have more dish than others, and as regards plumb spoke, why, that simply means a level tire, that is, a tire resting level on the ground, whether the spoke is plumb or not.

The gather should be enough to insure that the revolving wheel runs to the shoulders of the spindle in front, and does not carry dust or mud outside, at the hind part of the tire on the ground. Those who work with wheels have to be governed by the dish in the wheel. For instance, if we have a buggy axle to repair, and one wheel has more dish than the other, then the spindle in the dished wheel must have more gather than the other, so as to overcome the dish, and the point must be set lower, to get a level tire. My way of doing this is as follows:

Take a wheel with a half inch dish, axle one and a half at shoulder, seven-eighths at point of arm, six inches long, straight on bottom, and with the center line at the point dropped an eighth of an inch. This will give a four-foot wheel, with a half inch dish and plumb under spoke, the rim standing out from the carriage one inch more at the top than at the bottom. In this example the front part of the wheel should stand in more than the back side at hight of axle exactly half an inch—no more, no less—though allowance may be made for deflections when at work. In the above example there are no extremes or ill proportions, and no good point thrown away. The more dish the more gather,

and the lower the spindle or arm. Properly setting axles re
quires practice and no little study, but a spindle that has to
much gather will not run as easily as one that has not enough
The first thing to do is to get the hind axle square with th
wheels or pull.—*By* M. T.

No Gather for Wheels.

I think a wheel or axle should have *no* gather, that is, th
front and back of a spindle should be beveled the same, s
that the rims of the wheel on an axle will be the same dis
tance apart at the front as at the back. By setting them i
this way the wheel will run straight forward without press
ing against the shoulder or nut; neither will there be an
slipping on the ground, as is the case when the front of th
wheel is set in or out more than the back.

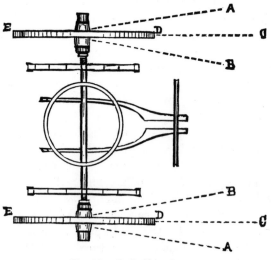

Fig. 15.   J. S. N.'s theory.

Fig. 15 will serve to make my meaning perfectly clear. I
the point of the spindle were set back too far, the wheel

would run in the direction indicated by *a*, if the nuts did not pull them in. If the spindle were set forward too much, the wheels would run toward *b*, if the shoulders did not push them out. In both these cases there is friction, in one against the nut, in the other against the shoulder, and besides the tire slips on the ground, causing the wagon to run heavily. But if the spindles are beveled as much in front as at the back, the wheels will run straight forward toward *c*, and there will be no slipping on the ground or pressure on nuts or shoulders.—*By* J. S. N.

The Gather of Wheels.

The theory that a wheel should have no gather, would be without fault if wheels were built straight, like a wheelbar-

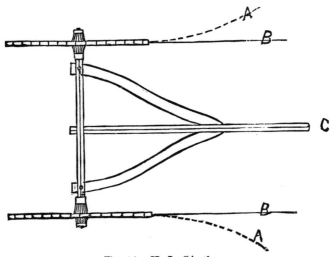

Fig. 16.   H. L. C.'s theory.

row wheel, and the boxes were straight instead of tapering, but such not being the case, we must counteract these peculiarities by giving a gather.

To explain my theory, suppose you start a hoop rolling,

you will notice as long as it keeps in a perpendicular position it will roll on a straight line, but as soon as it leans to one side, it will form a circle toward that side. Now the same principle applies to a wheel built with a dish. When it is set on the axle with the spokes square under the axle, the top of the wheel will stand out, consequently the wheel will follow the line A, Fig. 16 (page 27); or, in other words, it would form a circle if the nut did not hold it in. Again, the front of the spindle is higher than the shoulder, which will make a wheel, when loaded, incline to push out against the nut, but by giving gather enough to counteract those two forces, the wheel will follow the line B. If J. S. N. will take the hind gearing of a wagon and place a dished wheel at C, set it on a true stroke without gather, and then push the gearing from behind, that wheel will describe a circle, or I will give up my theory. It will be found that the more dish the front wheel has the smaller the circle will be. I set new wheels with three-eighths of an inch gather to the wheel.—By H. L. C.

CHAPTER II.

Making Neck Yokes.

NECK YOKES are an important factor in the wagon shop. They can always be purchased of dealers, but the wagonmaker who has power and lathes can make it profitable to produce them in his own place. Yokes for wagons vary in diameter from two and an eighth to three and a half inches in the center and thirty-four to fifty-four inches in length, the gradations being by one-eighth of an inch in diameter and two inches in length. The bulk of farm wagon yokes are thirty-eight inches in length and two and a half inches in diameter in the center. The long yokes are either for heavy draft teams or for light trotting.

The following table gives the proportional diameters of centers and ends, also the width of pole strap collar:

Center.	Strap.	Ends.
1 3-8 inch	2 5-8 inch	7-8 inch
1 1-2 "	2 5-8 "	15-16 "
1 5-8 "	2 3-4 "	1 "
1 3-4 "	3 "	1 1-16 "
1 7-8 "	3 "	1 1-8 "
2 "	3 "	1 3-16 "
2 1-8 "	3 "	1 1-4 "
2 1-4 "	3 "	1 5-16 "

Yokes made for the trade are generally turned green, and the result is that they are seldom true. A better plan is to **block** out the green stuff and turn up when seasoned. Blocks should be about a quarter inch larger in diameter than the yoke is to be when finished. With the proper appliances, turning is rapid work. A good workman can turn from one hundred and twenty-five to one hundred and fifty a day.

The patterns are a matter of taste, but it is necessary to maintain correct proportions. To facilitate the work, scratch

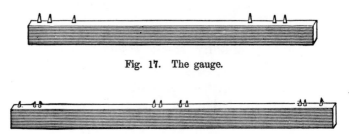

Fig. 17.   The gauge.

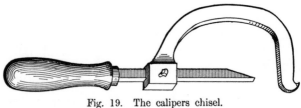

Fig. 18.   A gauge used for small work.

gauges, Fig. 17 for wagon yokes and Fig. 18 for small work, are a great assistance, and as they are little trouble to make, one should be on hand for all lengths. If an extra scratch point be in the center, it will aid materially in quickening the work.

The timber used should be of the toughest kind of second growth hickory or white oak—split, not sawed. The tools used do not necessarily differ materially from the regular turning tools, but a few special ones can be used to advan-

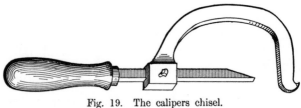

Fig. 19.   The calipers chisel.

tage, as the calipers chisel, Fig. 19. This is specially advantageous for turning the ferrule parts. If two are used, absolute uniformity can be obtained in much less time than in any other way.

Fig. 20.   A popular style of yoke.

Fig. 21.   Another popular yoke.

Figs. 20 and 21 show popular patterns for farm wagon yokes, but in turning care should be taken not to cut below the bead at the collar. A little nick at that point will greatly weaken the yoke. The large majority of yokes are weakened by the spur cut, as indicated by *A A*, Fig. 22, and a still

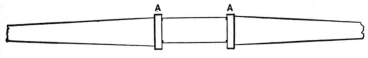

Fig. 22.   The spur cut.

greater number by being too small at *A*, Fig. 22. When too small at that point, the whole strain is concentrated there, and when a break does occur, it is apt to be at that point. The wood there should not only be larger, but there should also be no square corners. A slight concave from the collar will not only give a good finish, but it will also secure greater strength.

Figs. 23, 24, 25 (page 32) show three styles of buggy yokes. Fig. 24 is the most showy, but Fig. 23 is the best. The beads, &c., weaken without adding to the beauty. The color of the hickory does not materially affect the durability, but where they are to be finished in wood, white hickory must be entirely free from stains.

Care must be taken in seasoning to prevent springing.

Fig. 23.   A popular neck yoke for a buggy.

Fig. 24.   Another popular yoke.

Fig. 25.   A yoke for tips.

After turning, it is a good plan to dip the newly turned wood into warm linseed oil.   This will prevent checking, and will increase the durability.

An Improved Whiffletree.

The following is a description of a new whiffletree, made by myself.   It seems to be a decided improvement on all others.

Fig. 26.   W. G. T.'s improved Whiffletree—wooden part.

Fig. 26 shows the wooden part complete, ready for the irons.   Fig. 27 represents the irons.   *A* is the staple, which is welded on.   Fig. 28 shows the improvement embodied in the complete whiffletree.   The wooden part acts simply as a spreader, and there is therefore no strain in the center, where a break generally occurs.

I make the iron work in the following manner : I take the size of iron that is in due proportion to the whiffletree to be made—one-half or one-quarter inch, half round—and cut off a piece long enough to go the entire length of the

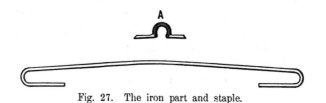

Fig. 27.   The iron part and staple.

back of the whiffletree, and take the hooks at the ends, and also the bolts shown in Fig. 28, and cut the piece off long enough to upset at the center, where the staple is in Fig. 28, so that it may be heavy enough for a weld there without becoming smaller. I punch two quarter inch holes for the bolts, and then bend, as shown in the cut. I then forge

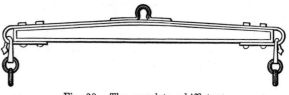

Fig. 28.   The complete whiffletree.

out the staple *A*, and weld it on in two heats. I next bolt the irons on at the ends, and the job is completed.

There is no patent on this that I am aware of. I invented it myself, and have never seen or heard of anything like it. When drawing a load the iron in the center is pulled away from the wood.—*By* W. G. T.

Making Whiffletrees.

Owing to stocks of whiffletrees kept by dealers, wagonmakers need not, from necessity, make up any of the rounds; bnt for heavy wagons rounds are too heavy and clumsy if the diameter is sufficiently large to give the required strength. It is necessary therefore that the wagonmaker be prepared to make such as he may need and cannot buy. Then too there is a serious objection to many of the ready-made, particularly the ovals. They are turned from sawed stock, and are therefore weaker than they should be, owing to the cutting across of the grains and the positions of the grains themselves.

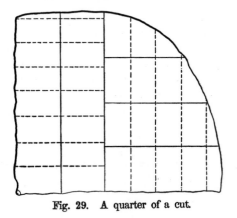

Fig. 29.   A quarter of a cut.

Fig. 29 shows the method of sawing from a qnarter section, Fig. 30 from a rived piece, and Fig. 31 from a half log. The best results are from Fig. 30, but even in it many of the pieces have the grain inclined to edgewise, but as riving out. Such large pieces cause great waste. It is an advantage to saw as shown by Fig. 31.

The timber should be fine second growth hickory or white oak. Occasionally forest oak can be found of quality sufficiently good for doubletrees and the heavier singletrees, but nothing but butt logs should be used. One point to be considered is the density, straightness, and uniformity of the grain.

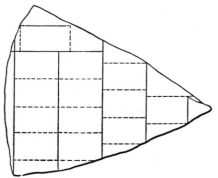

Fig. 30. How a cut is split into seven or eight pieces.

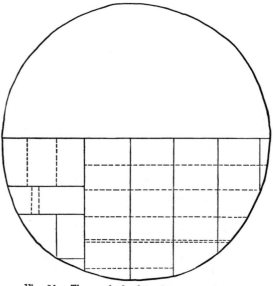

Fig. 31. The method of sawing a round stick.

It is exceedingly important that buggy singletrees should

be sawed properly and split, especially if they have been turned green. If not done properly, the ends will be all kinds of sizes and shapes. In fact, not the ends only, but the whole singletree will shrink in seasoning so as to make a variety of shapes and sizes. Many of them will be ill-shaped, scarcely resembling the original design. The grain should be uniform—that is, it should cross each singletree the same way. If this point is not attended to, the shrinkage tending so much more to decrease the circle of the grain than to contract it, will have results well known to the trade. It is better to have the grain cross each singletree in the same direction, even if they are to be seasoned before turning. I do not say they will be stronger from the arrangement referred to, but it will certainly prevent much warping and twisting if the grain is either square across—what is better known as a bastard—or if the grain crosses the singletree the thin way up and down. Both ways are

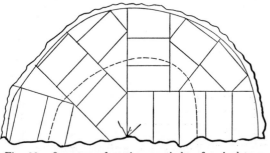

Fig. 32.   One way of cutting up timber for singletrees.

shown in Figs. 32 and 33, which represent two halves of a stick of timber. The circular, dotted lines separate the white from the red wood. If the timber has, say three inches of white, then Fig. 33 represents much the better way, as it can be noticed that the white is used to greater advantage. Fig. 32 is from a half of a cut—two less all-white singletrees than in Fig. 33.

The timber should be thoroughly seasoned, without steaming or artificial heat of any kind. If split or sawed, the pieces should be piled up under a shed, protected from sun or rain, and not nearer the ground than two feet. After being piled up for six months, the pieces may be rough

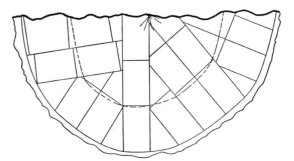

Fig. 33.   A better method of cutting.

turned and assorted. If dipped immediately after turning into hot linseed oil, no damage will afterward result from worms.

Very few small shops have facilities for turning, particularly for turning ovals, and as these can be purchased turned, there is no particular necessity for incurring the expense of putting in machinery. But if power is to be had, an emery belt, as shown by Fig. 34 (page 38), is the thing.

A very common and quite an objectionable custom with many manufacturers is that of turning their timber green and seasoning it afterward. This practice results in the production of a variety of shapes, some round, others too flat, others oblong or of the ellipsis shape. This is occasioned by the grain crossing the singletree in various ways, sometimes parallel to the flat part, at other times diagonally, as it may happen. There is but little shrinkage from the bark to the heart. A very coarse, thrifty growth stick will shrink more than a brush stick or one of a spongy appearance,

Figs. 35 and 36 represent the ends of two singletrees, one turned green, the other from seasoned timber. The contrast will be more noticeable after the ferrule is cut.

Buggy singletrees are made from one and three-eighths inch wide across the face or flat part to two and a half inches by

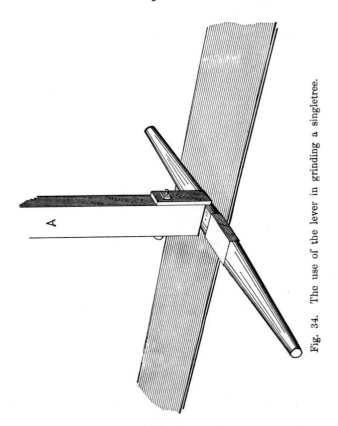

Fig. 34. The use of the lever in grinding a singletree.

one-eighth inch. The leading sizes are one and three-quarters and two inches, principally forty inches long, although some are made only thirty-six and thirty-eight. A very good proportion for a one and three-quarter inch singletree is one and three-quarter inch wide by one and three-eighths inch thick, by one inch round at point, perfectly straight on the back.

There are quite a variety of patterns to suit the different ideas of the purchaser. The square center and square ends are quite popular on the Pacific coast. They make a neat singletree. Then there is the sword point singletree, with the end tapered down to one-half by one and one-eighths or one and a quarter.

Fig. 35.   The end of a singletree cut from green timber.

Fig. 36.   The end of a singletree cut from seasoned timber.

A well shaped singletree has a taper on three sides. The top or back of the singletree should be straight. A medium sized singletree is one and three-quarter inch wide across the flat part of the center by one inch at point, making three-eighths taper on each side of the point, flatwise of the singletree. It should be one and three-eighths inch thick at the center, three-eighths taper from the point to the center on the bottom side.

Making a Runner Barrow.

I have an article in use of my own invention that may be of service to others. I call it a runner barrow. It is made of one and a quarter inch plank, eleven inches wide, and planed at the lower edge to fit the shoe to be used. The

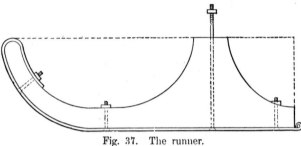

Fig. 37.   The runner.

runner can be sawed out, as shown in Fig. 37, or can be left in the shape indicated by the dotted lines. The length of the runner is twenty-six inches; the ground bearing is twenty-one inches. The main bolt is one-half inch iron, and is ten inches from the back end. The arm of the axle is made as

Fig. 38.   The axle arm.

shown in Fig. 38, the material being one and one-half inch plank, two and a half inches at center and tapering at the end, to take the ferrule, as on a wheel. A slot on the flat side in the center fits the top of the panel, the main bolt running through fastens them together when hung at *B*, as shown in Fig. 39. This throws a large part of the load on the runner. Or you can exchange the runner for the wheel in the wheelbarrow, and you will have an article that is far ahead of any sled for winter work. It will run in foot-path or sleigh-path with ease and without turning over, and will carry a heavy load. The axle on mine is eighteen inches long. You can make it any length you wish.—*By* E. W. J.

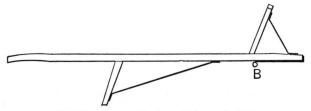

Fig. 39.   The application of the main bolt.

Making Wooden Emery Wheels.

To prepare wooden emery wheels, I procure a suitable block of wood for making the wheel—pine wood is good for the purpose—and bore a seven-eighths inch hole through the center. I then turn in the lathe a wooden mandrel of a size to fit tightly in the hole. I next drive the mandrel into the hole, the block is again placed upon the lathe centers and turned truly and with a parallel face. I next saw across the

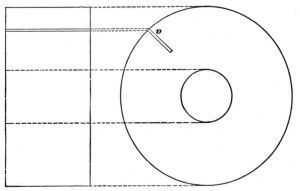

Fig. 40.   E. H. W.'s method of making wooden emery wheels.

face of the wheel to a depth of a half inch, as at *a* in Fig. 40,

Then cut emery paper (cloth is better), into strips the width of the face of the wheel, and of a length sufficient to reach around the wheel and into the kerf. The ends of the paper are secured in the kerf by small wooden wedges. The circumference of the wheel should be proportioned so there will be no waste of paper. When one piece of the paper is worn out, another can be quickly inserted.

This device can be used on the lathe for polishing after the rough grinding is done on the grindstone. It is very serviceable and cheap, but probably will not answer the requirements of a commercial scale of business.—*By* E. H. W.

Melting and Using Glue.

Glue, as received from the factory, is dry and brittle. It, however, absorbs moisture readily, and is quickly affected by atmospheric heat, and because of this buyers are often deceived as to its quality, condemning it if it breaks easily, and approving it if it will bend and show a white line on the fold. These tests are of little value, owing to the causes above mentioned.

In warm, humid weather a piece could be bent double without breaking, while in dry, cold weather, the same piece would break into a score of pieces, if bent. The only absolute test is in melting. The glue then being reduced to a liquid state, develops its adhesive properties so plainly that the merest novice can satisfy himself as to its quality. If, when boiling, there is the slightest disagreeable odor, it is evidence of decomposition, and where that exists, it is a sure indication of weakness.

The one test, when dry, is clearness. If, on holding a piece up to the light, it appears clear and free from spots, it is a pretty sure guarantee that the quality is good, but if there are dark spots, they indicate the presence of foreign matter, and are proof positive of an inferior quality. But it matters little how good the glue may be, if it is not melted properly. To do this, break the glue up in small pieces, put it into an iron kettle, and cover it with clean water. If the broken glue is thus covered, it will absorb the entire amount of water in about twelve hours, and have the appearance of a thick jelly. Then boil, without additional water, the glue kettle being set into the outside water kettle. It will not do to melt over a dry heat, as heat from the fire or from a lamp direct upon the kettle holding the glue tends to dry and harden that part in direct contact with the iron, and thus destroy all its adhesive properties.

After the glue is melted, it is a good plan to pour off a portion into an air tight box, and set it aside for future use, though, except in winter, we would not recommend keeping it more than twenty-four hours.

Before using the melted glue, dilute with clean, boiling water, reducing it very thin. Most woodworkers use glue too thick, so thick that it spreads over the surface and does not penetrate the wood, and when two pieces are glued together, there is a film of glue between them, whereas the surfaces of the wood should come in contact and adhesion be secured by the hold the glue has in the fibers. Just how much water glue will require to give it the requisite strength, is a matter that must be determined by the workman, as there is a great difference in glues in this respect; but it is safe to affirm that more trouble arises from having the glue too thick than too thin. While using the glue, if it stands long enough to thicken, dilute with hot water. Every time water is added, up to a certain point, new strength is imparted.

Quick drying glue is not to be recommended. It is, as a rule, the weakest when dry, and is liable to get set while using and before the joints are properly drawn together. Some workers heat the wood before applying the glue. This is wrong, as there is a liability, particularly when the surface glued is large, that the heated wood will too quickly absorb the moisture before the glue penetrates the wood. The surface of the wood may be moistened with hot water. This should always be done when putting on large panels. Apply the glue to both surfaces, but not more than can be taken up, except in cases where the surplus may escape when pressure is applied.

Glue exposed to the atmosphere loses its strength very rapidly, even when boiling. Every user of glue knows how quickly the surface of hot glue becomes covered with a thin film, which must be removed. This film is produced by the action of the air upon the boiling glue, and no matter how often it is removed, a new film will form immediately. To overcome this trouble in part, the kettle should be provided with a lid.

Glue brushes should be of different sizes and of good strong bristles. The fiber brushes are poor substitutes for those of bristles, as the fiber breaks easily and sheds the broken hairs, thus fouling the glue.

Never melt fresh glue in a kettle containing any old cooked glue, as the latter will surely injnre the new. A dirty glue kettle is the rule; but the man who gets the best results, will be as careful of his glue pot as he is of his dinner plate.

To Determine the Location of the Front Carriage and the Length of the Perch.

Many bodymakers, not conversant with the French or square rule, experience difficulty in finding the proper cut-under, or obtaining the required location of the king bolt. Fig. 41 illustrates a simple rule, one that can be readily understood by any workman, and one that will not fail them. To lay off, draw line *A*. Then with the compass strike a circle *B*, the full size of the wheel. Next draw line *C*, representing half of the length of the axle and arm at the tread of the felloe at *D*. Then ascertain the dish of the wheel, and the location of the top of the rim at *E*. With the point of the dividers set at *a*, which represents the center of the king bolt, and the pencil point at *D*, strike line *b* up to where it intersects line *A*. Then, without moving the point,

set the pencil at *G*, and strike line *c*, carrying the circle up
to line *A*, and extending a parallel line from that point to
line *H*. This gives the swing of the outside of the rim at
center of its hight. Next, without removing the point, strike
line *d* from *E*, the top of the wheel, carrying the straight
line up to line *M*. The three points thus ascertained, give
b the line traversed by the tread of the wheel. The line *d*,
followed by the back of the wheel, is at its center, and the
line *c*, described by the wheel at its topmost point. Having

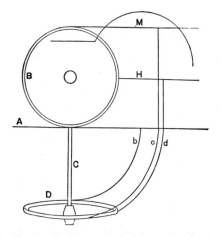

Fig. 41. A simple rule to determine the location of the front carriage and
the length of the perch.

these three points together, with the hight of the wheel,
there need be no difficulty in locating the cut-under or the
front carriage or length of perch. Fig. 42 (page 46) will,
however, serve to make the application plainer. In this the
bottom line of the *A* boot, the cut-under *B*, and a portion
of the coupé pillar *c*, are shown, together with the wheel *D*
and the axle *E*, in their respective positions, when the body
is hung off. Added to this is given the ground plan, with
center line of body, the outside of the boot *G*, the nick *H*,

and the side sweep *K*. Having these arbitrary lines established, the workman applies the rule as above. Placing the
point of his dividers at *a*, which represents the center of the
king bolt at the center of the axle, he strikes the dotted line
b, and discovers that the top of the wheel will strike the
cut-under *B* at 1. He next, from the same center, strikes
the dotted line, which describes the segment of the circle
made by the back of the rim at its central point from the
ground, and learns that it will come in contact with the

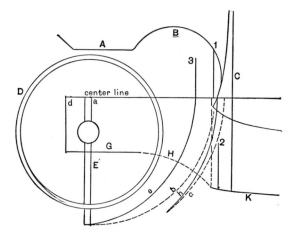

Fig. 42. A more detailed illustration of the same rule.

lower line of the cut-under at 2. These lines show that the
body cannot be hung off in that manner. Either the carriage part must be carried forward enough to allow the wheels
to pass under the cut-under, without coming in contact with
the body, or the king bolt must be placed further forward.
As it is desirable to have the carriage part as short as possible, the change is made by using bent beds, and thus throw
the central or turning point forward of the axle. To determine just how much this point must be moved forward, place
the point of the dividers on the center line at *d*. Then set

the marking point as before, and strike line *e*, which describes the line traversed by the top of the wheel. Terminating at 3, it leaves ample room for the wheel, without endangering its contact with the body. Then from the point *d* describe line *h*, the line traversed by the back of the felloe at its central point, this line being clear of either the elevation or plan lines of the body. This bend of the bed is equivalent to four inches; if moved forward six inches, lines *e* and *h* will be moved forward and give greater clearing space without liability of interfering with the front of the boot.

This rule can be applied to all vehicles, and with a knowledge of it, no carriage blacksmith can have an excuse for the wheel striking the body.

A Hint about Grinding Tools.

Good tools are an absolute necessity if the workman is to perform his work in a satisfactory manner and in good time. By "good tools" is meant those of which the cutting parts are made of the best quality of steel, and the wood portion of correct shape. Ornamental work and high polishing are not necessary. A saw blade of fine quality is just as serviceable, set onto a good beechwood handle as on a rosewood handle. So too with any other tool. Correct shape, proper weight, and fine steel are the essentials for the respective parts; but even with all these, if the cutting edges are not properly ground, the tools are of little service.

The carriage bodymaker is called on to work all kinds of wood, hard and soft, and for convenience sake he must grind the various tools to a bevel which will insure the easiest working with all kinds of woods. With the exception of chisels, no two bodymakers will agree as to what is the correct bevel. This is due to the fact that scarcely any two can be found who carry the tools alike, and the position in which the tool is held, must govern to a certain extent the bevel of the cutting edge.

For general use chisels should have a bevel of about forty-five degrees. The broad, firmer trimming up chisels may have a little more, as they are seldom subjected to blows from the mallet, but mortising chisels should have less, for if ground too thin, they are liable to break in the mortise. It is therefore impossible to lay down any fixed rule for the bevel, but the workman soon learns which bevel best suits his position and manner of holding, and having learned that, the next point to be ascertained is to grind in such a manner as to retain the standard bevels. To do this, it is necessary to provide rests for supporting the tools. These rests consist of sliding bars placed upon grooved uprights, the bars having at least two inches in depth upon which the tool rests. When the bevel is upon the stone, with such a rest, the workman has but to hold the tool firmly in place until the required amount of metal is cut away. In all cases grind with the edge toward the line of revolution, and unless there are nicks or other defects, do not grind so as to turn the edge of the metal.

The grindstone should not be allowed to run in a trough of water, as the action of the water tends to wash off all loosened particles, while the stone is in motion, and to soften that portion which is allowed to stand in the water when not in use. A bucket with a spicket so arranged that it will supply the necessary amount of water when in use, and which can be moved when not needed, is far the best plan.

In selecting a grindstone, choose one that gives off fine granules, when being cut down, instead of muddy particles. See that it is free from coarse or hard streaks, and provided with a circular instead of a square hole in the center. This is an important matter when selecting a stone to be run by power, as it removes all danger of bursting, if the stone is otherwise perfect. Do not allow a stone to stand where it is exposed to the sun's rays, as the heat is sure to harden the exposed side, causing, long before it is half worn out, a hard shell of from an eighth to a quarter of an inch in thickness.

Rule for Framing Stick Seats.

The stick or slot seat, though used but little at the present time, is an article that every bodymaker is likely to be called upon to make, and one which few know how to lay off. The following is a rule that was used by bodymakers years ago, when the stick was an important part of the buggy body. It has stood the test of time on account of its accuracy and simplicity:

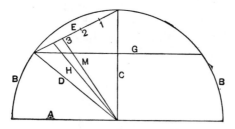

Fig. 43. Rule for framing stick seats.

To lay off the rule, draw a diagram as shown by Fig. 43. Strike the parallel line A, and strike the half circle B of any diameter; then draw the perpendicular line C from the central point on A to the circular line B. Then set the bevel to the angle desired for the flare of the seat, and strike line D. Then draw line E from the points where lines C and D intersect the circle. Then draw line G parallel with line A. Set the dividers with one point on line C, where it intersects the circle B, and ascertain half the space above line D on line C. Set the dividers at that space, and with one point resting on line B, where lines G and D intersect it, and the other point on line E, from which point draw line H. Next set one point of the dividers on line B, at the point where E and C intersect it, and space off on line E three spaces, and from the third draw line M. This gives the diagram complete.

To work it, dress up the pillars to the bevel determined by lines *A* and *M*. Cut the shoulders by the bevel set to *A* and *H*, and lay off the mortises in the seat frames to the bevel obtained by *A D*.

After a little practice the workman can quickly draw his diagrams for any flare of seat and lay off the bevels for shoulders and sides of pillars.

Handy Tools.

The woodworker often finds himself compelled to secure nut heads or to hold or turn on nuts in positions where it is extremely difficult to reach with any of the ordinary appliances, and much time is lost in devising means to overcome the difficulty.

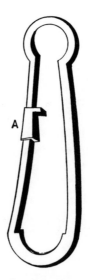

Fig. 44. An adjustable wrench.

Figs. 44 and 45 illustrate two convenient tools for the purpose, while Fig. 44 also answers for an adjustable wrench, one that would be found very handy as a wagon wrench.

This is made of a square three-eighths to a five-eighths inch square bar, the smaller one being sufficiently strong for a wrench from four to five inches long, the larger for one from six to ten inches long. The slide block *A* has a face which runs parallel with that of the opposite bar, and a small off-set to prevent the nut slipping. This slide plays freely upon the bar, and when in use it is tightened up to the nut by blows from a hammer.

Fig. 45. A clamp for holding bolt heads to prevent them from turning.

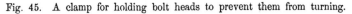

The opening at *B* should be such as to permit the working of a nut three-eighths of an inch square. At *C* the opening may be sufficiently large to grip a nut one and a quarter inch square. All that is required is that the face of the slide block be on a parallel line with the opposite bar. This is a simple tool, and, as before said, it is one that could be used to good advantage as a wagon wrench. All that is required is that the ends be spaced so as to accommodate the smallest and largest nuts.

Fig. 45 is designed more especially as a clamp for holding bolt heads or nuts to prevent their turning. It is made of heavy iron, and has a flange upon each arm, upon which the slide block *A* can be placed, the block being fitted to both sides. As with Fig. 44, the face of the slide block must be on a parallel line with the face of the opposite, so that no matter what the size of the square to be held, the grip will be firm. The block is set with a hammer.

There are so many places where a tool of this kind can be used to advantage that no woodworker should be without one.

Strengthening Seat and Body Corners.

The weakest parts of square bodies and panel seats are the corners. These, when square, must be mitered in order to give a good, clean, smooth job, and a mitered joint, unsupported, is a weak joint. It is necessary therefore to use corner blocks whenever they do not interfere too much with the trimming.

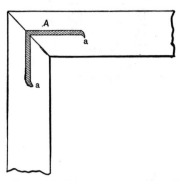

Fig. 46. Top view of a panel seat corner, strengthened without the use of corner blocks.

Fig. 46 gives a top view of a panel seat corner, strengthened without the use of corner blocks, *A* being an angle iron of light band iron, having the edges turned and sharpened, as shown at *a a*. In making this corner, fit up the miter in the usual manner, and after both pieces are fitted, saw into each end for the iron. When machinery is employed, this can be cut in by a circular saw to a uniform depth, and at the proper gauge from the edge. Then glue up, and when calls and thumbscrews are in place, and the glue soft, drive in the angle iron, which should be about one-quarter of an inch shorter than the full hight of the seat panel. Set it in so that there will be one-eighth of an inch space, top and bottom, to allow for planing or fitting up.

The iron may be put in after the glue is hard, but there is danger of breaking the joint. If driven in after the seat panels are finished, they should be securely fastened to the seat frame by a corner block fitted against the outside, and held in place by thumbscrews. First, however, clean all the glue out of the saw kerf by running through a keyhole saw. In all cases coat the iron with white lead before driving it in. If the iron fits well, this makes a strong corner, the strongest that can be made.

The same plan may be followed with corners of bodies, but as there is always room enough for corner blocks, they may be used instead.

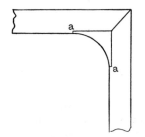

Fig. 47. A body secured by a corner block.

Fig. 47 shows a body corner secured by a corner block, the foot of which should be lapped upon the sills. The panel is cut away at *a a* to the depth of an eighth of an inch, which leaves enough wood at the edges, when lightened out, to give a good finish, and leave nothing to sliver up, as is too

often the case when the block is placed against the inside of
the panel and finished to a feather edge.

A Gauge for a Mortise Chisel.

In many places the stub mortise is much better than one
cut entirely through, but woodworkers prefer to make the
latter because of their inability to make a quick stub mortise.
To overcome this difficulty the woodworker should be pro-

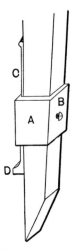

Fig. 48. The gauge secured to the chisel by the screw *B.*

vided with a gauge or stop, such as shown by Figs. 48 and
49. This consists of the block secured to the chisel by the
screw *B*, Fig. 48. To make this absolutely secure, a small
hole should be drilled into the chisel, into which the screw
foot can enter. Unless this is done, there is liability of the
block slipping from the repeated blows from the hammer.

The gauge is shown by *C*, Fig. 49. It consists of a piece
of spring steel, having the foot as a square offset of about a
quarter of an inch. The inside of the block *A* is nicked
out on the inside, to allow the steel gauge to work without

loosening the block. The face of the gauge is provided with a number of low pins, *a a a*, which fit into the holes *b b b*, drilled through the face of the block. The spurs must be short enough to allow of their passing through the recess

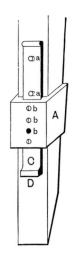

Fig. 49. The gauge *C.*

where the gauge piece is flat against the chisel face, the spring given being sufficient to hold the pin in the hole and prevent the gauge slipping. The pins must be set far enough apart so that but one will be under the box at a time.

CHAPTER III.

Striking Ovals.—Corner Blocks.—Connecting Sweeps.—Transferring Drawings.
—Directions for making Corner Pillar and Top Rail Patterns.—Standing
Pillar for a Phaeton.—How to frame a light Standing Pillar.

Striking Ovals.

THE ellipsis, or what is generally termed the oval, is used
to a considerable extent by carriage bodymakers, either as a
whole or in parts, and is generally looked upon as one of the
most difficult forms which the bodymaker is expected to construct. One of the oldest methods of striking is by the use
of a string and a pencil. With care, a fairly correct outline
may be obtained in this manner; but, at the best, it is un-
certain. The manner of working is to first determine the
length and width of oval required, and strike lines A B, Fig.
50, for the length, and designate at the center the points
C D for the width. Then set pins E E at equal distances
from the center, and locate them so that when the looped
string is passed around them, the pencil point will rest at
the end A or B, and when carried upward at point C. The
lines a a a indicate the string when in the latter position,
and lines b b b the same string when the pencil is on its way
from the center line. With the string of the proper length,
and the pins E E in a correct position, the operator sets a
pencil against the inside of the string, and pressing hard
against it, moves it entirely around the pins to the starting
point. To secure a correct line, it is necessary that the string
be one that will not stretch, and perfectly smooth.

Another method is shown by Fig. 51, which represents a quarter section. This is a useful guide, particularly for making curves of an irregular sweep. By it the workman can

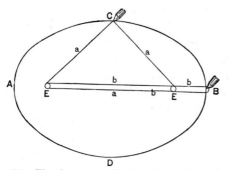

Fig. 50. The first step. Finding the striking lines.

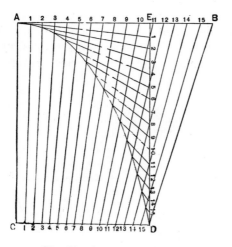

Fig. 51. A quarter section.

lay out a true section of an ellipsis, or he can modify it so that the center may be raised or flattened. To lay off this, strike lines *A C* and *C D* for half the length and width of the desired oval; square up by striking lines *D E* and *A B* for the other side and end. Next divide lines *C D* and *D E* into an equal number of spaces; then begin at *A* and divide line *A B* into spaces the same width of those on *D E.* Number the lines as designated, and strike the lines connecting *A B* and *C D.* Then, with the straightedge held at the corner *A,* as a central point, strike the lines as spaced on *E D,* each to form a point where it intersects the line bearing a similar number, these lines and points being made plain by the illustration. When these points are designated, it is a simple matter to produce a correct segment of a circle, the curve.

If desirable to change the sweep, say at the center, instead of retaining the central point at *A,* move it up to line No. I, and strike a line from that—No. 9 on line *E D.* Then move up to No. 2, and strike a line from No. 10, and so on to the end. By thus changing the location of the central point, almost any degree of curvature can be outlined.

By the use of the compass, curves and ovals may be struck of almost any degree of curvature, and geometrically perfect. Ovals can be struck in this way quicker than by any other, after the workman has learned the rules governing the ob-

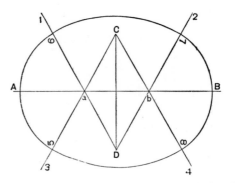

Fig. 52. An oval the width of which is one-half of its length.

taining of pivotal points. Fig. 52 represents an oval, the

width of which is half its length. To lay off this, first strike line *A B*, and bisect with perpendicular line *C D*. Next divide line *A B* into three equal parts, as designated by *A a*, *a b*, and *b B*. Then point off on line *C D* from *a C* or *a D*, the same distance as from *A a*. Next strike lines *D* 1, *D* 2, *C* 3 and *C* 4, being careful to intersect the lines at the centers, *a* and *b*. Then, with the point of the compass at *a*, strike the arc of the circle 5 6, and with the point at *b*, strike the arc 7 8. Then set the point at *D C*, and strike the arcs 6 7 and 5 8. If all lines are correctly centered, the oval will be absolutely perfect.

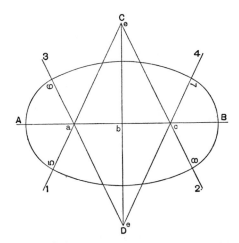

Fig. 53. An oval the width of which is one-fifth of its length.

Fig. 53 shows an oval the width of which is three-fifths the length. To lay off for the pivotal points for an oval of this character, strike lines *A B*, and bisect with line *C D*. Then divide line *A B* into four equal parts, *A a*, *a b*, *b c*, and *C B*. Then, with the point of the compass at the intersection of the main lines, strike a half circle, the center at the end of the oval, on line *A B*, and the ends at *e e*, on line *C D*.

Then strike lines C 1, C 2, and lines D 3 and D 4, being
careful that they intersect on line C D at a and C. Then,
with the point of the compass at a, strike the arc 5 6, and
at C strike the arc 7 8. Next, with the point at E, strike
the arcs 6 7 and 5 8.

It will be seen that the same method for striking the curves
is adopted in both cases, the difference in methods being the
locating of the pivotal points, the result being such that the
curves partake of forms which intersect without breaking
the line.

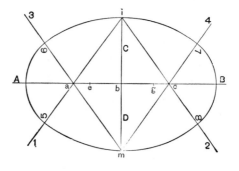

Fig. 54.   An oval the width of which is two-thirds of its length.

Fig. 54 represents an oval the width of which is two-thirds
its length. To obtain the pivotal points of this, strike the
lines A B and C D as directed in regard to Figs. 52 and 53.
Then divide the line A B into four equal parts, A a, a b,
b c, c B. The space line A B into three equal parts, as
designated A E, e g, and g B. Set the compass to either of
the spaces thus obtained, and with one point at the intersection of the main lines designating points i m on line C D.
Then strike lines i 1, i 2, m 3, and m 4, passing through
pivotal points a c on line A B. Then, with the compass

point on center *a*, strike the arc 5 6, and with point on *c*, strike arc 7 and 8. Then set the compass point on *i* and *m*, and strike the arcs 6 7 and 5 8.

A little study will enable the workman to lay off points for almost any form when the proportions are divided by regular proportions. As before said, the laying off of curves by geometrical rules will enable the workman to produce sweeps or curves for various parts of the body in much less time and with greater accuracy than can be secured in any other way. In pattern making sweeps thus obtained will be found of great service, and every bodymaker should provide himself with several different sizes and forms.

In the preceding directions the rules given have been for ovals of fixed proportions, that is, those where the width was one-half, three-fifths, and one-third the length, all of which have their place, and are so simple that any workman should be able to use them to advantage.

There is another rule which can be made applicable to all

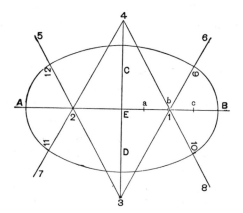

Fig. 55. Illustrating a rule which is applicable to all forms of ovals

forms of ovals. Fig. 55 is made by this rule. To make this it is necessary to know the length and width of oval required.

Then strike line *A B* and bisect with line *C D*, the two lines being at perfect right angles. Then, on line *A B*, lay off the exact width of the oval, as designated by space between *A a*. Next divide the space between *a* and the end of the oval at *B* into three equal parts, as *a b c*. Then from *E*, where the main lines cross, set off two of these parts on each side, as *E* 1 and *E* 2, and from 1 or 2 designate the space between 1 and 2 on line *E D*, at points 3 and 4. Next, from point 3, draw lines 3 5 and 3 6, and from point 4 draw lines 4 7 and 4 8. Then from point 1 describe the arc 9 10, and from point 2, as a center, describe the arc 11 12. Then, with point 3 as a center, describe the arc 12 9, and from point 4 as a center, describe the arc 7 10. With this, as with the preceding diagrams, it is absolutely necessary that lines be perfect, and that the exact centers be maintained in all cases; otherwise the side will be irregular and the points where the long and short curves intersect them will be a break in the lines.

In one particular this rule is superior to those previously given, as it is adapted to all proportions, the foundation being a knowledge of the length and width of oval required.

Corner Blocks.

Fashion, ever changing, makes necessary a line of instruction that under other circumstances might never be needed. The round corners to bodies, so fashionable a few years ago, are not made by first class builders at present, but a change may occur at any time, when they will be required.

One of the chief objections to them by manufacturers was their weakness, a defect which was more the result of a want of knowledge as to their proper construction than the existence of any mechanical difficulty. For round cornered seats, these corners would often represent the arc of a circle of six to eight inches diameter, and for bodies, a circle of two inches. In both cases the panels were cut away as illustrated by Figs. 56 and 57, Fig. 56 representing the seat and 57 the body, the panels of the former being three-quarters of an inch thick and those of the latter three-eighths of an inch. These illustrations are reduced from drawings representing the full size, and are consequently correct in their proportions. *A A* represent the panels and *B* the corner blocks, the lines *C C* the joints of the panels. It will be seen that in perfecting the corner it is necessary to cut away so much of the panels that a portion of the corner block itself must be exposed to complete the surface. Now, as generally made, the corner blocks are cut from straight grained wood, the grain

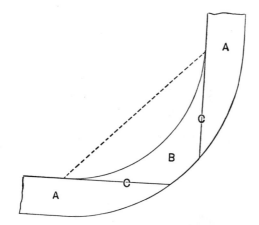

Fig. 56. An arc of a circle representing the seat.

of which runs parallel, as shown by Fig. 58, the ends of the block being in the exact reverse position of that of the ends of the panels. When therefore the corner is fully rounded, the grain of the corners runs from top to bottom of the side, while that of the panel runs from end to end, as shown by Fig. 59 (page 64), the panels terminating at *A A*, leaving between these two points a thin section so weak that unless protected by corner irons it could be easily split by the hands; and the strain upon the side and end panels is lia-

ble at any time to split the block before the glue will lose
its hold. When the blocks and panels are joined, and even
when the arc of the circle is much smaller than that shown,

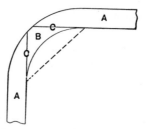

Fig. 57.   An arc of a circle representing the body.

Fig. 58.   The run of the grain in the wood used for corner blocks.

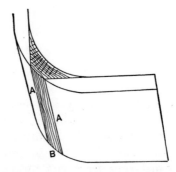

Fig. 59.   The run of the grain in wood used for panels.

the little left of the panel serves to increase rather than di-
minish the weakness of the corner. If it were absolutely

necessary to put in the corner block, as shown, there would be an excuse for many weak corners, but there is no excuse for thus weakening the body.

Whitewood is preferred for corners for many reasons. 1st, it holds glue well. 2d, it paints smooth. It is also more easily worked, and no more liable to split than ash, unless the latter is coarse grained, and too hard to be easily worked true.

It is necessary, in order that the glue may get a good hold, that the side, not the end, of the fiber be in contact with the panel; and because of that the grain is run lengthwise. The same result, however, may be attained by cutting the

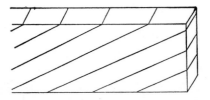

Fig. 60. The block cut with grain running on the bias.

blocks on a bias, as shown by Fig. 60. These blocks present the side of the grain to the panels, when in position, while the grains run sufficiently diagonally across the center to make it impossible to split the latter without completely destroying the body; in fact, the blocks, when cut in this way and glued in position, cannot be split from top to bottom. The gluing surface is just as good as that of the blocks cut straight, and it requires but little if any more work to true them off outside or in. It may waste a little wood to cut plank in this way, but the result is so much better that no careful bodymaker will refuse to adopt the strongest plan.

Connecting Sweeps.

It is often necessary when making patterns, and also when

working, to change the curvature.   To effect this, a knowledge
of one general principle of joining each sweep at a common tan-

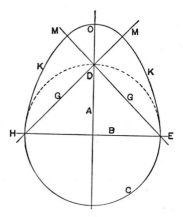

Fig. 61.   Illustrating a method of joining curvatures.

gent is all that is required.   Fig. 61 shows the method.   Supposing that a sweep is to be made in which a full segment
of a circle is to be continued as an oval.   First strike line
A, and intersect it with line *B*.   Set the point of the compass at the point where the two lines *A* and *B* cross each
other, and strike the circle *C*, half of which is indicated by
the dotted line *C a*.   Then use the point *D*, where the circle crosses line *A*, as one point, and *E* where the line *B* and
the circle *C* intersect, as a second point, and strike line *G*.
Then set the point of the compass on line *B*, and spread
them until the pencil point touches the circle at *H*, and
strike the segment *K*, terminating the line at the point where
it intersects line *G*.   Then set the compass at point *D*, where
the various lines intersect the circle line *C a*, and extend the
points until the pencil intersects the line *A* at *M*, and strike
the segment *O*.   This, as will be seen by the illustration,
gives a perfect oval—not an ellipsis.   By a little care and
study the arrangement of the lines and the arcs starting from

the semi-circle may be made to describe tangents, which, continued, can be formed to a variety of sweeps, all clean and true.

The drawing is made to represent a full oval, as it is necessary in order to illustrate the point in full; but on a draft board the workman can proceed from a central point, and make one side only.

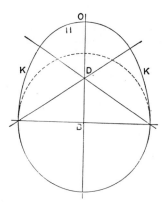

Fig. 62.   Illustrating how the lines of Fig. 61 may be modified.

Fig. 62 illustrates how the lines may be modified. In it the same diameter of semi-circle is used, but the point of intersection of radial lines is changed, as at *D*, by which the space between *B* and *O* is decreased, terminating the lines *K* at a point nearer the center, and increasing the diameter of the semi-circle *H*.

Transferring Drawings.

The bodymaker who has not learned the French rule, is often at a loss how to proceed when desiring to place upon the draft board a body of which he has secured a correct half inch or other scale drawing. The main lines are easily obtained, but when making the sweeps great difficulty is experienced in getting them to appear as graceful as they do in the small illustration. A simple plan whereby this difficulty can be surmounted is to line the small drawing, as shown by

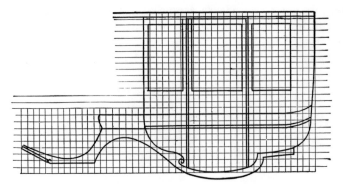

Fig. 63. A simple rule to place the drawing of a body on a blackboard.

Fig. 63, placing the lines at perfect right angles with each other, and if the drawing is to a half inch scale, place the lines an eighth of an inch apart. Having the small drawing lined, proceed to make the transfer to the draft board. First strike the line *A*, Fig. 64, representing the back end of the top rail. Then measure off the required space between this line and the inner or face line of the hinge pillar *B*. Then measure off for the door, and strike line *C*, which represents the inner or face line of the lock pillar. Next measure off for the front quarter and strike line *D*, which represents the front pillar, and then the line *E*, representing the end of the top rail. These lines being established, strike the horizontal line *S* as a base line, it representing the extreme lowest point of the bottom side. Then strike horizontal line *G*, which represents the top side of the top rail at its highest point. Having established the square into which the body is to be drawn, space off lines *A* and *D*, beginning at the base line *E*, into sections of three inches each, these being the equivalents of the one-eighth inch spaces on the small drawing and strike the intermediate lines between *E* and *G*.

Then divide off line *E* into three-inch spaces, and with a square strike the perpendicular lines. This being completed number the lines on the scale drawing and on the draftboard one, two, three, &c. Next indicate by *X*, Fig. 64, the points on the large draft, where the lines of the body intersect the

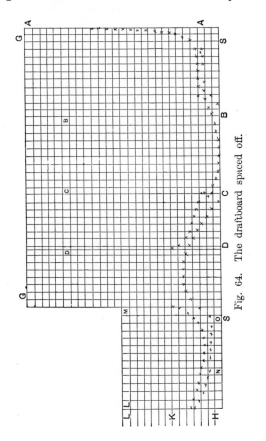

Fig. 64. The draftboard spaced off.

guide lines on the small drawing. These points being carefully marked, the bodymaker will experience little difficulty in perfecting the sweeps so as to secure the same character of curves as those indicated in the small drawing. Having made the bottom side and corner pillar patterns, measure up from the base line *E*, and strike the horizontal line *H*, as the line of the tread of the front of the rocker.   Next strike line *K* for the seat line.   Then strike the perpendicular lines *L M O P*, as indicating the respective points in the scale drawing.   Extend the horizontal lines, or as many as are necessary, across the outside seat, and also mark the necessary number of perpendicular lines to cover the space occupied by the cut-under, and in the same manner as directed for the body, indicate the points for the outlines of the rocker.

Having the outlines secured, wipe off all the cross lines, having first set pointers to obviate the possibility of changing the position of the patterns, and trace out on the draftboard a clean drawing, after which mark off the arm rails and make the patterns, and the patterns and drawing are completed.   The workman has but to remember, when spacing off, that to a half-inch scale drawing every one-eighth of an inch represents three inches when transferred to the draftboard.

Directions for Making Corner Pillar and Top Rail Patterns.

There is no part of the bodymaker's business which causes so much trouble to those not fully acquainted with the French rule, as the making of the top rail and standing pillar pattern, so that they will work together without trouble, and which are sufficiently accurate to enable the bodymaker to select timber of the right thickness; also to locate the position of the corner pillars.   A simple rule, one which can be understood by any bodymaker, is as follows:

Procure a clean, whitewood board, a half inch thick and five feet long.   If the turn-under of the standing pillar is two and a half inches, the board must be three inches wide. Straighten both edges; then strike line 1, Fig. 65, across one end of the board.   Then measure up from this line the thickness of the bottom side, and strike line 2.   Measure up from

line 2 the desired point for the arm rail, commonly about
ten inches, and strike line 3. About six inches above the
arm rail line strike line 4, the topmost point of the side
sweep. Then measure off on line 1 seven-eighths of an inch
for the tenon, and one and an eighth inch for the foot,
making two and an eighth inches in all, which point represents the extreme outside of the bottom line, when dressed

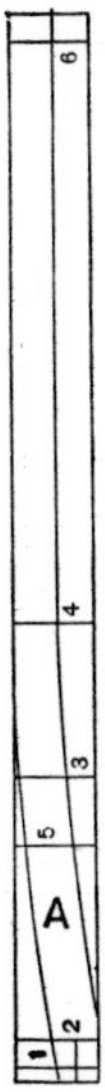

Fig. 65. The pattern for a corner pillar.

off. Then, with an easy sweep, strike the turn-under line of
the pillar from line 4 to line 1. Then measure off on line 6
from the outside an eighth of an inch, and strike the outside
line of the pillar from line 4 to line 6. This completes the
outside, which is the guide line.

To shape the inside, measure up from line 1, to which is
added the depth of the rocker in the center, a distance sufficient to make the entire distance—from the bottom of the
rocker to the top of the seat rail—twelve inches, and strike

line 5, which locates the top of the seat rail. Measure off
on this line, from the outside, two inches, and on line 5
three inches, and use the three points thus obtained as guide
lines for the inside of the pillar. Then space off on line 6
one and one-eighth inch from the outeredge, and strike the
line from 4 to 6 on the inside. This finishes the outlines of
the pillar. Dress up to these lines and across the edges,
mark with a cutting marker the various lines designated by
Figs. 1, &c., and the standing pillar will be completed.

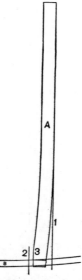

Fig. 66.   The pattern as it should appear when ready to lay on the draftboard.

When completed, lay the pattern upon the draftboard (Fig.
66, page 72). *A* the pillar, *B* the bottom side, line 1
the face of the pillar, when framed into the bottom side,
line 2 the face of the bottom side, line 3 the face of the
tenon of the pillar. The space between lines 2 and 3 being
one inch, be sure that the face line 3 is on an exact parallel
with line 1.

Then select a good, clean, well seasoned piece of white-wood for the top rail pattern, a half inch thick, long enough to take both corner pillars and about four inches wide.

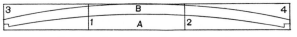

Fig. 67. The pattern for the top rail.

Straighten the edge *A*, Fig. 67. Then strike lines 1 and 2 to represent the inside faces of the door pillars. Then measure off from lines 1 and 2 the required lengths for the quarters, and strike lines 3 and 4. Then, with a compass, determine the distance between lines 1 and 2, Fig. 66, and prick off on lines 1 and 2, Fig. 67, from the face line. Next measure off on lines 3 and 4, Fig. 67, one and a quarter inch for corner pillars, and by the four points thus designated, sweep off the outside of the top rail pattern. Then sweep off the inside, leaving it the width of the door pillars on lines 1 and 2. If a flatter top rail is required, retain the points on lines 1 and 2, but increase the distance on lines 3 and 4. If the top rail is straightened to a considerable extent, the corner pillar will have to be thicker than at first shown, or it will have to be set as much further from the face of the rocker as there is difference in the sweep. If the back end of the rail is swept more than when made as directed, a new face line must be made and the sweep increased. For ordinary rockaway work, the proportions designated by the drawings herewith will be all that is required.

Standing Pillar for a Phaeton.

Phaëtons with standing tops make very desirable summer carriages, but if the pillars are not attached very firmly at the bottom, they soon give way, owing to the trembling and swaying of the top. The front pillar being straight, can be secured by a foot iron to the bracket or toe bar, and the

back one to the seat corner, being stiffened by the arm rail
and the back bar. The most troublesome pillar to secure is
the center one, which is affixed to the seat panel at the front

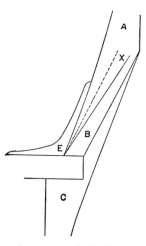

Fig. 68. A neat and secure method of fastening a phaëton pillar.

end. Fig. 68 shows a method of fastening that is neat and
secure. *A*, the pillar, is cut with a foot to correspond with
the flare of the seat end *B*. It is boxed into the seat end,
as shown by the line *X*, the bottom being flush with the
seat panel, the two being secured by glue and wooden screws.
These bodies generally have the stanhope pillar *C*, which,
being firmly glued to the panel, aids materially to strengthen
the pillar and seat end, while the foot iron *E* renders the
pillar perfectly secure.

How to Frame a Light Standing Pillar.

In many standing top bodies the pillars are so light that
unless extra care is taken they are liable to break at the
bottom shoulder, or to spring, and thus check the panel.
This can be overcome if the shoulder is cut and fastened as

shown by Fig. 69. *A* is the pillar, *B* the bottom side, as it would appear cut off at the side of the pillar, *C* the panel grooved in between the pillar and the molding. Ordinarily the tenon *E* is cut with a shoulder, as indicated by the dotted line *H*. This leaves the joint on a line with the grain in the panel, and as it is not secured, the springing of the pillar will open the joint and check the panel. To overcome this difficulty, instead of cutting a square shoulder, the V-

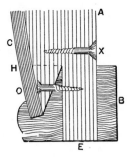

Fig. 69. Method of framing the pillars to prevent their breaking or the panels springing.

shaped section is left on the pillar extending down to the bottom of the panel groove, leaving another V-shaped section between that of the pillar and the tenon. When in place, the screw *O* is run in, binding the lower ends, while the screw *X* prevents the pillar splitting. When the panel is in place, the whole is so firmly secured that the pillar is as strong there, if not stronger, than at any other place.

CHAPTER IV.

CARRIAGE WOODWORK.

Hints on Drafting, Drafting Tools and Appliances, Practical Body Making, Wheel Making, and Sleigh Making.

NOTWITHSTANDING the advantages arising from a knowledge of the French rule of carriage drafting, a large proportion, say four-fifths, of carriage woodworkmen have no idea of it whatever, and two-thirds of the remaining fifth, while able to work to it, when a complete draft and a full set of patterns are placed before them, are not able to lay off a draftboard or make a set of patterns. That this is so, is due to several causes, first among them being the lack of incentive, due to the subdivision of labor whereby a man can learn enough of the trade to enable him to earn living wages without spending years of time to learn the trade. Another barrier is the apparent complexity of the rule, which frightens the younger workmen, where they are so situated that they must study without the aid of a teacher. A third is the limited opportunities offered in a majority of the shops to apply the rule to the class of work built. Yet, despite all these barriers, workmen would best study their own interests by learning the rule in all its details, if possible, but where not, they should master the primary elements. To encourage this, and thus induce the workman to advance himself in the higher branches of the rule as applied to carriage drafting, the following instructions, based upon the rule, and in keeping with it, should be read and heeded. Beginning with a plain buggy body, the lessons carry the woodworker along through the various kinds of work, step by step, until the Brougham is reached. Effort has been made to make the instruction complete, but to so simplify it that the apprentice as well as the journeyman can understand it. As a preliminary to the working instructions, a chapter is devoted to drafting and to tools and materials. To further add to the value of the book, chapters are added giving details regarding the making of wheels and carriage parts. These too are simple and plain. Another chapter takes up the construction of sleighs, a branch of the business that interests a large number of woodworkmen.

It may not be amiss to state that in the selection of styles the choice has been made of those that are representative of the respective classes, but there is nothing to prevent the rules and principles laid down being applied to bodies of different outlines.

A Lesson in Carriage Drafting.

The carriage draftsman must not only be able to make a good clean drawing, but he must, in order to make that drawing practical, be thoroughly conversant with the foundation rules upon which proportions are based. These exist in the body and all other parts must be subordinated thereto.

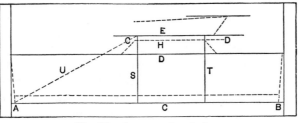

Fig. 70. A square box body.

To illustrate, take a square box body, Fig. 70, as a representative of the buggy class. The arbitrary proportions necessary to secure comfort to the rider are hight of seat between the top of the seat bottom and the inside of the bottom board on line S, which must be twelve inches at least. The next line is that from the front edge of the seat frame to the lower front corner of the body, as indicated by line U. This must be twenty-four inches in the clear, but twenty-six inches is better. The depth of the seat is the next point. This must be sixteen inches as a minimum. Having these points established, the other proportions are based upon taste and a correct idea as to balance. The depth of the side panel is solely a matter of taste. The length of the body is dictated by judgment in securing a proper balance. If too short or too long, the entire effect of the ill proportion is shown back of the front line of the seat frame, as in front of that point the length is arbitrary. A good proportion is to make the central point of the extreme length of the body one inch back of the front edge of the seat frame.

Having established these points, strike line C as the base line of the bottom. Then line D as the top of the panel, line E as top of seat bottom, upright lines A and B for end panels. Then flare the ends as shown by dotted lines, and lines S and T as outside lines of seat pillars, and dotted line H as top of seat riser. All square box and straight sill bodies for one seat can be laid out on these lines.

The phaëton, Fig. 71, is another class. The rules governing its proportions cover the same grounds, except so far as regards the length back of the seat, as the body has no projection back of the back pillars. Line A represents the base and line B the top of the seat board. The distance between these on line D should be thirteen inches from the point where B and D intersect. The distance should be twenty-six inches as the minimum. The seat on line B must be sixteen to eighteen inches, and the flare of the corner pillars five to six inches. In making a drawing of this body strike line A for the base, B seat, E D and F for end and center lines, H five to six inches below B for bottom of quarter panel, M top of back rail, C top of quarter line at line D.

These points being determined, the draftsman next dots off outlines as shown. The lines indicated by x x represent the portions of the rocker which are not flush with the panel

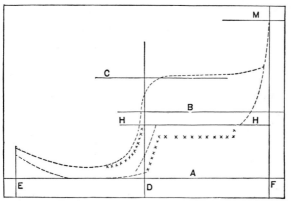

Fig. 71.   The phaëton body.

outlines. There is nothing about the outlines that is arbitrary. All that is required is to keep the cardinal points unimpaired.

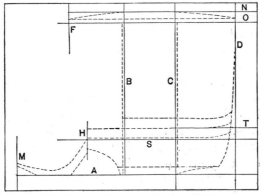

Fig. 72.   A simple standing top body.

Fig. 72 represents one of the simplest of standing top

bodies, but by it the arbitrary points can be illustrated. These are length, front of outside or front seat, which should be twenty-six to twenty-eight inches, as the distance between the top of the seat board and the foot board cannot as a rule exceed eleven inches. The second point is the location of the seat rail, twelve inches above the base line A. The width of the door, not less than twenty inches, and the hight of the top, which must be three feet six inches in the clear, between the front seat bottom and the underside of the top curve. This measurement must in all cases be made between the front seat bottom and the curve, as, with the exception of straight bodies, this seat is higher than the inside seat, sometimes as much as six inches. Carelessness in making this measurement leads to so many ill looking rockaways, wherein the riders on the outside are compelled to sit half bent. The remaining point is the back quarter, which should be sixteen and a half to seventeen inches on a parallel line with the top of the seat rail, back of the line representing the back edge of the seat. The pillar should cant at least one and a quarter inch. The under curve below this line is a matter of taste. In making a drawing therefore of a rockaway, strike line A for a base; then lines B and C for faces of standing pillars; then line H for front of front seat; M end of bracket, D back end of top rail, O bottom line of top rail, N top of curves in the center. The form of the wheelhouse is governed by the class of carriage part used, and the taste of the designer. If a perch carriage is used, the proportions are not arbitrary, but if a platform carriage is used, then the wheelhouse must be of such proportions as will admit of the wheel turning under without coming in contact with the body. The dotted lines indicate one style of body, but they are in no wise arbitrary.

These three styles serve to illustrate the foundation principles governing carriage drafting, and if thoroughly understood, they do not interfere with the draftsman work.

To make satisfactory drawings, good tools are necessary.

These can be purchased, but it is false economy which induces any one to be governed in selection by the price. Cheap tools soon wear, become loose in the joints, the springs fail, and the most skilled workman finds it impossible to depend upon them for accurate drawings. German silver with hardened bearings and steel points cost more than the ordinary brass and steel tools, but they are accurate and retain their accuracy for a long time. Nine distinct tools make a very

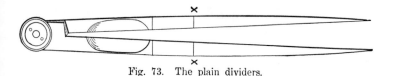

Fig. 73. The plain dividers.

complete set. These consist first of the plain dividers, Fig. 73. The joint and top above $x\ x$ is of German silver, with a steel washer in the joint to insure equality in the wear and durability. The joints must be smooth, so that while loose enough to work freely, they will not slip nor spring in any way. The operator often finds it necessary to set the points with one hand, and unless they work smoothly, much annoyance is caused by the jumping when working the points, and they are apt also to change location while working. The points below $x\ x$ are of finely tempered steel, hard enough to insure good points, but not so hard as to break easily. The joints are set by the use of a two-point key, by which the little nut at the outside of the joint is loosened or tightened.

Where great accuracy is required, the hair spring dividers,

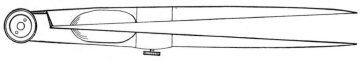

Fig. 74. The adjustable dividers.

Fig. 74, will be found useful. These are constructed with

joint top and one point similar to the corresponding parts of
the plain dividers. The other arm has an adjustable point,
secured by a set screw. This arrangement permits the use
of a splice or extension piece, which can be used to increase
the spacing points, either with a point, pen, or pencil.

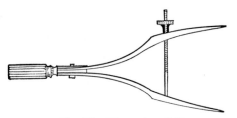

Fig. 75.   The spring dividers.

Fig. 75 shows a set of spring dividers. The legs are of
steel, the upper ends being flattened to act as springs. The
handle is of metal, with a roughened top, by which the compasses can be operated by being clasped between the thumb
and finger. A bar and set screw holds the arms in place,
and permits a fine adjustment of the points.

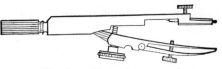

Fig. 76.   The spring pen point.

Fig. 76 represents a spring pen point. The pen is attached
to the main point by a steel rivet, which enters the body
and extends up to the handle. It is regulated by a set screw,
which holds it firmly in place. The top portion of the pen
point hinging the lower is stationary. A set screw through
the two bodies of the pen determines the width of line to be
made by the ink. The point proper has a needle point, which
passes through the small tube at the end. A set screw holds
the point in place. The top is roughened so that the pen

can be operated by grasping the top between the thumb and first finger.

Figs. 77, 78, 79, 80, and 81 show the parts of the changeable dividers. Fig. 77 is the main joint, with steel points

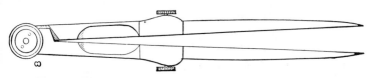

Fig. 77. The parts of the changeable dividers. The main joint.

Fig. 78. The adjustable point.

Fig. 79. The pencil holder.

Fig. 80. The pen point.

Fig. 81. A lengthening arm.

in place. These points are held in position by the set screws shown near the center of the legs. These points can be removed, and any one of the other parts put in. Fig. 78 is the adjustable point, the top section of which can be secured firmly in the body and held by the set screw. The lower part hinges firmly into the body, the joint working close, but loose enough to be moved by the hand. The lower end is provided with a point holder similar to that on Fig. 77. Fig. 79 is a pencil holder similar in all parts, except at the bottom end, to the point holder. At the lower end the body is split and made hollow. The pencil is inserted into this hollow space and held in place by the set screw. Fig. 80 is the pen point. It is made of two pieces of steel, the points of which can be closed or separated by the set screw; the ink is placed between the blades, and the width of the line is determined by the space between the points. The blades of the pen are attached to the body by a joint, by which the position can be regulated at will, it being desirable to carry the pen point as nearly perpendicular as possible. Fig. 81 shows a lengthening arm, one end of which can be attached to the joint arm, and the pen or any other of the adjustable pieces can be inserted into the socket at the lower end and held there by a set screw.

```
13
```

Fig. 82. The nut wrench.

Fig 82 shows the nut wrench for tightening the joints.

This makes a set of drawing tools by itself, but as it is necessary to use the different parts at the same time, it will not do to attempt to perform all the work with the one tool.

Fig. 83. The hand pen point.

Fig. 83 is a hand pen. The pen point is made the same

as the other pen point, but it is attached to a handle of ivory or wood instead of a compass joint. In using this pen, carry it perpendicular so that the two points will bear upon the paper with equal pressure, and slightly inclined on the parallel line.

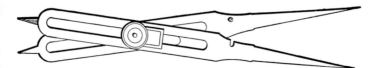

Fig. 84. The proportionate compasses, with two arms and movable set screw.

The proportioning compass, Fig. 84, is one of the most desirable tools. It consists of two arms, with a movable set screw, by which the central pivot can be changed. The upper section of the arms is slotted to hold the pivot slide.

Fig. 85. The reverse arm.

The reverse arm, Fig. 85, is spaced off to a scale showing the relative position of points. A cross line on the slide, moved to any one of the scale points, centers the pivot at a point where, when the long points are placed into a given position, the short arms will be in a position representing a relative proportionate distance. Thus, if the long points were four inches apart, and the pivot point set so that the line on the slide was opposite the line marked one-quarter on the body, the short points would be one inch apart.

For enlarging or reducing scale drawings, the proportioning compass is accurate and convenient.

The T square, Fig. 86, is an indispensable part of a drafts-man's kit. It should be of wood, light and thin. Two or three sizes will be found useful. Fig. 87 shows one with an adjustable cross head, which will also be needed. It has a split cross head. One section is set square on the slot, the other is held in place by a set screw, and can be moved to any desired angle. Straightedges, rules, &c., must be provided. These can be had of wood, rubber, ivory, and metal.

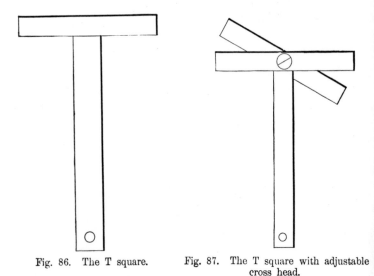

Fig. 86. The T square.   Fig. 87. The T square with adjustable cross head.

The harder substances are the best, as they are reliable; the edges do not lose their perfection.

Scales are necessary. The finest are too high priced for most carriage draftsmen. The paper scales answer equally well, and are cheap. They are put up in packages or sets, of six, one-quarter, one-half, three-quarters, one and a half, and three inches to the foot for series A, and three-thirty-seconds, one-eighth, three-sixteenths, five-sixteenths, three-eighths, and seven-eighths to the foot for series B, and ten, twenty, thirty, forty, fifty, and sixty parts of an inch for series C.

A full set of sweeps are absolutely necessary, for while free hand drawing is to be recommended as a trainer, yet the sweeps must be depended upon to give perfect lines. These may be purchased, made of wood, rubber, and bone. Those of apple wood are the best of the wood sweeps; those of rubber are more durable, but the color, black, is against them. The bone sweeps are only to be recommended for the small sizes. German silver sweeps, nickel plated, are superior to all others. A set will last for generations. They do not wear on the edges, and are light and convenient. For carriage drafting to a scale one inch and under, it is difficult to find suitable sweeps, the curves and combinations being unsuited, particularly reverse or S curves, and those having a long, straight arm, and a short, quick curve at the end.

The patterns herein illustrated (pages 88, 89) nineteen, twenty, twenty-one, twenty-two, twenty-three, twenty-four, twenty-five, and twenty-six, on a reduced scale, serve the purpose well, but every draftsman can, after a short time, discover new forms which will materially assist him in his labor. If he is not mechanic enough to perfect the sweeps, he can draw the lines and leave their completion to some one who can fit them up carefully.

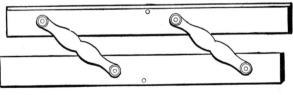

Fig. 88. Parallel rule.

The parallel rule, Fig. 88, is a most convenient tool, as by its use a series of parallel lines can be laid off without the use of the square. It is composed of two short wood rules,

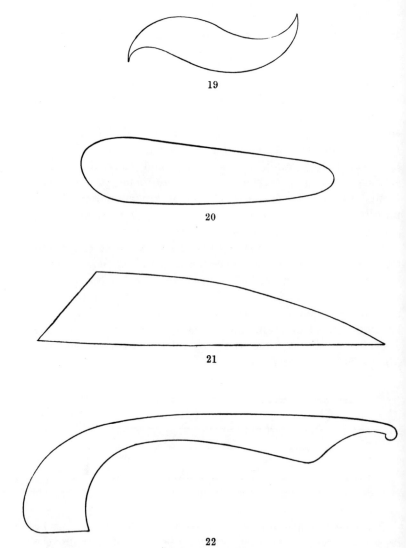

19

20

21

22
A set of sweeps.

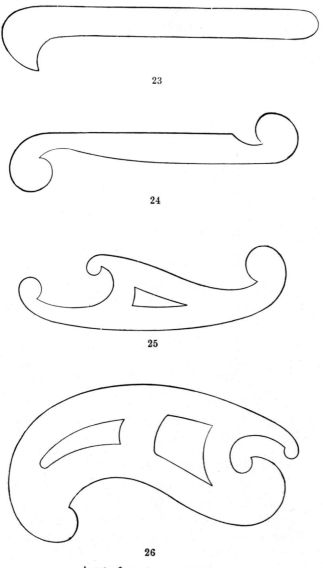

23

24

25

26

A set of sweeps—concluded.

joined by two brass arms, which carry the loose rule on a parallel line. The little pins at the edge of the rules furnish points which enable the operator to hold the rules in place to move the adjustable arm.

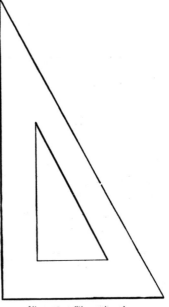

Fig. 89.   The triangle.

The triangle, Fig. 89, is one of the accessories which serve a convenient purpose for angles, &c.

Drafting Room and Draftboards.

Draftboards, both black and plain, the former for general drawing and pattern making, the latter as a working board, are conveniences, and where any attempt at accuracy is aimed at, they are necessities. There is no factory so small that room cannot be found for a blackboard. If not one of a size sufficiently large for a coach, a smaller one may be set up.

A board ten feet long and eight feet high will answer for buggies and light rockaways. The hight is not absolutely necessary for buggies, but it is always best to draw the top, set up, indicating the location of bows and joints. When space will permit, the draft room should be twenty by twenty-five feet. In a room of that size the draftboards can be hinged at the ends and run in grooves, or they may be hung upon hooks or wheels in such a manner as to permit their being reversed or changed in desirable positions. The manner of supporting them depends in a measure upon the situation of the room. Almost every draftsman in the large factories has his own plan, the points kept in view being good light and easy working of the boards, so as to prevent handling the surfaces.

In small shops space is a more important matter, and if more than one stationary board is used, recourse must be had to sectional boards, ranged together in a manner that will permit them being easily handled, and when not in use, not to occupy much space. This can be done by making the board up in sections, two or three for a ten-foot board, and four, if greater length is required.

Fig. 90 (page 92) illustrates the manner of hinging—*A B C*, the top or bottom of the board, *D* the hinge arms, secured to the cleats on the boards by bolts or screws, *E* stump joint hinges.

Fig. 91 shows the board when being folded up, the lettering corresponding with that on Fig. 92.

Square slide bolts are used to keep the boards in position, when spread at full length. The bottom should be provided with hinges, carefully hung upon the same centers as those of the top, and also a full set of socket rollers. To close the board, remove the bolts and pull out the respective sections until they are far enough out to clear each other; then carry them to the left or right, whichever way they may be hinged, until they are placed as shown by Fig. 92. By this arrangement a draftboard ten feet long can be folded into a

space three feet six inches by eight inches, and both sides
be made available.

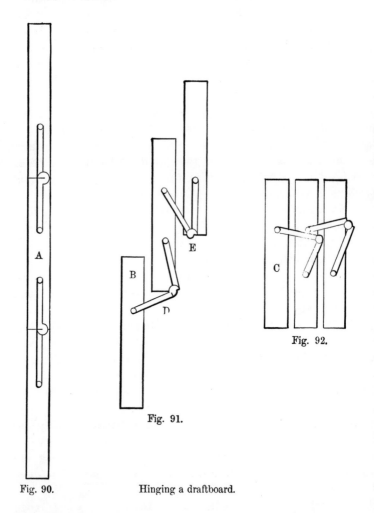

Fig. 90.   Hinging a draftboard.

The draftboard, whether made whole or in sections, must
be of clear, thoroughly seasoned white wood boards, an inch
thick, if one thickness only is used, and of half-inch boards,

if two thicknesses. The boards should not be more than twelve inches wide, and all joints be tongued and grooved. Much care is required in gluing up, but it is economy to construct the blackboard in a first-class manner. The surface must be well painted.

Small boards for working drafts need not be more than seven feet long and twenty-four inches wide. They must be of thoroughly seasoned white wood, the ends cleated to prevent splitting. Both edges should be straight and the width absolutely uniform.

Owing to the inclination of wood to shrink and expand when subjected to heat or moisture, it is absolutely necessary for the workman to test the accuracy of the lines upon the draftboard whenever laying off the frame work of a body.

All lines representing shoulders, bevels, &c., should be made with a cutting marker instead of a scratch awl, as the latter breaks the fiber and broadens the line, making it possible for a workman to change a bevel sufficiently to throw the entire frame work out of its true line. The outside guide lines can be made with a pencil, but all working lines must be made fine and distinct.

CHAPTER V.

Cut-Down Front Buggy.

THE bodymaker, whether he builds one or one hundred bodies, should be provided with good draftboards and patterns. A good trestle is also indispensable. It must be sufficiently large to give support to the body, and heavy enough to be firm, as there are times when work must be done on the body when it is on the trestle. An adjustable bar that can be raised or lowered is a valuable adjunct.

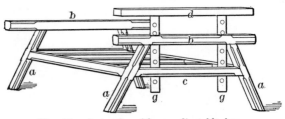

Fig. 93.   A trestle with an adjustable bar.

Fig. 93 illustrates a trestle with an adjustable bar. The parts *a* should be two and a half inches square, eighteen inches long. The bar *b* two and an eighth by two and a quarter inches square and forty-six inches long; bar *c* two and a quarter by two and a half inches square and forty-two inches long between shoulders. Bar *d* two by two and a quarter inches square and forty-six inches long. The arms, *g g* seven-eighths by three inches, bottom boards a half inch thick. Bar a must have two mortises, three inches by seven-eighths of an inch for the arms g g to move in, the lower ends of the arms running through like mortises in bar c. A good supply of wood handscrews and iron thumbscrews completes the floor outfit. A makeshift of a workman will manage to get along without these extras, but at a sacrifice of time that no thoughtful man would submit to have charged up against him.

Having all things ready, let it be supposed the bodymaker wants to put up a full-sized cut-down front body to be hung upon elliptic springs, the whole vehicle sufficiently large to accommodate two full-grown persons. The dimensions of such a body are: Four feet two inches long on the bottom and twenty-six inches wide, inside of the panels, and flare of each side one-half inch, between the bottom and the seat riser. The flare of the corners of the body is much a matter of taste, but a good outline is secured by three inches at the back corner and one inch at the front. Cut the sills A, Fig. 94 (page 98) of good, close grained forest ash, with the annular layers in the position shown by Fig. 95. The uprights B, Fig. 94, two and one-half by five-eighths inch, the riser C one and five-eighths inch; these pieces of good, close grained, strong forest ash; D, the corner, of good whitewood or soft ash, one inch square. In setting up the seat risers dove-tail in the laps, cutting a shoulder an eighth inch, as shown by A, Fig. 97.

Fig. 95 shows the end of sills A. Dotted line C, which indicates the inside round corner; B the rabbet as cut away for the bottom boards. In dressing up, make the top, inside, and bottom square, and bevel the outside to the required extent, to secure a half inch flare to the side.

The position of the grain is a matter of more importance than most persons imagine. In the first place, a bar one and a half inch deep and one and a fourth wide, with grain running as shown in Fig. 95, will support as great a strain—weight applied top or bottom—as a bar of equal width and

one-fourth of an inch greater depth, with the grain running
the opposite direction. Then too timber splits much more

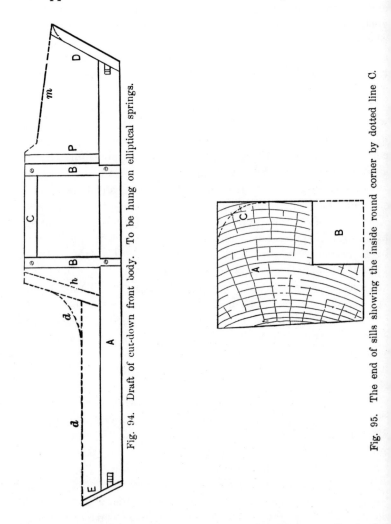

Fig. 94. Draft of cut-down front body. To be hung on elliptical springs.

Fig. 95. The end of sills showing the inside round corner by dotted line C.

easily on lines radiating outward from the heart to the bark,
than parallel with the layers, an item not to be overlooked

in connection with the nailing in of bottom boards and bolting on the various irons.

The cross bars should be tenoned and the sills mortised instead of being lapped. The mortises should exceed by a trifle one-third the full depth of the bar.

The corners of the panels being mitered, the corner blocks play a very important part, as there must be surface enough to hold the panel. When the deck is covered, a full square block can be used, but when open, the block must be cut away to give a good clean finish inside.

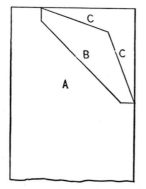

Fig. 96. One form of block. *A*, sill. *B*, inside face of corner block. *C C*, lines of shoulder.

Fig. 96 shows one form of block, *A* the end of the sill, *B* the inside face of the corner blocks, *C C* the lines of the shoulders where the block is lapped against the corner, the intervening space between lines *B* and *C C* the shoulder bearing upon the sill.

The panel is to be cut to the form indicated by the dotted lines seen in Fig. 94. If cut square at the front, a strip half the thickness of the panel should be let in, as indicated by dotted lines *H*, to prevent the panel checking at the corner. If cut to a sweep, as per line *D*, there is no necessity of letting in the strip. If the deck is paneled, the back seat riser should be moved back to line *P,* and the cross piece of whitewood cut to fit against the pillar and fill up the offset of the panel. Nail the deck panel against the underside of the cross bar. The side panels should be of full half-inch whitewood. Dress them off perfectly true on the inside; also dress off the frame work perfectly true. Prepare freshly cooked glue, and have it as hot as it can be made in a double glue kettle. Moisten the wood of the frame and the panels, where they come in contact with the frame, with hot water, apply the glue quickly to both sides, place them on the frames, place the sides together—frames out—and clamp firmly together. Clean away all surplus glue from the inside and set the sides to dry. They should not be disturbed under twenty-four hours.

While the sides are getting in order, make the seat frame, the corner of which is shown by *A A,* Fig. 100. The frames should be of good fine-grained ash or cherry, three inches wide and seven-eighths of an inch thick. Lap and miter the corners as shown. The lap on the long bar should be cut away from the top.

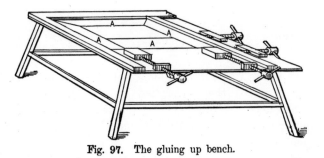

Fig. 97. The gluing up bench.

A gluing-up bench is a great convenience. By its use much time can be saved and greater accuracy secured. Fig. 97 shows such a bench with a seat frame, *A,* compressed into position. All that is required is to glue the joints, lay the strips in their proper positions, and tighten the screws.

When the seat frame joints are all properly secured and the glue cold, clean off and true up the top. Plane the back to a slight sweep, say one-sixteenth of an inch at each end, then dress off the ends. In all cases the front end of the end panels of seats is lower than the back at the corner. If the seat frame is left square, the seat will measure wider across the top when finished than it does across the front.

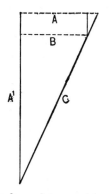

Fig. 98. Triangle used to ascertain plan of seat.

To correct this, lay off a triangle as shown by Fig. 98. *A* the perpendicular, *C* the seat flare, *A* the top line of the back corner, *B* the top line of the front corner. The difference between the length of these lines gives the width necessary to be removed from each end at the back corners to make the finished seat of the same width, back and front.

Having shaped this frame correctly, gauge off one and three-quarters inch from the outside and rabbet out the recess *C* to the depth of one-eighth of an inch. Next bevel off the back seat panel, gauge off seven-eighths of an inch and dress off the edge to a square with the bottom edge bevel. Secure it in place by a screw near each end. Mark off on each side for bevel of curves; miter. Remove the panel, cut the miters, and with a coarse saw run in a slot,

as shown at *B*, Fig. 99. Screw the panel in position and
fit the ends. Glue the corners, remove the panels, and saw
into the end panels the continuation of the slot *B*. Have
the corners firmly secured by corner clamps and drive a
glued strip of good ash into the slot *B* and set away to dry.
By this time the body will be ready to clean off. Each side
should be well cleaned off on the bench and the corner bevels
cut for the end panels. Glue in the end bars, and square
up the body; then fit in the end panels and glue them in
place. It is a good plan to fit in the balance piece at the
top of the seat risers before gluing in end panels, as this
piece will hold the sides in their proper position.

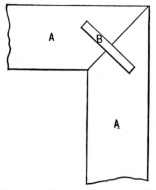

Fig. 99.   The slot in seat panels.

In clearing off the panels, give them a slight fullness, as
the tendency is to shrink and give a hollow appearance to
the side. A perfectly straight flat side will appear slightly
convexed under certain lights. As a rule bodymakers depend
too much on the file and sandpaper. The truing up should
be done with the plane, the file and sandpaper being used
to good advantage for this purpose and for removing file
scratches.

Corner plates for the bottom and corner irons for the top
of panels at corners cost but a trifle, and they should not be

omitted. Those for the top of the panels are best secured by long wire nails, but whether secured by nails or screws, they should be thoroughly trued up before being secured to the body, as it is almost impossible to fit up the irons on the panels without causing some of the screws to jump out or to get loose.

Nothing has been said about plugs, &c., simply because there is no necessity for using screws to secure the panels, if the glue is of good quality, properly tempered and hot when applied. When panels are molded, nails or very small head screws may be used, as they can be covered by the

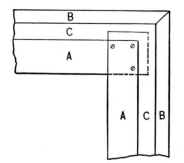

Fig. 100. Method of making seat frame corner.

moldings, but they are not absolutely necessary. No wood-worker has yet been able to put in plugs over screw heads that will not reveal themselves after the vehicle is painted. If the bodymaker is willing to do the necessary work, he can rabbet out the sills and end bars one-half inch, and thus secure a double joint for the bottom of the panels, which may be further secured by nails or screws run up into the panels through the hard wood, the heads being on the under side. The screws or nails, however, should be put in after the body is cleaned off.

It is well right here to caution woodworkers against extra

tight mortises and tenons, also against fitting joints so that
the wood is bruised or the grain breaks in any way.

Panels.

One of the most troublesome features of bodymaking is the
settling of panels between the supporting pieces of the frame.
It matters not whether the panel be that of a square box
body or the thin panels covering the framework of heavy
bodies, the result is the same. But when the panel is flat,
the effect is more injurious than when bent. The common
belief is that this sinking is due entirely to the panels not
being seasoned. This is a mistake. Seasoned panels will sink
as well as those not seasoned, of course not to the same extent, but sufficient to prove injurious.

The fault often lies with the bodymaker. When making a
square box body he takes it for granted that a level surface
once secured, will remain, provided the panel is dry. But
he takes no steps toward protecting the panel from injury.
If the well-established fact was fully recognized that wood
shrinks every time a new surface is exposed, there would be
far less trouble from the settling of panels. He prepares his
frame, and then cuts out and planes up his panels, and immediately glues them to the frame. The frame itself may
be perfectly level, but when he puts on the panels he clamps
them too tight, and uses wide clamps which overhang the
pillar, and the result is that the panel is drawn down inside,
a little, it may be, but that little is sufficient to cause the
panel to settle when the screws are removed. Then, when
the panels are finally cleaned off, a new surface is exposed
and shrinkage occurs, the panel being firmly glued to the
frame on the inside.

The shrinkage by reason of the new surface operates to
force the panel in lengthwise, and to concave it between the
supports. To prevent this, the entire framework should be
trued off so that there will be a slight fullness on all inner
edges of such pieces as are not central on the panel.

Fig. 101 shows the side frame of a square box wagon, *a a a* the edges which should be the highest. The fullness is slight, no more than necessary to throw the straightedge out about an eighth of an inch at a point corresponding with the top edge of the panel.

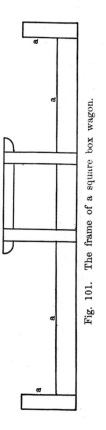

Fig. 101. The frame of a square box wagon.

Fig. 102 (page 104) represents an end view. *A* is the sill, *B* the panel line when set up square, and *C* the line described by the straightedge. The corner posts must be set up square on to the required flare of the body. The sill can be faced

off at the joint; the seat posts being central and the strain
from the panel being equal on both sides, they can be set
out a little more than is required for the body flare. But
even all this precaution will avail nothing if care is not used
in gluing the panels upon the frame. The most common
method is to lay the two sides together—frames outside—and
dispense with "calls." This will prove satisfactory if care is
taken to retain the handscrews in a correct position, but if

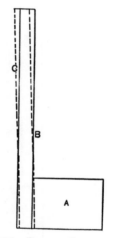

Fig. 102.   Representing an end view.

too wide or open at the back, the frame will be twisted, and
whatever gain would naturally result from the flaring of the
face of the frame pieces will be lost. Unless care is taken
in this respect, it is best to use "calls," but they should be
so placed upon the panel that the inner edges will be back
of the edges of the post, instead of being, as is most commonly the case, inside.

Fig. 103 shows the correct and incorrect position of a
"call." A the corner post, B the sill, dotted line C the
proper location for the inside edge of the "call," and D the
common location.

In the final dressing off of the panel there should be a slight fullness lengthwise and crosswise, not enough to be perceptible to the eye, but which would amount to one-sixteenth of an inch in length, say in four feet two inches, and about a thirty-second of an inch in the width of the panel. A panel dressed up in this way will appear flat and straight, and if shrinkage causes it to settle, the depression will hardly be perceptible.

Thin panels having no central supports, or when the supports are far apart, are almost certain to settle unless great care is taken, but when they are bent, then sinking is due entirely to faulty workmanship. This assertion may be modified as regards ogee and other double sweep bends, as slight

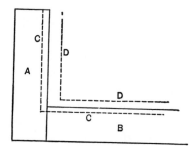

Fig. 103. The correct and incorrect position of a "call."

differences in the thicknesses, or in the texture of the wood may cause one bend to run into the other, and thus change both. This is particularly noticeable in the old style ogee back panels, the lower or concave bend of which is very short and the panel is planed very thin to enable the workman to give it the required shape. If bent over forms and allowed to dry before being put into the grooves, these panels would hold their shape as well as others.

Wherever practicable, forms should be used for all panels where there is much bend, and in all cases these forms should be provided with pressure screws, so that the grains are upset instead of being stretched or separated, as is the universal practice with timber bent the other way of the grain, and the bend should be a little in excess of the actual requirements.

Quarter panels and others when the bend is comparatively slight in each, and when it is put in at the time of being glued into place, must be treated differently from those panels that can be bent over forms. Lower quarter panels must be bent to a certain extent both ways of the grain, and as the edges are supported by being inserted into grooves, it is necessary to use panels somewhat thicker than the grooves, and to reduce them by planing the edge down to the required thickness on the outer side. These should never be glued in. The only places where glue should be used is on the standing pillar and grooves in the arm rail, when the latter is not finished with a solid molding. These panels must always be supported by strainers, but gluing the panels to these strainers is a great mistake. Instead of glue in the grooves, use the best white lead reduced to the consistency of soft putty, by linseed oil. Apply this freely to the edges of the panel and in the groove; then drive the panel up to its place and remove the surplus lead. As the panel must be moist when driven in, it will necessarily shrink on drying. The lead will not set as quickly as glue, so that if the panel shrinks a little it will do no harm, but if glue is used in the grooves and on the strainers, the shrinkage will either check the panel or the panel will settle between the strainers and show the entire outline, even after the vehicle has been painted.

Do not use glue or lead upon the strainers. Treat lower back panels in the same way, and be sure that the edges are all strongly supported, and the panel set out to its fullest point in the center. This will operate to prevent settling so as to be too low when seasoned. Upper quarter panels are stayed by strainers, but we often see those that have settled to such an extent as to show the entire outline of the strainers. This can be avoided entirely by bending the panels a little more than is necessary, and when gluing them on securing the edges, first allowing the panel to bulge in the center, as shown by Fig. 104. *A* is the top rail, *B* the panel and *C* the strainer, which is straighter than the top rail, but which has lighter bends, when it is set up in place. It will do no harm if the panel bilges from the top rail a quarter of an inch at the center after the edges are secured. When set down the wood upsets, and any shrinkage that may occur after the panel has become dry, is taken up by the expansion of the fiber, without changing the form of the panel in the least.

Blocking up so as to give a solid backing to the panel is

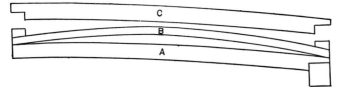

Fig. 104. The panel bilging in the center.

unnecessary when good whitewood panels are used, and when care is taken in putting them in properly. It may be necessary with some woods, but it certainly is not with whitewood. Flat panels should be allowed to become thoroughly dry outside before applying the canvas. Bent panels may be canvased after they have been in twenty-four hours, but they should not be canvased immediately after bendings, as they often are, as the canvas when thoroughly dry prevents any change to the surface covered by it, and throws all strain upon the exposed surface.

If this frame work is properly made, very little planing will be necessary to give the proper surface to the outside, and bodymakers will find it to their advantage to use fine set, concave face (from end to end) for cleaning off. If these are of the proper form, much better results can be reached by their use than by depending upon the straight-face plane and sandpaper.—*By* W. N. F.

Ladies' Phaeton.

This class of carriage is preferred in many localities to the square box, cutaway front buggies for a two-passenger vehicle. The body is hung off on an elliptic spring carriage part,

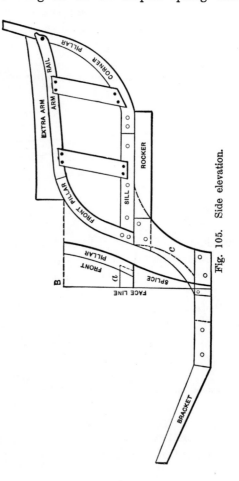

Fig. 105.   Side elevation.

making it a plain as well as a serviceable vehicle, one that is within the range of any workman of intelligence.

With this a draftboard is indispensable. The first drawing to be made is the side elevation, as shown by Fig. 105. In laying out this, strike lines horizontal and perpendicular, and establish certain points that are arbitrary in this body. These are the depth from top of the seat rail to the inside of the bottom board. This must be twelve inches as the minimum and thirteen inches as the maximum. The second point is on a line extending diagonally from the top of the seat rail to the line of the bottom intersecting the latter at a point that will give not less than twenty inches on the diagonal line. This will give the location of the front heel bar. The bracket piece should extend ten inches forward of this point. If a shorter bracket is desired, then the front heel bar must be further from the seat rail.

With these points established, the draft for the side elevation is easily made. For the side sweeps, three patterns are necessary, viz., front pillar, arm rail and corner pillar. When these are made, correct the draft on the board by them. A top rail sweep is necessary, as this body has but little sweep. The front corner pillar also has but little—not to exceed a fourth of an inch.

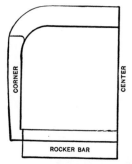

Fig. 106. Half of the back.

Fig. 106 shows half of the back, and Fig. 108 half of the

front view. Fig. 107 shows half of the ground plan. The drawings of these will greatly assist the bodymaker, but he can dispense with Figs. 106 and 108 if he desires. Fig. 107, showing the center line of the ground plan, gives the loca-

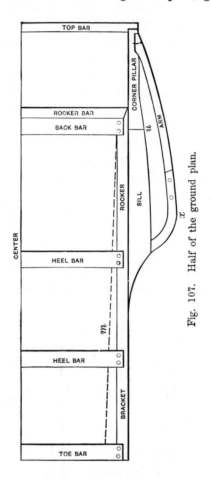

Fig. 107. Half of the ground plan.

tion and length of bars, sills, corner pillars, &c. This drawing shows the bottom bars of one length, but in many cases it is desirable to shorten the front bar. When this is done, this view becomes more valuable than when square. Make the contraction by changing the face line of the rocker, as shown by dotted line *M.*

Having the drafts made, it is an easy matter to determine the thickness of every piece of timber that will be used. The sectional drawing *B,* Fig. 106, shows the front elevation of the front corner, the "face line" being the outside face of the rockers, the width of the sill, which in this case is three inches. Draw a straight line from the top to the bottom of the corner pillar on the inside, and the measurement across at the broadest point gives the thickness of the timber for the corner pillar—one and a half inch.

The thickness for the arm rail is ascertained by drawing a straight line on the arm rail, Fig. 107, inside from the back corner forward to the point of the arm at *X.* This will require a piece one and a half inch thick. When dressed up and lightened out inside, the front corner pillar and the arm rail should not be lighter than one inch. The thickness required for the corner pillar is ascertained by measuring across the foot line *u.* It can be cut from two-inch timber. The rockers are made up of four pieces each. These should be cut out of one and one-fourth inch ash, so that when dressed up they will not vary much from one and one-eighth inch in thickness. The top bar for the back should be of three-eighths inch thickness, and cut wider. All heel bars should be one inch thick. The back bar need not be more than one inch thick in this body, as the rocker bar which is two and a half inches deep and seven-eighths inch thick, gives all the stiffness required. This bar extends up to the inside edge of the corner pillar molding, the bottom of the back panel being secured to it instead of being grooved in.

In lapping the rocker pieces make the shortest lap the shoulders outside, unless the shoulder joint is to be covered. In that case make the laps so that the grain of the panel or other piece will cross the shoulder lap at right angles.

Frame the rockers up square and flat; rabbet out for the

toe and foot boards a half inch. For the heel and back rocker bottom, one-fourth inch is heavy enough. Dress up the sills square on the top, bottom, and face. Mark off the front corner pillar by the pattern on the face side. Dress off at each end to the bevel of the cant; then mark across at each end the required bevel; lay on the pattern, moving it up so that the indicating points inside shall be at the bevel marks outside. Mark off and dress up to the outside and inside marks.

If the bodymaker is not far enough advanced to lay off these corner pillars, he can first set up his corner pillars, then lap together the front corner pillar and the arm rails, and set them up, being careful to give all the outward cant. Then lay the rocker and quarter down flat on the draft-board, and with a square, the head of which rests upon the draftboard, and the arm against the pillar, he can get the cross lines which will guide him in shifting his pattern, so that when the front corner pillars are dressed up, a straight-edge laid across from each side will bear upon the outside of the pillar as though it was square.

Set the back corner pillar up square, lap the foot to the sill, and secure by two screws. When the frame is put up, dress off the outside true, using a convex sweep of the required convexity, to secure the proper level to the outside of the molding. When this is done, gauge off the molding nine-sixteenths inch on the bottom of the sill, and on the back corner pillar half way up to the arm. From that point taper to three-eighths of an inch at the arm. Make the arm and front corner pillar molding a half inch, slightly tapered at the back end of the arm. Frame in the top back bar, mold off pillars and back bar, glue and screw the sill and back corner pillar together, and secure them to the rockers, glue the front corner pillar and arm rail at the splice, set them up in their place, screw, but don't glue them into their place; then fit and dress off the strainers, mark off, and fit in the panel. Set the panel into the sill and back corner pillar groove, slip in the strainers and put on the arm rail and front pillar, glue the joints well and screw them up firmly. If the panel has been well fitted, no trouble will be experienced in getting all joints snug and in proper position. Next fit in the "splice" of whitewood, shaped to follow the outlines of the rocker up to where it intersects the back piece of the rocker. From that point the sweep must be continued as shown by the dotted lines on Fig. 105. This piece must come out flush with the outside of the sill molding. Secure it to the rocker by a few screws and glue.

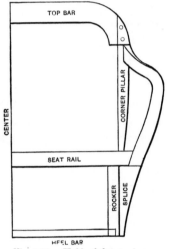

Fig. 108.   Half of front view.

When dry dress off to a sweep, as shown by Fig. 108. The rocker forward of the "splice" may be paneled if desired, worked off smooth, and finish the "splice" as well as the panel with a narrow molding near each edge. The dotted line *C* indicates the edge of the rocker as sometimes made, in which case the splice is dressed out to within an eighth of an inch of the outside, the object being to give a lighter appearance to the front.

After the panels and all glued joints are dry, clean off each side, as it is much handier to do so before being put together than afterward. Then set up the frame and fit in the back panel. The toe bar and the front heel bar may be glued and screwed into place before the back panel is fitted in; but in either case the rocker plates must be put on before setting up. In putting in the back panel, bend it a little more than is necessary and press up from the bottom all it will bear before nailing the bottom edge to the bar. If this is done, the panel will not sink in when dry, nor will strainers be necessary. When strainers are used, they should not be glued to the panels, as the glue will hold that part of the panel so that it cannot move when shrinking, and the panel will settle between the strainers. Secure the front seat rail into position, and put in the seat bottom boards, giving the seat about a fourth of an inch slope backward. Then fit on the extra arms, which should be of one and a fourth inch white-wood. Allow this arm to extend over the other about an eighth of an inch, and screw it firmly into position. This being done, turn over the body and put in the bottom boards the last thing.

Most bodymakers put in the bottom boards as soon as possible after the frame is up. They make a mistake by so doing, as the boards interfere materially when putting in the back panel and doing other work from the top.

The bodymaker, although not making the rocker plates, should be able to give instruction concerning them, as a failure on their part means a failure of the body. For a phaëton of this character the plate should be of one and a fourth by three-eighth-inch iron, the ends drawn down. The front end, owing to its width, can be of one-fourth by one-inch iron, welded on the wider iron at the point designated by X, Fig. 109, an inside view of rocker and rocker plate. The back should be drawn to one-eighth inch at the end, beginning at i. Avoid all square corners and leave the iron full thickness and width at the bends. The bodymaker should

mark off for the screws, placing them to either side of tl
joints in the rockers, and in a position where they w.
strengthen the laps. In all crooked work there are places
where the grain of the wood runs crosswise. In marking off
for screws, the rule is to set them near the edges of the

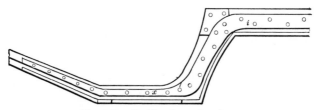

Fig. 109.   Inside view of rocker.

plates, alternating to either edge. When the cross grain section is reached, it is often necessary to change the situation
of the screws to avoid two being on a direct line with the
grain. Use heavy screws, nothing lighter than No. 12, and
wherever possible No. 16.

Four-Passenger Rockaway.

With standing top, as well as with other classes of work,
the object is to give a representation of a class, selecting a
popular form of body, and one that contains within itself the
requisites necessary to make all points clear. The particular
sweep of the bottom sides, quarter panels, or other outlines
are not arbitrary.

This paper will relate entirely to the building of a curtain
quarter, cut-under rockaway, one of the simplest of its class,
at the same time a very complete and comfortable vehicle.
The draftboard for this should be large enough to take the
full body, as shown by Fig. 110 (page 116). If long enough
to take Figs. 111 and 112, the workman will find it advantageous.

The first thing to be done is to draw the side elevation

and then make the patterns.   These are standing pillar, corner pillar, bottom side, top rail, pieces 1, 2, 3, and 4 of
rocker, in Fig. 110, back bar top rail, and arm of quarter
rail.   The standing and quarter pillars, though apparently
straight above the position, turn under, and should have a
fullness of about an eighth of an inch between the quarter
rail and the top.

For a rockaway of this class the standing pillar should
have a turn-under of three inches, and the top rail a sweep

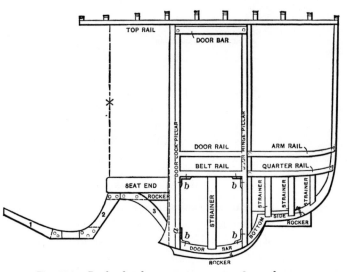

Fig. 110.   Draft of a four-passenger, cut-under rockaway.

of three and a half inches.   Flatten the sweep of the top
rail forward of the front pillar.   The hight of the top must
be determined by the front seat.   Three feet six inches is
the minimum hight between the bottom of the front seat
and the under side of the curve, on dotted line X, Fig. 110.
Too many rockaway tops are located by the measurement
from the back seat rail regardless of the difference of hight
of the front seat.   The result is the occupant of the front

seat, unless of diminutive stature, sits in a stooped position. The objection to raising the top so as to give the full measurement at the front seat, is the apparent disproportion of the hight to the length of the carriage. Three to five inches may convey the idea of a top-heavy job on the draftboard, but it would not be noticed on the street, while the loss of that space would give discomfiture to the driver and cause him to assume an ungainly position.

In a factory where there are few patterns to help the draftsman in making a set of any particular kind, a large

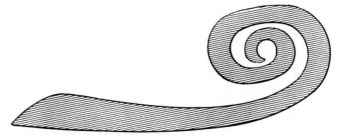

Fig. 111. Large scroll sweep.

scroll sweep of the general character as that shown by Fig. 111, will prove valuable. Though made by a compass, there is no true compass sweep in its entire outline. It is made by setting a compass wide enough to strike a six-foot circle. Place the pointed end in position and strike a line with the pencil end, say eight inches long. Then move the pointed end a few inches on a line parallel with the pencil line, and and move the pencil a few inches. The length of the pencil line as well as the sweep is determined by the distance the pointer is made each time. When the sharp bend is reached, the pointer is moved in the opposite direction of the pencil, and as heretofore the curve of the pencil line is determined by the movement of the pointer. In no case must the pointer be moved enough nor the pencil line made long enough to cause a sudden bend or flattening. The pencil point should not leave the board until the sweep is made. The sweep is the result of an ever changing center. When the sweep is sawed out and trued up, it is a good plan to canvas the sides to prevent splitting. Another good assistant is a strip of lead one-quarter by one-half inch square and three or four feet long. This can be laid upon the draft, bent to the sweep and then laid upon the pattern board and the sweep transferred thereon.

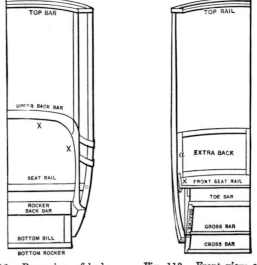

Fig. 112.   Rear view of body.   Fig. 113.   Front view of frame.

In making all sectional patterns, such as pieces 1, 2, 3, and 4 of rockers, make them full length, and indicate on them the location of the shoulders. Having the patterns made, the next step is the selection of timber. For the rockers use good tough ash, one and three-eighths inch thick, bottom sides three inches, corner pillars two and a half inches, top rail three inches, hinge pillars one and an eighth inch, lock

pillars one and three-eighths inch, arm rails two inches, upper back bar one inch. These are the dressed thicknesses.

The door cuts through to form the continuation of the
bottom side. The bottom side used is the piece back of the
face of the hinge pillar.   The coupé pillar is of one and
three-eighths inch stuff with a spliced foot of whitewood, as

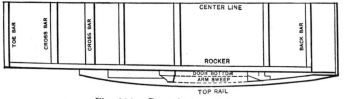

Fig. 114. Ground plan of frame.

shown by *B*, Fig. 116. The side view *A*, the lap on the
pillar, which is five-eighths of an inch, the full depth of the
rabbet, the dotted line *x*, Fig. 116, which shows the face of
the ash pillar, the part front of that being a projection of
uniform thickness. This pillar foot is solely an ornamental
feature, and may be omitted if desired. In lapping the rockers make as far as possible all joints so that whatever covers
them on the outside will strengthen them, and where not
covered, the joint exposed will be short. Be careful to glue
up the rockers square and true.

The body is contracted at the front end six inches forward
of the hinge pillar. An experienced bodymaker will provide
for this by framing the back piece of the rocker so that the
face will be straight while all forward of it will correspond
to the lines of the contraction. An easy way for an inexperienced bodymaker is to frame the rockers as though the
width was alike at both ends, and then dress off the outside of
the back piece to a line corresponding to the straight center
line of the body. In this case the back end of the rocker
piece will be scant five-eighths of an inch. This will leave
the rocker three-fourths of an inch thick at the back end.

This plan is drawn for a sawed corner pillar with the foot bottom to the end of the bottom side, the form of the lap and shoulder being shown if a bent pillar is used. The top portion of the pillar is lapped at the arm by a lap not less than four inches long and the bottom end extended forward to the drop of the bottom side, where it is lapped to that piece. This makes a much better job than the sawed pillar, but bent pieces are not always accessible to the smaller manufacturers, and no man can bend them properly without an upsetting bender.

The face of the coupé pillar must be long enough to bear

Fig. 115.   Coupé pillar.

against the rocker up to the top. In Fig. 115 *a* shows the face to the coupé pillar, and *b* the face of the hinge pillar. Heavy screws pass through the rocker into the pillars.

Lap in the quarter rail and secure both ends by a screw. It must project the full thickness of the molding outside of the hinge pillar. Dress off the bottom side and corner pillar to the sweep of the top rail at the point directly over these pieces, using a concave sweep made to the convex line of the top rail.

In order to secure a perfect quarter, it is necessary to make what is known as the cheat line, a line having a convexity at the point where the corner pillar and bottom side join of an eighth of an inch to the foot, increasing the cut-under that much at the point designated. The geometrical rule fully explains the cause of this, but it is out of place in this article. .

The quarter molding on the bottom side and corner pillar should be full one-quarter of an inch thick, five-eighths of an inch wide at the bottom and three-eighths of an inch at the top of the quarter. Above the quarter rail the molding on the corner pillar should be a quarter of an inch wide and full an eighth of an inch deep. The molding on the coupé pillar must be of the same proportions at the bottom as that on the bottom side, gradually tapering in width to three-eighths of an inch at the top rail. The rabbet for the door should be five-eighths by one-quarter inch.

The upper back bar should be mortised into the corner pillar and the molding boxed out to the shape shown by the inside line x, Fig. 112. The foot of the panel rests on the top of the back bar of the rocker.

Fig. 113 gives a front view of the frame; x, the seat end, shows the plan of this piece and its projection over the rocker, together with the skirt. As this drawing shows the frame not paneled, the workman will understand that the actual overhang is less than that shown by the thickness of the panel.

Fig. 116.   Pillar with spliced foot.

It is desirable at times to have this carriage partially closed up in front, and for that purpose an extra back is made. It consists of two frames, meeting in the center, where they are hinged. The outside bar is provided with two dowels which fit into holes in the pillars. To set up the back, spring the hinges at the center, enter the dowels into the holes in each pillar, and press the back up straight. Two strong, flat bolts keep the back from springing when set up. As all the pressure comes against it from the outside or driver's seat, the beams must be so hinged that, to spring it open, the center must be moved toward the front. This is the simplest extra front that is made.

There is no part of the body which requires more care than

the making of the doors. They must fit in every way, and yet be entirely free so as not to bind or rattle. The pillars must be of forest ash, fine and tough, ash that will not spring. The belt rail and door rail are best tenoned in. The bottom bar, which in this body retains the sweep of the bottom side, should be lapped on and secured by two screws to each pillar. The top bar may be lapped or tenoned. After the door is all framed, dress it up so as to leave a plump one-sixteenth of an inch between the body and the door hinge pillars, and the same space between the outside of the rabbet of the lock pillars, and one-eighth of an inch on the inside, one-quarter of an inch between the face of the bottom door bar and the rocker, and one-eighth of an inch at the top. The lock pillar must project one-sixteenth of an inch outside of the coupé pillar, and the hinge pillar must be hung to project the same distance outside of the body lock pillar. A little spring may be given to the door, so that when the top is against the rabbet, the bottom will be off one-eighth of an inch. A little gather may also be given to the face of the rabbet on the door pillar to obviate the possibility of the centers coming in contact before the ends. Hang the door with three butt hinges, so placed that the pins of all are on a perpendicular line. Doors, where no glass frames are used, can be made up square, but where there are glass frames, the lock pillars must have an outside bevel to correspond with the segment of a circle made by the door, with the hinges as the pivot. Corner irons, as shown by *b b b b*, on the door frame, Fig. 110, add greatly to the strength of the door and cost but a trifle.

Fig. 117 shows the rocker plate. It should be of five-eighths by two and a quarter inch iron, using the full width where the rockers will admit of it. The screws should be one and a half, No. 18, except at the front, where No. 12 will answer. The screws should not be more than three inches apart, and they must be set well in to hold the plate firmly against the rocker.

The dimensions of this body are forty-two inches on the back seat rail over all, front bar thirty-five inches, back thirty-six inches, boot panels three-eighths of an inch thick,

Fig. 117.   The rocker plate.

quarter panels, door panels and back panels five-sixteenths of an inch thick, bottom boards on tread a full half inch, others three-eighths of an inch, top boards a quarter of an inch.

Extension Top Phaeton.

The class of carriages known as extension top phaëtons find favor in every part of our country. They are essentially democratic, neat and comfortable in appearance, and can be produced at a price which brings them within the range of a large number of persons who could not afford to possess a four-passenger vehicle if the cost was high.

The bodies partake of a variety of forms. Some have straight bottoms, low-cut sides, no doors; others straight bottoms, high sides and doors; others again with cut-unders for wheels and bottom sides with more or less sweep, with and without doors. Those having straight bottom sides are, as a rule, hung upon side-bar gears. Those with sweep lines on three elliptic springs or upon plain platform gears.

The fact that forms are so numerous and the manner of hanging so varied makes it possible for the woodworkman to exercise his skill in designing without much fear of clashing against fixed styles or features of construction.

In this series of articles it would be folly to attempt to give any special style as a guide. I have therefore selected style of body which can be hung upon an elliptic spring gear on a platform, with or without doors. The only gear that cannot be used is the side bar; for that the straight bottom side is absolutely necessary if the vehicle is to be at all tasty in appearance.

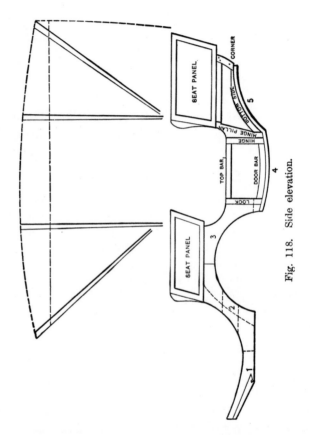

Fig. 118. Side elevation.

Fig. 118 gives side elevation of a four-passenger phaëton, one extremely simple in its construction. The rockers are of one and three-eighths inch ash, in five pieces, viz., the bracket piece, 1; the riser, 2; the arch, 3; the door piece, 4; and the back piece, 5. In splicing make all outside joints perpendicular, and put in the screws from the inside. The only piece that can be designated as a bottom side is the under piece of the back quarter. This is of one and a quarter-inch ash, "jacked" off to one and an eighth on the bottom. The bottom bar of the door continues the line of the bottom side. It is one and an eighth of an inch thinner, as there must be at least an eighth of an inch between the face of the door bar and the face of the bottom side.

The hinge pillar is of one and a half inch ash, cut down to one and an eighth inch on the bottom end. It is secured to the rocker by one bolt and two No. 20 screws. The back corner pillar is of one and a quarter inch ash. The outside joints in the back quarter frame are all perpendicular. When the quarter frame is glued up, it must be dressed off perfectly true on the outside, as the panel is put on without screws, nails or moldings, and unless the frame is true, the panel will not fit and the glue will not keep it in place. The back end of the panel must project a fourth of an inch beyond the corner pillar, as the back end panel miters to the corner. The door frame is no heavier than is absolutely necessary to enable it to hold the hinges and lock. It is paneled outside the same as the quarter. Inside the panel must be fitted inside of the frame. An eighth inch lining is all that is required. The seats are made of one inch whitewood, with a three-quarter inch molding worked on the wood. This is a little more work than to nail the moldings on, but the absence of nail holes more than compensates for the extra work. Some prefer round corners to the back of the seats. When these are used the top and bottom moldings extend entirely around the seat, the corner moldings being omitted. If round corners are used, half spindles give a very neat finish to the seat panels.

Forward of the door a piece of whitewood is fitted to the rocker, following the latter's outlines. The straight side next the door takes the place of the lock pillar, and is rabbeted out for the guard. The pillar on the line of the door is finished flush with it, and forward of this it is lightened off by an easy sweep to one-quarter of an inch at a point a little forward of the back corner of the front seat. Here the front panel is mitered to it. The deck panel should be mitered, but some are put on and the ends left about a half inch from the outside of the rocker. These are rounded to give the appearance of a molding.

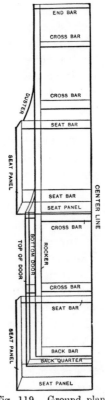

Fig. 119. Ground plan.

Fig. 119 gives a view of the ground plan, the various bars,

&c., being specified. All the cross bars to the bottom should be lapped into the rabbet for the bottom boards, and secured by at least three No. 16 screws at each end. In putting in the wheelhouse panel, instead of making a perfect joint at the ends of the panel, round the end from the outside down close to the edge, and also round the edge of the rabbet. This, when finished, gives the appearance of a molding, and no trouble arises from the joint showing when the carriage is painted. Clamp the panel in if possible. By so doing the use of many nails is dispensed with, and the panel is less liable to become checked. For bottom board at the front and back tread use full half inch pine. The other panels may be of three-eighths inch whitewood. The front duster is shown by the line in front of the forward seat, in Fig. 119, and by the dotted line on the rocker under the forward seat in Fig. 118. This must be of whitewood, about two inches thick, lightened down to a quarter inch at the bottom. It is finished without moldings.

As the seats project well over the sides of the panels it is necessary to use wide end bars for the seat frames. There being no skirtings, the under sides must be well finished. The seat panels are screwed against the seat frames, and it is necessary to plug over the screw heads. Unless the plugs are put in carefully, they will show after the vehicle is painted. Most bodymakers commit a serious error by putting in the plugs too tight, as driving them in breaks the fiber of the panel and carries the wood down. It afterward yields a little and the full outline of the plug is exposed. The plugs should be of the same wood as the panel and snugly fitted, so that a slight tap by the hammer will set them in. The screw head should be sunken a little below the bottom of the plug hole, so that the plug will come in contact with wood, not metal, when it is driven in. After the body has been cleaned off, moisten the plug and wood around it so as to raise the grain, and when thoroughly dry, clean off again. This will decrease the chances of the plug showing.

Fig. 120 shows the view of the front end location of bars and projection of sides and seats, and Fig. 121 that of the back.

These carriages have, as a rule, tops with four bows. More are sometimes used, but they are not necessary. The setting of these bows is generally left to the trimmer, but I contend that the bodymaker should control this part of the work. In setting the bows be careful to have the face sides of the two door bows perfectly plumb. Set the back bow so that it projects at least one and a half inch back of the seat back, and the front one six inches forward of the front seat bar. These bows are subjected to a severe strain, and I favor the tubu-

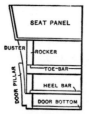

Fig. 120.   Front end elevation.

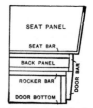

Fig. 121.   Back end elevation.

lar socket or the long slat. The short slat irons do not give the necessary support to insure the bows retaining their shape. Round the bows nicely over if they are to be covered, as they are exposed, and unless well finished, mar the appearance of the vehicle.

The rocker plates should be of one and a half by three-eighths inch iron, all corners bent round as possible. Secure them by No. 18 screws, placed not more than two inches apart. Stay the cross bars at the ends with corner irons.— *By* W. N. F.

A Tub Phaeton.

The plain phaëton has long been a favorite vehicle with those who desire a carriage that is easy of access, and roomy and comfortable when trimmed, features that are unknown to the square box body and those of kindred pattern. Body-makers who are not familiar with the French rule have a dread of putting up a framework body of this form. That they could succeed better were they thus informed, than when ignorant of all rules of the kind, none will dispute. But a workman who possesses sufficient knowledge of his business to claim the right to be recognized as a journeyman bodymaker, can with a little trouble lay off a skeleton frame upon a draftboard that will contain enough of the essential points to enable him to frame up the body correctly, and in a short time acquire the information that will insure his building a good job.

The first thing to be done is to lay off the elevation plan as shown by Fig. 122 (page 130). A represents the bottom side and B the corner pillar; or the two may be of one bent piece. They can be purchased of wood benders, and though costing a trifle more than when worked out solid, they are better. But if sawed stock is preferred, the bottom side A must be cut long enough to allow for a good tenon to the point b, and the corner B to lap the point a. These are formed together, as shown by the sectional drawing, Fig. 123. The end of the tenon on the corner pillar is cut as shown by the dotted line e, and the shoulders cut as shown at g and h. By this method all the joints are backed by solid wood, and the liability of opening is decreased. In putting the pieces together, glue the tenon mortise well, draw up by clamps, and pin after the glue is set.

The front pillar is the most difficult piece to set up. There are several rules governing the work, but all are too compli-cated for the beginner, or for the bodymaker who has no knowledge of the French rule. I should therefore advise the bodymaker to frame it up so that the straight back line C, Fig. 122, will range with the corresponding line on the draft-board. Cant it outward, as indicated by line d, Fig. 124— line g indicating the perpendicular position and the curved line *i* the radius described by the pillar on reaching the cant, the length on the line *g* being that required for the pillar.

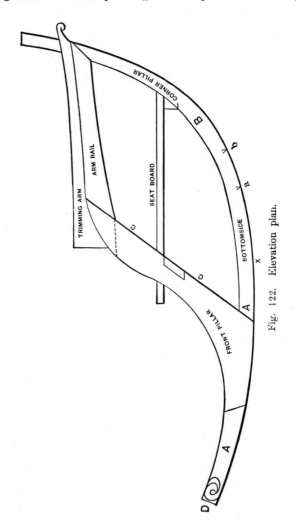

Fig. 122. Elevation plan.

If preferred, the pillar may be cut of timber of sufficient

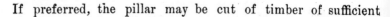

thickness to allow of its being framed up square on the inside, and swept off outside to the required shape, then lightened up from the inside, as the cant is seldom more than four inches. The latter plan may prove the easiest to the novice. If the first plan is followed, the bodymaker should have a thin pattern of the quarter, just as it appears on the draftboard, by which the front line of the pillar can be marked off. When the pillar is in place and properly dressed off, lap on the arm rail as shown, cutting the front pillar

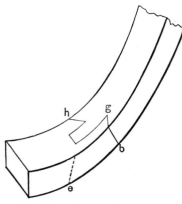

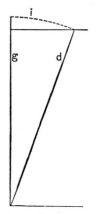

Fig. 123. Corner pillar.   Fig. 124. Outward cant.

lap from the inside, and allowing the back end to miter at the corner pillar. Screw all parts together without gluing, and sweep off the side; then gauge off the moldings, separate the several pieces, and frame up the back to the draft shown by Fig. 125 (page 132). Frame the back bar into the bottom side, a trifle forward of the foot of the corner pillar. The cross bar should be on a line with the bottom of the seat, and the back rail at the required hight. Mortise in the cross bar flush with the corner pillar. After the back is framed up, sweep off the moldings as shown by lines *a* and *b*, Fig. 125. Next lay off the seat rail and toe bar as shown by Fig. 126. Then cut the bars as shown by the half-bottom plan, Fig. 127.

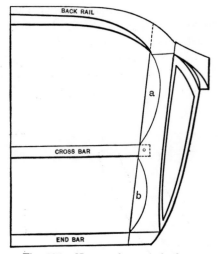

Fig. 125.   How to frame up back.

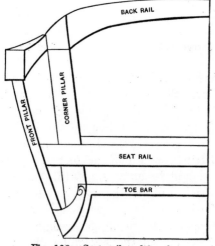

Fig. 126.   Seat rail and toe bar.

After the framing up is completed, box out for the moldings, making one on the bottom side three-quarters of an inch

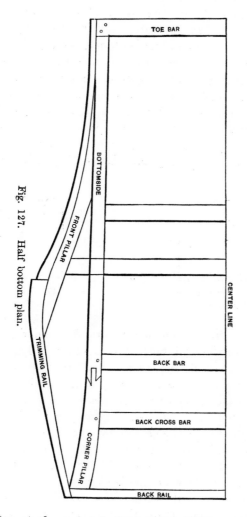

Fig. 127. Half bottom plan.

at the center at the point indicated by *X*, Fig. 122. Taper
up to scant five-eighths of an inch at the arm rail on the

corner pillar, and to half the thickness of the bottom side at the scroll *D*, carry the molding up the front pillar and along the arm rail a uniform width of five-eighths of an inch.

After the moldings are all worked on and rounded, as shown by Fig. 128, or fluted and beaded, as per Fig. 129, glue the corner pillars and bottom sides together. It is well to leave a little fullness to the moldings at the joints, to allow for truing off after gluing. Set up the frame and fit the quarter panels, placing strainers as shown by the dotted lines *O O*, Fig. 122. Put the strainers and panels in place and glue up. Do not glue the panels to the strainers. In point of fact, it is a good plan to glue the frame only, using white lead for the panels where they enter the grooves.

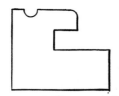

Fig. 128. Moldings worked on and rounded.

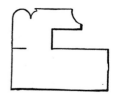

Fig. 129. Moldings fluted and beaded.

After the frame and panels are dry and the glue hard, true off the sides and finish the moldings. Then set up the back and put in all the cross bars. Having previously rabbeted out for the bottom boards, bend, mark off, and fit in the back panels; put them in place and glue all the cross framework together, and before gluing in the bottom boards.

Use clean, fine grained ash for the frame, whitewood for panels, and whitewood or pine for the bottom boards. The popular notion calls for cross moldings. When these are used, there should be three on the back and two on each quarter, if they extend the full width of the panel, or three if a parallel molding is put across the side quarters.—*By* W. N. F.

A Six-Passenger Rockaway.

The rockaway is distinctively an American vehicle. It is built nowhere else, and exceeds in number used any other pleasure carriage for four or six persons. Since its introduction it has undergone many changes in form, but its family feature has been maintained. The most popular outline is that known as the coupé, but in securing this, simplicity of construction has kept down the cost, and made it possible for workmen who could not build a brougham or landau body to build the rockaway.

The pattern selected for this paper is an English quarter coupé, six-seat rockaway, with glass and panel quarters, high door, paneled partition, and closed back, as this makes it possible in a single paper to cover all the points for a closed vehicle for six passengers, and the necessary points not previously given for a four passenger rockaway.

A large draftboard is indispensable, as the workman must have before him the entire plan of the framework. In making the drawing for the side elevation, strike the lines for the faces of the door pillars not less than twenty-two inches apart, measure off from the hinge, or back door pillar, twenty-six inches, and strike a line for the extreme width of the back quarter, measure off from the face of the coupé pillar eighteen inches, and strike a line for the front pillar. These give the necessary guides for the four uprights. The base line, which represents the lowest point of the bottom side at the center of the door, being determined, measure up from it six inches as the minimum, eight inches as the maximum, and strike at the front end a parallel line with the base line, for the base line of the bracket. Measure up from this line fourteen inches as the top of the outside seat bottom. From this last line measure on a line parallel with the standing pillars three feet six inches for head room on the front seat under the roof curves. The curve in the front should have a sweep of one inch, and as the top rail should be two and three-fourths inches deep, deduct three and three-fourths inches from the three feet six inches, and strike a line parallel with the base line as the bottom line of the top rail.

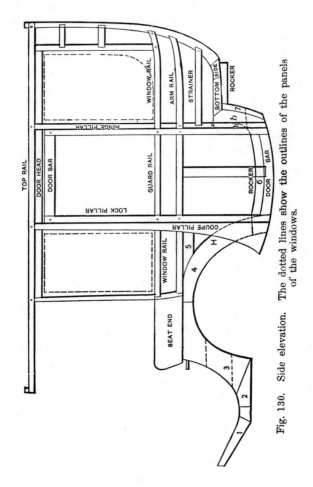

Fig. 130. Side elevation. The dotted lines show the outlines of the panels of the windows.

The square is now formed into which the body is constructed, with the exception of the extension front of the forward pillar. As the body is very long, it is desirable to shorten

the front as much as possible without cramping the leg or
seat room. Eighteen inches is a good depth for the latter,
but as the seat boards can be extended three inches forward
of the side end of the seat panel, an additional perpendicular line can be struck, which will indicate the front end of
the rocker at the front seat, and which will also serve as a
guide for locating the heel bar of the bracket. The latter
should never be back of this line; neither should it exceed

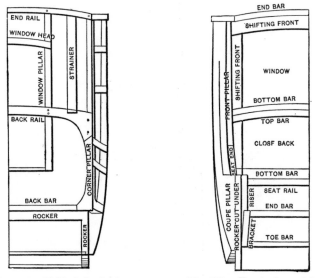

Fig. 131.   Half of the back.   Fig. 132.   Front view of front
part of body.

four inches in front of it. In this design the two points are
in a horizontal line with each other. If the leg room is less
than fourteen inches on the perpendicular line, the toe bar
should be at least twenty-eight inches forward of the end of
the rocker on a straight line. If the depth is fourteen inches,
the front can be shortened two inches. The tread should
not be less than fifteen inches, and the use of the toe bracket

not to exceed nine inches, as these carriages require a leather dash.

With these additional lines the fixed points of outline are

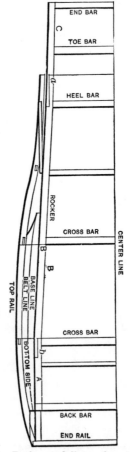

Fig. 133.   Rocker and lines of contraction.

secured. The location of the belt rail, window bars, and door guard are now to be determined. The drop of the center below the bottom line of the back quarter should be

one foot, and the width of the back quarter panel one foot.
This will locate the bottom of the belt line twenty-four inches
above the base line. The end of the front seat should be
eight inches deep. Its bottom line and the bottom line of

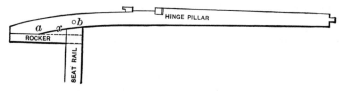

Fig. 134.   Difference in length of coupé and hinge pillars.

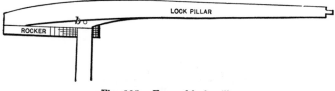

Fig. 135.   Face of lock pillar.

the front quarter must be parallel with the line of the back
quarter at the hinge pillar. The door guard bar must also
be on the same line. The location of the head bar of the
door is determined by the distance between the door guard
and the bottom bar of the door, so that the glass frame,
which, when down, should if possible fall to the level of the
door guard, and when up extend a fourth of an inch above
the bottom line of the top bar of the door. This bar should
be two and a fourth inches wide. The door being shorter
when open, a door head is necessary. There is no fixed rule
for its width; that must be governed entirely by the necessities of the case. The bottom of the rocker between the
corner pillar and the hinge pillar should have a slight upward curve, enough to decrease the width of the quarter panel
a trifle at that point. The sweep of the back corner pillar

is a matter of taste, but the governing points must be twenty-
six inches at the top rail, and twenty-one inches at the back
end of the bottom side. The top rail should extend fifteen
inches forward of the front end of the rocker. From the
points indicated, strike all the other lines, harmonizing sweeps,
and maintaining material enough to secure strength.

The standing pillar turn-under is the next thing to be determined, three inches being a good sweep below the arm

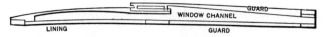

Fig. 136.   Inside of door pillar.

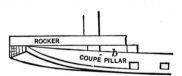

Fig. 137.   Front view of coupé pillar molding, rocker, and location of arm-pieces.

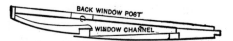

Fig. 138.   Window pillar boxed out.

rail. In this body the pillars face on the rocker. The bottom end should be seven-eighths of an inch thick, after being lightened for the panel, one and a half inch wide at the
top, and not less than two and an eighth inches at the seat
rail. The face on the coupé pillar is long; that on the
hinge pillar is shorter, as it is set in front of the bottom side,
and boxed out between a and b, Fig. 133, to line x. The
rocker cut is shown by dotted line e, Fig. 130. The face of
the lock pillar is shown in Fig. 135, the top line being at H,

Fig. 130. It is boxed out to line *b*, Fig. 135, to the depth of one inch.

Fig. 131 shows half of the back, and as all the pieces are indicated, no special mention of the frame is necessary. The back window must be large, and made to drop. The frame for this is the window pillar, the window head, and the back rail. The pillar is of seven-eighths inch ash, boxed out as shown by Fig. 138, the guard *x* being solid. The guard *a* is a strip of whitewood a half inch thick, glued and nailed against the ash pillar, and allowed to project a half inch. The inside cross guard *a* is of hard wood; the lower and top linings as well as the inside guards are whitewood.

Fig. 132 shows a front view of the front of the body. The various bars, together with the contraction of the rockers, are plainly indicated.

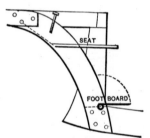

Fig. 139. Inside of rocker and seat and foot board.

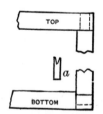

Fig. 140. Plan for framing the glass for closed carriages.

The six-passenger rockaway is provided with a movable partition dividing the front inside seat from the outside or driver's seat. In some cases the entire partition is movable. In others only the upper half can be taken out. In both cases, however, the partition is made in two parts, the lower section being closely paneled and trimmed; the upper section, with one or two windows, is framed and painted. In making the front, use whitewood for the side pillars. It must be thick enough to sit up, so that the inside space is of equal width, top and bottom, and have at least one inch wood at the bottom end of the pillar. It must be two and a fourth inches thick at the corner rails to allow ample room for the guards and grooves. The top must be lengthened down from the inside one and three-fourths inch. Make the front up solid, and saw apart on the line between the bottom and top center bars. If two windows are used, there must be a center pillar one and an eighth inch thick, boxed out for the frames on each side, the same as the face sides of the end pillars. If the front is made up with the bottom section permanent, dowel the upper into the lower sections at the pillars, and use thumb bolts to secure the top. If both sections are movable, dowel the bottom of the parts as well as the center. Secure the top of the lower section by sliding bolts into the body pillars. The boxing out for the window frames is similar to that for the door pillars. It is desirable to have an extra bar to cover the opening into the

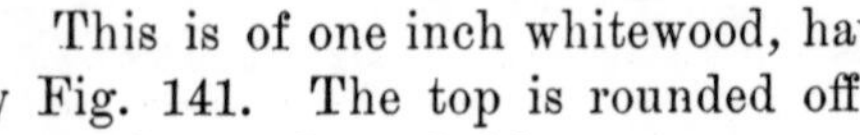

Fig. 141.   The extra bar desired.

top of the bottom section when the section and glass frames are removed. This is of one inch whitewood, having tongues, as shown by Fig. 141. The top is rounded off and painted and trimmed to give a clean finish.

Fig. 136 shows the inside of the door pillar, with guards, channels, &c. The door bar guard rail should be tenoned in the pillars, the shoulder on the outside only. The top door bar may be tenoned or lapped. The window channel must be boxed out to the depth of a fourth of an inch at least. In boxing out use a "trial strip" the full length and thickness of the window frame, and cut away the guards below the guard rail, to allow full play of the "trial strip."

It is important that the door pillars be of good ash. If

possible, have the "layers" edgewise; that is, from the out to inside. Placed in this way, the pillar will be less liable to spring than when the layers run in the opposite direction. The springing of the door pillars often causes much trouble. Second growth ash will spring, no matter how well seasoned, otherwise it would be better than forest ash, as it is much stronger, and the strain upon door pillars is very severe. In selecting, choose the best forest ash—close, fine grained, but "live;" that is, with the porous stratas firm and not inclined to "powder" when dressed. Hard maple has been used to advantage. It is a wood that, when well and properly seasoned, never springs, and is much more rigid than ash. It is close grained, and therefore paints well. The drawback to maple is in its seasoning; the sap is more fully charged with sugar than that of other hard woods, and, unless the seasoning is steady and quick, fermentation takes place and the fiber is ruined. Steaming kills it, and renders the grain harsh.

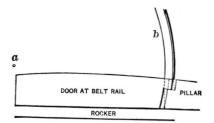

Fig. 142. The advantages of a bevel for the body and door lock pillars.

The faces of the body and door lock pillars must be dressed to a bevel to insure the door closing without binding. Fig. 142 illustrates the advantages of the bevel more plainly than a column of words. The point *a* indicates the pivotal point of the hinges, from which the door describes the circle indicated by lines *b*. It will be seen by this that if the rabbet or face side of the pillars are straight, the edges of the door pillar would come in contact with those of the body pillar, unless the opening between the two is greatly enlarged, and when fully in place the inner edges would touch. The bevel to the back pillar must be given on the rabbet side, leaving the inside square, otherwise a new trouble would arise by the interference with the glass frame.

Close carriages require glass frames. These should be of hard wood. If varnished or otherwise finished, without being covered, they should be three-eighths of an inch thick. A good width is one and a half inch for the sides and top end, and one and a quarter inch for the bottom bar. Frame them as shown by Fig. 140, the tenon on the side pieces for the top, and on the end piece for the bottom. If the frames are finished in the wood, the glass groove must be of uniform width, and three-sixteenths of an inch deep. If covered, the groove must be shaped as shown by a, Fig. 140, in order to provide for the cloth, the edges of which are pasted into the groove.

Fig. 139 shows the inside of the rocker at the front quarter, giving seat bottom and an extra seat board; the latter is folded up when not in use. The object is to get the seat board up where a fair width can be obtained. When it is placed high, the leg-room is increased so much as to require an extra rest for the feet. Placed as shown, this cushion can be extended back at the bevel indicated by the dotted lines, thus securing ample width. If the seat bottom is put on a level with that of the back seat, the cushion will be too narrow for comfort.

The dotted lines in the quarters on Fig. 130 indicate the outlines of the panels of the windows.

The rockers should be of one and a half inch ash, the bottom sides three inches thick, corner pillars two and a quarter inches, door pillars one and a quarter and one and a half inch, body hinge pillars one and a quarter inch to point x, Fig. 130. The section b is a part of the bottom side, but may be added to the foot of the pillar if so desired. In that case the pillar must be cut of four and a half inch ash. The coupé pillars are of four and a half inch ash, seven and a half inches wide, top rails three inches deep, arm rails of two inch ash, bottom cross bars one and an eighth inch thick, back bar two inches thick, back rail seven-eighth inch. The strainers of the back quarters are set in parallel with the arm rail, as the grain of the quarter panels runs parallel with the standing pillars.

The moldings should be three-quarter inch at the bottom and a half inch at the arm rails. The door pillar moldings should be seven-eighths inch for the hinge pillars and one and an eighth inch for the back pillars, the cross moldings corresponding with the moldings on the quarters. The rocker panels should be three-eighths of an inch whitewood, the head panels for the bottom five-eighths of an inch; all others a quarter inch thick.

CHAPTER VI.

A Two-Wheeled Delivery Wagon.

DELIVERY WAGONS have become so much of a necessity that retailers in almost every line of trade find it convenient to make use of them, and in doing so they aim at making the best of the opportunity afforded for advertising, the large, close panels of the sides affording an excellent opportunity for display lettering and ornamenting.

The variety of styles is very great, including two as well as four-wheel gears, and in the latter, platform and perch carriage parts. The two-wheeled vehicle is popular, and much attention has been given to its construction in order to secure an evenly balanced and convenient wagon.

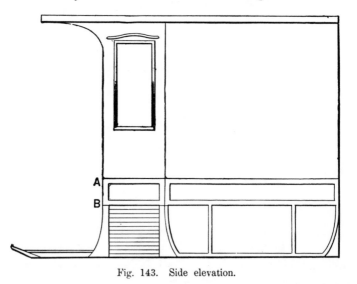

Fig. 143. Side elevation.

Fig. 143 shows the side elevation of a two-wheeled body

for light delivery. The outlines of the body are all square and straight. The relief is given by molding and paneling. The body is six feet long and three feet two inches to three feet four inches wide; full hight, four feet eight inches.

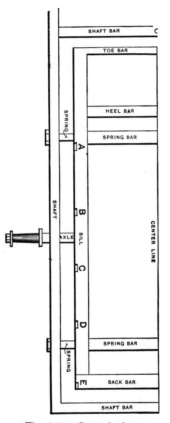

Fig. 144.   Ground plan.

The ground plan shows half of the framework of the body, together with one shaft, the shaft bars, location of axle and cross springs.

In framing, make the sills of two and a fourth by one and

a half inch ash, the back and heel bars of two and an eighth by one and a fourth inch ash, the spring bars of two by one inch ash, the toe bar of one and a fourth by one and a fourth inch ash. The supporting bars are seven-eighths by two inches, and are tenoned in between the heel and back bars, and cut flush with the under side of the sills. The rabbets for the bottom boards are cut in on the top of the sill and cross bars, so that when the half inch bottom board is in, the surface will be smooth. The posts *A B C D* and *E* are

Fig. 145. Half of back partition.   Fig. 146. Half of front partition.

of one and an eighth inch square ash and lapped into the sills. A dove-tail lap is the best form for strength. The inside shoulder of the pillar need not be more than three-eighths of an inch. Long rails are necessary at *A* and *B*, in Fig. 143. These are tenoned into the posts *A* and *E*, Fig. 144, and lapped to the others, the lap being cut from the outside of the rails and inside of the posts. This is best, as it removes the danger from splitting of the panel by parallel joints.

The back end, Fig. 145, has but one cross slot. This is framed into the corner pillars on a line flush with the bottom line of bar *B*, Fig. 143. A board bar answers the double purpose of an end rail and door head. The door pillars are of   one-eighth by one and one-fourth inch ash, and hung

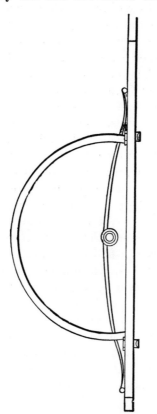

Fig. 147.   Side elevation, showing shaft and the method of hanging.

so that when paneled the surface will be flush with that of the end of the body.

Fig. 146 shows half of the front partition and the seat rail; the doors to this partition are of one and an eighth inch ash, an iron grating being used in place of a panel. This partition is set back against the pillar *B*, Fig. 144. The space *B*, Fig. 146, is filled by a panel seven-eighths of an inch thick, which serves as a seat back as well as a partition. Fig. 147 shows the spring hanging for the shafts and the location of the cross springs which support the body.

The shafts have the coupé bend at the front, and at the front cross bar they are one and a half by one and three-fourths inch, finished with a slightly oval top, round edges, and flat bottom. The cross bars are of the same size as the shafts, and finished in the same way.

Guard strips, one-half by one inch, are placed two inches apart between the posts. These, as well as the posts, are slightly rounded; the panels throughout are three-eighths of an inch thick; the curves are one by five-eighths inch, and placed five inches apart; the roof boards are of pine, one-fourth inch thick; the large panels are molded with thin, flat moldings, and wherever possible the moldings should cover joints in panels; the axles are one and a fourth inch steel, the shaft springs one and three-fourths, cross springs one and a half inch, spokes one and one-eighth, hubs four and three-fourths by seven inches, tire one and an eighth inch.

These vehicles depend in a great measure upon the lettering and ornamenting for effect.

The popular colors are red for gears and black for bodies, reversing the colors for striping. There is, however, no fixed rule for coloring, as the broadest limit is allowed. In fact, the vehicle does not fully answer its purpose if it is not made specially attractive by ornamentation and lettering.— *By* W. N. F.

Delivery Wagon.

The changed mode of doing business in recent years has called into use a number of vehicles for specific purposes. Among these is the delivery wagon, two and four-wheeled. The construction of the bodies of the two and four wheels being so similar, a description of one style of the 4-wheeler will suffice.   In fact, there are few who care to build the two-wheeler, unless they have had experience in that kind of work, special knowledge being requisite to enable the builder to hang the job correctly.   The basis of the body is the cut-under phaëton, but the body is bigger and heavier.   Simplicity is an important requisite, as the prices are always low.

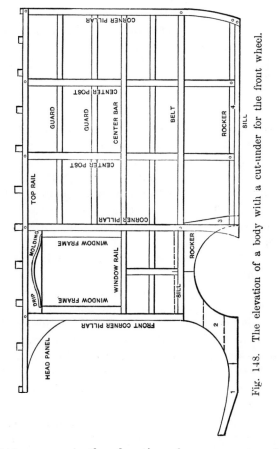

Fig. 148.   The elevation of a body with a cut-under for the front wheel.

Fig. 148 represents the elevation of a very neat and strong

body, having a cut-under for the front wheel, making the body suitable for a platform or a three-spring carriage part. The rocker is framed up square, and to provide for a contraction of the front, the forward part of the rocker has the face side against the inside of the back piece, which narrows the front three inches over all, the rockers being one and a half inch thick. The sill to the front quarter is on a line with the lower belt. In fact, it is a continuation of the belt. The belt is tenoned into the back and front corner pillars, and lapped to the coupé corner pillar. The corner and coupé pillars are grooved below the belt to admit a five-sixteenth inch panel and a molding a fourth of an inch thick. The front corner pillar and the front of the coupé pillar between the sill and window rail are grooved in a like manner. The center rail and posts are lightened to admit a three-eighths inch panel. The guards are strips of five-eighths inch by two inch strips, screwed against the inside of the pillars.

The panels are all grooved into the corner pillars, the edges nailed to the belt, and the rails and the joints covered with moldings one inch wide and a fourth of an inch thick, finished flush with the pillar moldings. The body here given is finished with three strips of panels, one below the belt a fourth of an inch thick, one between the belt and the center bar, and one from the center bar to the top rail three-eighths of an inch thick.

The front quarter is provided with a window with a stationary glass. The frame may be of dark wood, varnished. Over this window is a strip of whitewood, upon which is worked a drip molding. The head panel, which acts as a support to the extension of the top rail, is best when grooved into the pillar and top rail. It should be of hard wood, a half inch thick. The rocker is made up of four pieces, as shown on Fig. 148—1, 2, 3, 4. That portion front of the coupé pillar is paneled with a quarter inch panel. It is generally finished plain, as moldings are liable to get bruised or broken. Below the belt rail, on the inside, the body is lined with a quarter inch panel, well canvased before being nailed in. It is further strengthened by narrow strips of iron; there being but a small foothold for the back corner pillar, a corner iron binding it to the rocker is necessary.

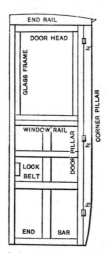

Fig. 149.   Half of the back end and one of the doors.

Fig. 149 shows half of the back end and one of the doors. The panels and moldings must correspond with those on the side of the body. The glass in the doors is stationary. The doors shut against the end bar and a guard on the end rail. The lock used is a heavy one, requiring a key to open it.

Fig. 150 shows a half view of the front end, locating the end bar rockers, seat back, &c. In some wagons a window partition is provided, filling in the space between the seat back and end rail at the coupé pillar. This partition consists of two frames hinged to the respective pillars so as to open in, and is secured by a key lock to the back seat bar. The glass in all the windows is heavy, and in some of the best it is beveled, which gives an ornamental appearance to the windows.

Fig. 151 gives a view from the top of half of the bottom, showing lap of rocker, cross bars, &c. The cross bars back of the wheelhouse are one and a fourth inch thick, tenoned

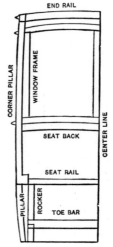

Fig. 150.   Half view of front end.

into the rocker flush with the bottom line. The parallel bars are lapped on the latter, and are seven-eighths of an inch thick, lapped flush with the top of the cross bars. A rabbet is taken out of the cross bar at the back of the wheelhouse, and out of the back bar, to admit a half inch board, and flush with the top of the rails and cross bars. The bottom boards are secured into their rabbets, resting upon the bars and strips, the joints of the boards being over the center of the strips. Strips of one inch band iron are screwed on over these joints, securing them in place and acting as a protection to the bottom boards. Forward of the coupé pillar the bottom boards are put in the usual way, the wheelhouse having a quarter inch panel, and the foot rest a half inch panel.

The rocker plate need not extend the full length of the

rocker, but it must have a good hold—of one foot at least—
back of the wheelhouse; three-eighths by two inches is sufficiently heavy. The body is three feet three inches over

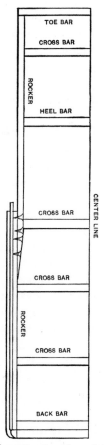

Fig. 151. View from the top of one-half to the bottom.

the rockers back of the wheelhouse, and three feet over all
at the front; the back corner pillars are two and a fourth
inches thick; the turn-under is one and a fourth inch, leav-

ing one inch at the foot. The coupé pillar must be of the same thickness and filled in on the face, to equalize the space produced by the offset at the rocker; above the rocker it can be cut to one and a fourth inch; the center parts are of one-fourth inch ash, one and a fourth inch square; the belt one and an eighth inch deep and one and a fourth thick; center bar one by one and an eighth inch. The doors should be lined between the windows and bottom bar, and finished smooth for painting. In some cases the top is lined and the boards neatly tongued and grooved, to give a smooth finish. All moldings are finished with round edges.—*By* W. N. F.

The Depot Wagon.

Vehicles for special uses, or those specially adapted for certain uses, receive names which designate them and by which they are made distinct. Among these is a vehicle known as the depot wagon. It belongs properly to the rockaway class, but is stronger and more roomy. The necessity of being able to turn around in a short space makes the wheelhouse a necessity. Where the platform carriage part is used, the carriage can be made to turn within its own length, but where the straight perch is used, very little advantage is derived from having a wheelhouse, as its costs but a trifle more to use a bent than a straight perch. Builders will find it to their advantage to use the crooked perch, the arch of which should not be less than six inches high.

The body selected for this paper is a four-passenger, square cut-under, with low doors and curtain quarters. It is extremely simple in its construction, yet strong, roomy, and comfortable.

The rockers are each of five pieces, Nos. 1, 2, 3, 4, 5, Fig. 152 (page 157). These are of one and three-eighths inch ash, strongly lapped together; the sills are of one and a half by one and three-eighths inch ash, the depth being a quarter of an inch less than the width; the pillars are lapped from the inside, bringing the faces flush with the rockers. That portion extending across the door is beveled up from the outside to the inside, as shown by Fig. 153, the door bar being cut to a bevel at the bottom. If preferred, the bottom side may

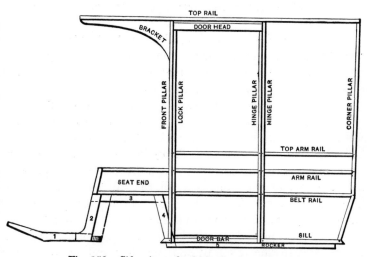

Fig. 152. Side view of a body for depot wagon.

Fig. 153. Bevel for door pillar and sill.

Fig. 154. Sectional view showing tenon of pillar and method of making secure.

be cut so that the face side is a fourth of an inch below the level of the top of the rocker, thus forming a shoulder for the door bar. The advantage of this is a closer door; the disadvantage is a liability to bind. The pillars are cut away a fourth of an inch in from the inner edge of the bevel, which forms the moldings, to take the panel, as shown by the end sectional view, Fig. 154. The same sketch shows the tenon of the pillar and the manner of securing the pillars, they being glued in place before the sills are screwed to the rockers.

The pillars are of good, fine, close grained ash, the lock pillar being one and a fourth inch thick, the hinge pillar one and an eighth inch; the rabbets to the lock pillars are three-eighths of an inch, measured from the outside, and full one-fourth of an inch deep, leaving ample space for the lock, without cutting into the rabbet guard; the belt rail is one and an eighth by one and an eighth inch square, lapped to the pillars, leaving an eighth of an inch projection to form a molding, making a complete finish from the back pillar to the front end of the front seat, all the rail being finished in the same manner. The inside corners of the pillars are rounded so as to paint smooth; the panels are put in with the grain running perpendicular instead of horizontal; the panels between the arm rail and the belt rail are a quarter of an inch, rabbeted in the two rails. The space between the top arm rail and the arm rail may be paneled in like manner or left open, whichever is preferred. The seat end is of cherry, worked out to assimilate a panel.

The top rail is one inch thick and two inches deep; the door moldings are an eighth of an inch thick and three-fourths of an inch wide. A storm bracket extends from the front pillar to the end of the top rail, of cherry, half an inch thick. In framing the rails they should be back from the inside a fourth of an inch, so as to take a panel, and finished flush with the inside. The door is finished in the same manner, in order to dispense with trimming. The top is finished on the inside with thin panels, and painted. In framing on the top rails, lap them to the pillars, cutting away an eighth of an inch from the inside of the rail, securing the rails to the pillars by screws.

Fig. 155 shows half of the back end. All the cross rails follow the line of the side rails, but if preferred, the arm rail piece may be omitted, leaving a full panel between the lazy back rail and the belt rail. The panels are all put in the same as the side panels, a molding extending across the bottom of the back, beveled in the same manner as the sill molding. From the bar to the seat, below the belt rail, the back is finished in the same manner as the inside of the quarters. Above this a rough lining will answer, as the back squab covers all that section.

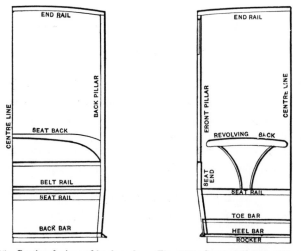

Fig. 155. Sectional view of back end. Fig. 156. Sectional view of front end.

Fig. 156 shows a view of the front end location of the seat rail, heel bar and toe bar, also the revolving back.

Fig. 157 (page 160) shows a half view of the bottom from the top. In this the back bar is framed into the sills, the rocker butting against the bar. All the other cross bars, with the exception of the toe bar, are lapped to the rockers from the underside. The wheelhouse cross bars to make a sweep for the wheelhouse back and front, the front bar being three

and a half inches wide, the back bar two and a half inches
wide, each three-fourths of an inch thick; the heel bar and
center cross bars are two and a half by three quarter inch;
the toe bar one and a fourth inch by the full size of the
front end of the bracket; the bottom boards are of half inch

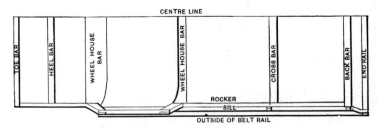

Fig. 157.　View of half of bottom as it appears looking downward.

whitewood; the wheelhouse panels a fourth inch whitewood.
These bodies require heavy rocker plates; they should not
be less than two and a half by three-eighths inch, the corners
to be bent as nearly round as possible. Secure them with
half inch No. 16 screws. A fourth inch bolt should be entered at each corner.—*By* W. N. F.

Light Express Wagons.

One of the most serviceable wagons for general light transportation is that known as the light express wagon. It is
light and very strong, besides being neat and attractive. The
body is not difficult to build, but care and judgment are required to make a perfect job. Many workmen look upon a
straight line square body as the simplest kind of work, when,
in fact, it is the most difficult in some respects, as long
straight lines, unless absolutely straight, always expose the
irregularity, while slight defects in curves are not readily
noticed. In a body where there are so many parallel pieces
close to each other, a deviation of one-thirty-second of an
inch will be apparent, and will appear as though it was twice

that amount out of the way. The workman therefore must
not expect to find all easy sailing because of the straight
lines. On the contrary, he must use extra care in cutting
all shoulders; otherwise he will find himself in trouble.

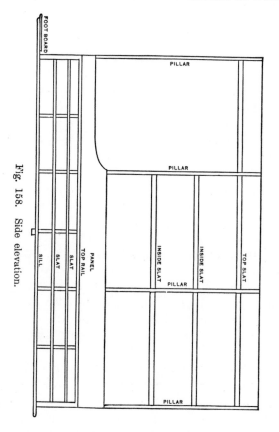

Fig. 158. Side elevation.

White oak has been proven by long use to be the best
wood for all parts of the framework, the fine, close grained
being the best. But it must be well seasoned, as it is one
of the woods which retain a large percentage of moisture even
when seasoned. The frame should not be fastened together

until at least twenty-four hours have passed since cutting the tenons, mortises and laps. Unless this is done, there is danger of "souring" and premature decay. White oak has the quality of resisting moisture after it is thoroughly seasoned, so that if all right when put together, very little trouble will arise thereafter.

For side panels whitewood is preferable to all others, and for bottom boards pine is undoubtedly the best. Red oak is sometimes used for frames, but it is the least desirable of all of our hard woods for all purposes where there are tenons, &c., and where all parts are not exposed. Next to white oak, I prefer fine, close grained, forest white ash. It deflects under the same pressure as oak, but it is less durable, unless thoroughly protected by paint, a quality that is detrimental where large surfaces, like the under side of an express body, are situated so that the sun's rays cannot reach it.

There is no absolute rule for the length or width of these bodies; accordingly I have selected one of medium size suited for transportation of small parcels. The body is seven feet long and three feet wide, outside to outside. The slat side is ten inches high over all, and the panel six inches high, except at the front, where it is cut down to three and a half inches in hight, and where there are but two slats above the sills. Fig. 158 shows the side elevation arrangement of top pillars or bows, the top slat, inside slats, and the upright body slats.

The sill should be cut twelve inches longer than the full length of the body, one and an eighth inch deep and two and a quarter inches wide, the corner posts one and three-quarters inch square, the top rail three-quarters inch deep and one inch wide, the parallel slats and the uprights five-eighths of an inch square, remembering, however, to make the front top slat the same size as the top rail of side. The pillars should be one and an eighth by one and a quarter inch. If a bow top is used, the bent bows must be spliced to the pillars, as there is no necessity of heavy bows, and

two short bows should be placed in each intervening space
between the pillars. The top should be covered with thin
boards down to the top slat. The inside slats should be one
and a quarter inch wide and three-quarters of an inch thick,
rounded on the inside.

In framing set the front corner pillar outside, nine inches
from the front end of the sill. Measure off seven feet from
that point for the back corner pillar, lay out the mortises
and space off for the side uprights, placing one exactly midway between the ends. Be careful to space off correctly.
After laying off the sills together, place the slats against one
sill and secure them with thumbscrews, and with a square
and cutting awl mark off for mortises and laps. In all cases
cut the lap away from the inside of the long slats. This is
recommended because of the fact that if cut from the outside, a pressure from the inside of the body will cause the
joints to open.

Tenon the ends of all the slats with the shoulder outside,
leaving a tenon half the thickness of the slat. Set all pillars,

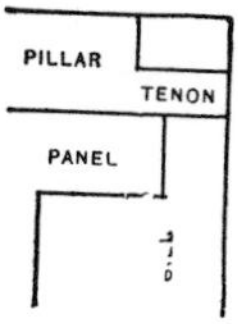

Fig. 159.   Cross section of sill of pillar.

slats, &c., flush with the outside of the sill. Fig. 159 shows
a cross section of the sill at a pillar, in which the sill is cut
away to leave a three-quarter inch molding outside and a
groove between the pillar and the shoulder of the recess for
the panel. This is not always done, but it makes a better
job than when the molding is full depth of the sill; but in
all cases a groove should be cut in for the panel.

Fig. 160 shows a half view of the back end, the entire space between the pillars being detached to form a drop tail board. This necessitates an extra rail at the bottom which, rests upon the cross bar, but all other slats must be in a line with those of the side. The panel is attached against an extra frame built up on the inside so that the outside of the panel, when in place, is flush with the outside of the top rail. To give strength to the corners at the back, strong corner irons are let into the cross bar and corner pillars.

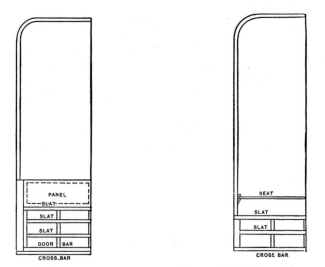

Fig. 160. Half view of back end.   Fig. 161. Half view of front end.

Fig. 161 shows a half section of the front end, giving, in addition to the location of the slats, the position of the seat. Chamfering the slats is a piece of work that must be carefully done. The form of the corners is shown by Fig. 163. The center should have a flat surface an eighth of an inch wide, and the chamfers so worked as to leave a neat scalloped section at the joints, extending down to a sixteenth of an inch from the panel side. A recess must be cut into the

corner pillars and top rail for the panels, which must be
securely screwed or nailed in and finished off flush with the
inside of the rail, the corner pillars being chamfered off inside between the shoulders of the recesses.

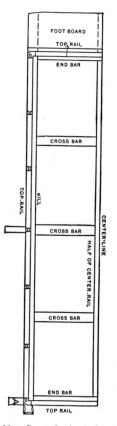

Fig. 162.   Ground plan of bottom.

Fig. 162 gives a view of a half section of the bottom from
the top side. The center rail and cross bars are framed
flush with the top of the sill. The cross bars are two inches
wide and three-quarters of an inch thick, set a half inch

below the bottom of the sill. A rabbet one-half by three-quarters of an inch is cut out of the end bars for the ends of the bottom boards, the other portion resting upon the cross bars, to which they are fastened by heavy screws. The front ends of the sills are used as a support for the foot-board, which should be of three-quarters of an inch ash, nine inches wide, and bolted to the sill.

In bodies of this kind the best results are attained by putting the woodwork together with white lead instead of glue.

In setting up the body, be careful to lay up the sills perfectly straight, putting the slat sides together before putting together with the end bars. Test them in every way to in-

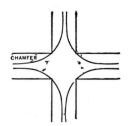

Fig. 163.   Form of corners and chamfer.

sure their being straight, flat, and out of "wind." After the slat portion of this body is set up, attach the standing pillars. They should extend down to the sills, the outsides cut away enough to allow the pillar to come flush with the outside of the body frame. Set the panel flush with the "top rail." Secure it by clamps, using the best of glue. When dry, run in screws from the inside, being careful not to allow them to go through the panel. The customary plan of putting the screws in from the outside and covering the heads with plugs gives no better result than the fastening from the inside, and insures a defect that cannot be hid—that of the plugs showing after the panels are painted.

The tail board is secured by three heavy strap hinges, a

guard chain being attached to prevent the board coming in contact with the gear when let down.

The inside of the body must be finished off smooth, and for greater security, thin strips of band iron are placed on the panels over each upright. An extra supporting bar is bolted to the back cross bar, the ends projecting as shown by *A*, Fig. 162. An iron brace from this to the top rail of the body gives additional support to the sides and prevents spreading.—*By* W. N. F.

Six-Passenger Phaeton.

The six-passenger phaeton is to open top carriages what the six-passenger rockaway is to closed or paneled tops. It is, however, much less expensive, and being lighter, is preferred by many who want a roomy carriage for summer use. It has another advantage in being simpler in construction, which is no inconsiderable item to carriage builders who are not so situated that they can build the more complicated vehicles. Any builder who can put up a four-passenger phaeton, can build one for six passengers. The most expensive are hung upon platform carriage parts, but the plain perch, three spring carriage can be used. In point of mechanical skill the most difficult part of a body of the kind shown is the putting up of the rockers, as these must be spliced in order to secure strength. In the design given, Fig. 164, the rocker is made of six pieces, namely: 1, the toe piece; 2, the seat riser; 3, the top arch piece; 4, the back arch; 5, the bottom piece; 6, the back quarter piece. These should be out of close grained, forest ash and dressed to one and three-eighths inch in thickness. The laps should be cut as follows : On toe piece from the outside, on seat riser from the inside, on top arch piece from the outside, on splice piece from inside at top arch piece, and from outside at bottom piece; bottom piece from inside, quarter piece from outside. This will locate all the joints where they will give the best results as to strength, and, what is most important, where they will be crossed by the grains of panels, &c. It is of the utmost importance that the rocker be absolutely true in every way, and I recommend inexperienced body-makers to dress off for laps and splice the rocker pieces to-gether before dressing up in full, as a deviation of even so little as one-thirty-second of an inch at any one of the cen-tral joints will throw the ends out of position and render patching up a necessity. This may not be considered good advice, but it is on the principle that it is better for a child to make its first attempt at walking by holding on to some

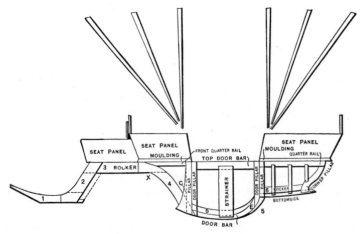

Fig. 164. Side elevation of phaëton.

movable object than to venture a first step without assistance.

Having the rocker pieces all glued and screwed together, dress them up, first facing the rocker its whole length, re-moving any springing or other irregularity. Then gauge to the required thickness, and dress up top and bottom.

Bodymakers too often act as though it was a waste of time to dress off the inside of rockers true, and they express sur-prise that the rockers are out of shape when the rocker plates are screwed on, a result that is sure to follow carelessness in truing up, as it is impossible for the blacksmith to fit plates where the surface to be fitted is out of shape, or has sharp, irregular indentations.

In this body there is no bottom side except at the back quarter. The bottom bar of the door forms the continuation of the bottom side from the quarter to the short front or lock pillar. This pillar is of whitewood or soft ash. By

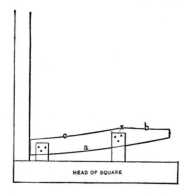

Fig. 165. Square set to the hinges.

dressing up as shown by Fig. 165, it will require a two and a half by six inch block. First dress up the face or rabbet side *a*, mark off the outside sweep, measure off one-eighth inch at the bottom, and strike the line *b* for the face; then lighten out the inside from *x*, as shown by line *c*. After dressing up, screw the pillar to the rocker in its proper position, as shown by Fig. 164, and fit the forward quarter rail, as shown by Figs. 164 and 165. Box out the forward edge of the lock pillar to the dotted line *C*, Fig. 164, leaving a seven-eighths inch molding on the outer edge.

The hinge pillar is dressed up to the same sweep as the lock pillar from the top, leaving the bottom one and three-quarter inch wide. Face up the foot the same as shown by Fig. 165.

Cut the back quarter bottom side out of close grained ash, two by one and an eighth inch, lap the end to the foot of the lock pillar, leaving the bottom side to extend to the face of the pillar. Cut the corner pillar out of two inch, fine, close grained ash, tenon it into the bottom side, leaving the shoulder outside, and cut as shown by Fig. 164. Lap the quarter rail to the two pillars, secure the bottom side to the rocker by screws from the outside, through the bottom side above the molding, dress off the quarter frame to the required sweep, leaving a molding on the bottom side and corner pillar three-quarters inch wide, tapering to five-eighths of an inch at the top of the corner pillar. After routing out for the panel, fit in and glue up the strainers and leave the frame to dry.

Make up the door frame, using one and a quarter inch stock for the lock pillars and one and an eighth inch for the hinge pillar. Cut the bottom bar out of one and a half inch ash, to the sweep indicated by line E, Fig. 164, as it forms the continuation of the outline of the bottom side, leaving the rocker to show three inches back of the bottom line sweep.

Fig. 166.   Half of ground plan.

Fig. 166 shows the view of half of the bottom from the top, giving the location of cross bars, seat frame, flare of panels, and sweep of body on the quarter line. The wheelhouse bars show the bottom bar on the foot rest and the top bar at the top of the arch. The bottom bar is of soft wood, and may be dispensed with if a half inch board is used for the arch bottom. A thin bar is also needed at the junction of the arch top and the "splice piece" panel at X, Fig. 164. The front quarter rail, forming the top line of the front quarter, is set in one and an eighth of an inch from the outside of the front or lock pillar. As there is a sweep and a turn-under to this section of the rocker, it is necessary to glue on a half inch piece of whitewood to the outside of the splice piece (4, Fig. 164), and when the glue is dry, dress off to a true sweep, finishing the lower edge at the original edge of the rocker. When this is completed the rocker panel can be glued on, allowing the end to extend under the molding on the lock pillar, nailing it to that pillar from the inside.

When the sides are put up as directed, set up the body, fit in all bars, top and bottom, without gluing. Then router out and mold the back corner pillar. This, on an O. G. pillar, is a nice piece of work, and where the workman is not an expert with the double router, it is best, after boxing out for the molding and groove, to work out the groove in the molding at the concave portion by boring with a three-sixteenths inch auger and trimming the edges with a chisel. Leave the molding seven-eighths inch wide at the bottom and five-eighths inch at the top. When the moldings are all finished, set up the back pillars, but do not glue them. Secure the bottom by a temporary bar, the ends screwed to the pillars on the inside as far down as possible, putting two screws in each end to prevent the possibility of the frame getting out of square. Remove the back pillars, turn over the body, remove the bars, and screw on the rocker plates, which should be of two and an eighth by three-eighths inch iron, tapered at the front ends, and secured by No. 20 screws. Then set up the body again, gluing and securing all the bars. Be careful at this stage to get the body level and square in every direction. After the bottom bars are all in, turn the body over, set up the hinge pillars and center seat rail, also the cross bars at the top of the seat risers and lock pillars. Test the body carefully to see that it is level and true, and secure it in position by hand screws to trestle and bench, and it is ready for the back panel. The positions of the various bars, as seen from the back end, are shown by Fig. 167, those of the front end by Fig. 168, each showing a half section of the respective ends.

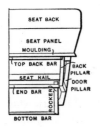

Fig. 167.   Half of back view.   Fig. 168.   Half of front view

The cutting of the panel of an O. G. back is a piece of workmanship which calls for care and skill. Very many workmen bend the panel and mark off with a crooked marker. If the bend is not too short, this is in all probability the quickest method for an expert workman, but a novice will be likely to split the panel when sawing off the ends or when putting the panel in the groove.

It is well to state just here that a panel once bent, unless it is bent over a mold, should be put in place as quickly as possible, as it hardens and straightens on drying, and when once dry, it is far more troublesome to get into the proper form than it was before being bent.

The best plan, taking all things into consideration, is to cut the panel to its required shape before bending. To do this, divide off the pillars at the bottom of the rabbet, as shown by Fig. 169, square. up the panel and strike two end lines, to represent the face of the pillars, whether square or otherwise, giving the exact space between the pillars when in place. Then with a compass determine the location for each line, resting the points of the compass upon the bottom of the rabbet, as indicated by line *a*, Fig. 169. Number the lines upon the pillars and strike, with a lead pencil, corresponding lines, numbered in like manner, lengthwise across the inside of the panel, as shown by Fig. 170. As will be seen, the spaces between the lines show a natural increase in width, as compared to the parallel lines across the outside of the corner pillar, an increase which is the result of the difference caused by the curves. Having established the lines, measure off with the compass upon each line the space between the face of the pillar and the inside edge of

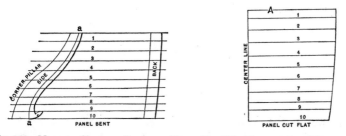

Fig. 169. Manner of laying off corner pillar.   Fig. 170 Manner of marking panel.

the molding. Then add a quarter of an inch to each of these spaces for the depth of the groove, and cut to these panels. Fit up the ends so that they will enter the grooves without binding, and the panel is ready for bending. When bending moisten the panel on the convex side—outside for the top and inside for the bottom. Moisten with hot water, and bend the bottom or small bend first, being careful to bend so that the sweep will correspond with that of the outside of the pillar. If the top sweep is not very sharp, the panel will warp enough without being heated, but if not, heat and bend to the required shape, keeping the bottom bend well moistened with hot water, on the convex side. Just as soon as the panel is bent to the required shape, insert it into its place in the pillars and glue them into their places on the rockers. Do not glue the panel, but block the edge top and bottom, so that the panel cannot straighten while drying. When dry, wedge up from the inside, gluing the wedges on the side next to the pillars. Then glue to the bottom and top bars, and canvas the inside with coarse crash. Next glue up the quarter rail and strainers, fit in and glue up the quarter panels, using white lead instead of glue in the grooves. Do not glue the panels to the strainers.

Frame up the doors and fit them up carefully, leaving an eighth of an inch in the clear next to the body pillars. Panel up and dress off to the sweep of the body. Fit up the lock pillar as shown by Fig. 171. If the pillar is not beveled as shown, the door will be sure to bind.

Fig. 171.   Door bottom.

Hanging the doors on a body of this kind calls for much care and skill. Butt hinges are used as a rule, and they must so set that the center line of the pivots are at direct right angles with the cross line of the body. The location of the hinges and the manner of deciding the right angle line are indicated by Fig. 165.

The seats are made in the same manner as ordinary board seats, using seven-eighths by three inch ash for the frames and seven-eighths cherry for the ends and sides. The high back to the front seat extends down to the seat frame, doing away with the necessity of any other back panel. As both the high backs to the middle seats have a slight outward pitch, the intervening space should be paneled to give a close finish.

The location of the bows is shown by Fig. 164. They must be stout, as the top is very heavy, and unless they are well stayed, they will bend outward, giving a bad appearance to the top.

Heavy Express Wagon.

Heavy wagons for freighting purposes are becoming a necessity in localities where a few years ago the common farm wagon was considered a marvel in size and freighting capacity. This is due to the extension of transportation facilities and the growth of business consequent thereto. The wagon builder therefore, even in small towns, finds a home demand for vehicles not before needed, and unless he meets this demand, some enterprising outsider steps in and secures the trade. The only excuse the home manufacturer can possibly have is that the building of these wagons is a business in which he has had no training, and that ordinary workmen cannot build the various parts. That there is reason in this plea is the justification for publishing primary instruction which the unskilled may understand. All that is required is to give the workman a start, get him interested, and, having learned his A B Cs, he will soon be master of the other problems.

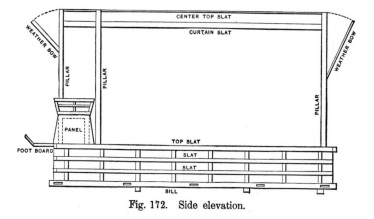

Fig. 172.   Side elevation.

The body shown by Fig. 172 is one of the heaviest used for general freight purposes. It has great strength, is very roomy, and is at the same time neat in appearance. The bodies vary in length from eight feet six inches to ten feet. The width also varies from three feet four inches to four feet; the latter is, however, an extreme width. The sides are thirteen and a half to fourteen and a half inches deep, and the riser for seat one foot deep; the seat ends six inches high, the seat being made without a back. It follows very naturally that a body of such great dimensions must be made extra heavy, and there is probably no form of body where the actual weight can be reduced as low in this pattern and possess the same strength, but the workmanship must be first-class. Uneven mortises, badly fitting tenons, bad laps, all tend to weaken the body.

By general consent white oak is accepted as the best timber, but it is doubtful if, where such great stiffness is required, whether it is as good as prime white ash. It is true that ash will break under less weight, the difference being about two per cent in favor of the oak, but oak deflects to the breaking gauge of ash under twenty per cent less pressure, so that whatever disadvantages there may be in the ash breaking under less weight, is counterbalanced by the inclination of oak to bend under less weight. When wagons are kept thoroughly painted all over, bottom as well as outside, I would favor prime ash for the frame. Where the timbers are so heavy, the reduction in weight in a body of this kind by using ash would be not far from twenty-five pounds, a no inconsiderable item when we take into account the fact that greater stiffness is obtained.

The side panels being narrow and well backed by the frame, need not be heavier than three-eighths inch. They should be of whitewood, it being sufficiently solid, and presents a much better surface for the painter than other soft woods. The seat riser panel should be of cherry, five-eighths inch thick.

The side frame should be as follows: Sills three and a half wide by two inches deep; top slat one and three-eighths by 7-

eighths inch; middle slats three-quarter inch square; uprights three-quarter inch square; seat riser battens one by five-eighths inch; foot board frame three-quarters by one and a quarter inch; boards three-quarters inch thick; seat frame three-quarters by three and a half inches; end slats

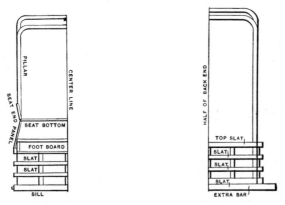

Fig. 173. Half of front end view.   Fig. 174. Half of back end view.

(Fig. 173) five-eighths inch square; end bars three and a half inches wide, two inches deep; girder bars two inches deep, two and a half wide; cross slats two and a half inches wide, seven-eighths inch deep; main top pillars one and three-quarters by one and a half inch; front pillars one and a quarter by seven-eighths inch; weather bows one by seven-eighths inch; curtain slat two by seven-eighths inch; center top slat one by three-quarters inch; additional slats seven-eighths by five-eighths inch; extra cross bars or bolsters two and a quarter by two inches; bottom slat of tail board (Fig. 174) two by one and three-eighths inch. All other slats the same as those of the sides.

In framing up the bottom, Fig. 175, place the front end bar flush with the upper framework, allow the sill to project one and three-quarters inch, set the back end bar two inches in from the outside end of the frame, as the tail board shuts against the bar, not on it; make the tenons of the end bars three-quarters inch thick, and allow them to project through the sills five-eighths of an inch, and finish off with side and edge chamfers. Tenon the cross slats with seven-eighths inch tenons, cutting the shoulders upon the upper sides, and finishing off the ends to correspond with the ends of the end bar tenons. Tenon the upright slats, top and bottom, with half inch tenons, shoulders on the outside. Lap the centers by cutting away from the inside of the long side slats and the outside of the short uprights. Set the end uprights six inches in from the ends of the sills, lap the front end cross slats to the side slats, and allow the ends to project five-eighths of an inch, and chamfer the ends as illustrated by

Fig. 175. Half of ground plan.

Fig. 176. The side panels at both ends extend to the ends of the slats, and are finished with a slight round. Box out of the inside lower corner of the top slat a recess a quarter inch wide and full thickness of the panel, and rabbet out a recess for the lower edge of the panel in the sill, as shown

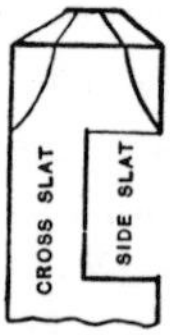

Fig. 176. End finish of slat.

by Fig. 177, a cross section of the side frame and panel.

The girders tenon into the end bars, and the cross slats pass through the girders full size.

Tenon the feet of the main pillars with one inch stub tenons, which set into mortises in the sills, the pillars being further secured by bolts through the top slat. The bow tops to the pillars should be sawed out and spliced to the pillars. The weather bows may be bent, but they are better sawed. Extra bows are not always used, but when they are, they are bent. The curtain slats are lapped against the bows from the inside and securely bolted. These tops are sometimes made adjustable. When that is the case, the feet of the pillars are secured by slat bolts, with nuts on the underside

Fig. 177. End view of slats.

of the sills. The weather bows are attached to the main pillars by bolts.

Chamfer the corners of the center slats, leaving a flat center a quarter inch wide and an eighth of an inch flat at the panel edge. Make the chamfer on the lower edge of the top slat of the same proportions as the chamfers on the center slats, and chamfer the upper edge of the sill in like manner. To harmonize the appearance, run a quarter inch bead along the outer edge of the top slats, and a three-eighths inch bead along the lower edge of the sills. The toe board frame, if of wood, is bolted against the end top slat, supported by iron braces. If of iron, the feet are bolted to the end uprights.

Finish the inside perfectly smooth and straighten by one inch band iron strips against the inside over each upright. Hinge the tail board to the end bar by heavy wrought iron slat hinges, securely bolted. Secure by screws to the girder bars strips of quarter inch band iron.

Use prime, first quality white lead when putting the framework together instead of glue; also lead the grooves when putting in the panels. Lap joints should be secured by screws from the inside, the screws being an eighth inch shorter than the thickness of the slats. Secure the panels also by screws. All tenon joints can be pinned. The seat riser panel may be molded if desired, but as a rule it is best plain, as it leaves a flat surface for the painter. The heel panel should be of three-quarter inch board, as it is likely to receive many heavy knocks.

The Farm Wagon.

The farm wagon, unlike other vehicles, must be treated as a whole, not, as a body and carriage part, separate. Its features are simplicity and great strength. While there has been little change in form of the farm wagon for many years, there has been a marked change in the construction. The weight has been reduced, friction overcome, so that the draft of a loaded farm wagon of the best make to-day is little if any more than the empty farm wagon of years ago. The old wood-arm and short-hub boxes are done away with, or, if the wood-arm is used, it runs into a pipe box, and the bearings are of metal. The old skein is obsolete. The improvements made were mainly by builders who aimed at a large business; not that they introduced all, but they adopted every improvement that gave evidence of being valuble. In this way they furnished a perfect wagon at a low price, and the country wagonmaker found his business sliding away from him—simply because he, instead of striving to improve his product, devoted his time to denouncing "machine-made wagons" and "store goods."

In giving details of construction, I have selected as a model one built by one of the most reputable farm wagon builders in this country, and of medium weight and size, giving also

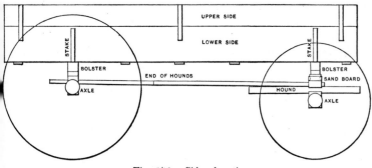

Fig. 178.   Side elevation.

two forms of gear. Fig. 178 shows the side elevation of woodwork only, and all in the block, but in correct proportions. The body is of poplar, from eleven feet six inches to twelve feet long, width thirty-eight to forty-two inches, side boards seven-eighths inch thick, lower side fourteen inches high, upper side six to nine inches high. Three outside cleats support each of the upper sides and keep them in place. The inside end cleats are of seven-eighths inch stock, three and a half inches wide, the boards, of Norway pine, one inch thick, secured to cross pieces of ash seven-eighths inch thick by three inches wide. The cleats or outside posts which support the upper side are of ash, one and a half by three-quarter inch. A toe board, nine inches wide and one inch thick, is attached to the body at the top of the lower side, supported by iron braces. The inside is stiffened and attached to the bottom by strap bolts, the straps being screwed to the inside of the body board, the bolt extending down through the bottom and bottom cross slats.

The front bolster is three and a quarter by four and a half inches, the full depth being maintained in the center, as shown by Fig. 179, leaving a bearing twelve inches long for the king bolt plate. The ends are lightened up to three inches; the stakes are three inches wide at the bottom and one and a half inch at the top, end one inch thick, the tenon at the bottom being seven-eighths by two and a quarter inches, the edge shoulder being on the outside. The sand board is three and a quarter inches deep by four wide, left straight on the top, except at the ends, which are light-

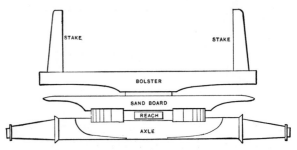

Fig. 179.   Front view of axle and bolster.

ened down as shown by Fig. 179. The underside is lightened up at the ends to one and an eighth inch. Between these points it is straight and full thickness, except where boxed out for the hounds, the boxing out being full width of the hounds and three-eighths of an inch in depth. The hounds, which are cut to a pattern, are of two inch stock, boxed out top and bottom for the sand board and axle to an extent that will leave a clear space between the sand board and axle of one and a half inch on the straight lines, the center of the two pieces being cut away enough to leave a clean two inch opening for the reach. The axle beds are of hickory or maple, four and a half by three and a quarter inches. Steel or some other form of thimble skeins are used, but as full directions are given by the manufacturers of these skeins, no directions are necessary here, as the methods differ in accordance with the pattern of skein used. The back axle corresponds in size with the front. The form, when finished, is shown by Fig. 180. The back bolster is three and a quarter by four and a quarter inches, ends lightened the same as those of the front bolster.

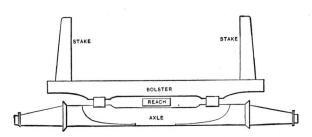

Fig. 180.   Back axle and bolster.

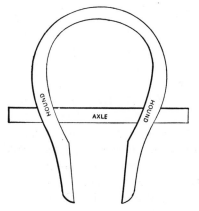

Fig. 181.   Bent hounds.

As two styles of poles are used—the drop and stiff—the forms of the hounds differ in front, the back ends being bent, as shown by Fig. 181, or straight, as shown by Fig. 182. The bent hounds may be in one piece, or of sawed fronts and bent backs. They are two inches thick at the axle and lightened to one and three-quarters inch at the back. For a drop pole they are placed as shown by Figs. 181 and 182, the front ends twelve inches apart, face for plate fifteen inches long, extreme length front of axle nineteen inches, back of axle twenty-six inches, spread on axle twenty-one inches from center to center, width at axle three and a quarter inches.

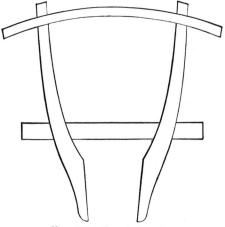

Fig. 182. Sawed hounds.

The straight hounds, Fig. 182, have the same proportions front. They are generally a little longer back, and in lieu of the bent end have a cross bar, bent or straight, connecting the ends, the bar and hounds being lapped together, leaving the top and bottom flush. The ends of the cross bar project from two to four inches beyond the hounds.

The stiff pole hounds are shown by Fig. 183, the ground plan of the undergear. They differ from the others only in form and position of the front ends, the outer ends being five inches apart, contracted at the heel to four inches. The faces are plated. These plates, together with those on the pole, reduce the opening to the size of the end of the pole.

The end of the drop pole, Fig. 184, has two hounds two

ches thick, the taper of the back ends being the same as
he taper between the face of the hounds. The bearing at
he poles should not be shorter than twelve inches. The
ack end of the pole is tapered to two inches, and the ends
f the hounds and pole are connected by a strip two inches
ide and three-quarters of an inch thick, extending entirely
hrough the hounds and pole. The pole is two by four inches
t the front end, and four by four at the back, between the
ounds. The stiff pole is of the same dimensions—full length
welve feet.

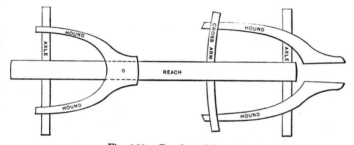

Fig. 183.   Reach and hounds.

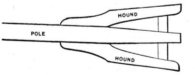

Fig. 184.   Pole and hounds.

The ground plan, Fig. 183, shows back as well as front
ounds, reach, and sections of the axles. The back hounds
e two inches thick, sawed to a pattern; the back ends are
vo inches wide and one and three-quarters inch thick at the
xle, boxed in a little, as shown by Fig. 180. The front
ids are placed four and a half inches apart and held in
osition by a top and a bottom plate of metal, through which

the connecting bolt passes, the reach passing between the bolster and the axle, which may be cut away, as shown by Fig. 180, or the two may be boxed out the width of the pole, leaving an opening sufficiently large to allow the pole to pass through without binding, as it is of the utmost importance that the gear of a farm wagon be made adjustable as to length. The reach is two by four and three-eighths inches; the front end extends about two inches forward of the front axle. There should be at least a half a dozen holes for the connecting bolt, not more than eight inches apart; the hounds should extend fully three feet forward of the back axle.

The timber used is prime white oak for hounds, reach, bolsters, and sand bars, oak for pillars and spokes, black New York mountain birch for hubs, white ash or black oak for poles. With the exception of the stake mortises and the mortises through the back of hound and pole, all joining pieces are put together by laps, in such a manner as to leave shoulders on all sides from an eighth to three-eighths of an inch deep, according to the location. It is of importance that all these fit accurately, as upon them depends the fixedness of the frame. Glue is not used in putting together, except for attaching the cleats to the ends of the side boards and to attach the cleats on the end boards. For all other joints white lead reduced by oil to the consistence of soft putty is applied wherever two pieces are joined. In the original cutting all joints should be fitted extra close, to allow for shrinkage. If this is not done, there is danger of loose joints. After all the pieces are shaped and finished and the frame work fitted, dip the various parts into warm, raw linseed oil; then put them away for a day or two to allow the oil to set in. This is not only a great advantage as a foundation for the paint, but it serves also to preserve the wood at joints and where iron is joined on.

In finishing up the various pieces, care should be taken to make all edges true, whether rounded or chamfered. The bolster ends should be rounded true, so that the band iron which binds the ends will fit. Round up the underside of the bolsters about an eighth of an inch on each edge; also the top of the sand board, except where the irons are secured; also the underside of the ends. A bead finish is neat and no more labor than the round or chamfer. It should be run upon each edge of all pieces, except the outside of the stakes, top of bolsters, and the pole. It should not be less than three-eighths inch.

The dimensions of wheels for this class of carriage are: Hubs nine by ten and a half inches, outer end four and a half inches, spokes two and a half inches, pillars, sawed, one and three-eighths inch, tread two and a half inches deep, wheels three feet eight inches and four feet six inches. The axles for a wagon of these dimensions are three inches, a size that has its equivalent in the three-quarter inch iron axle.

Seats are of plank; ends and back three-quarters inch thick, bottom one inch. The seat must be short enough to go between the box boards without touching. They are generally set upon light elliptic springs.

CHAPTER VII.

Carriage Part for Side Bar Buggies.

THE square box wagon hung upon side bars has the most
simple of any of the many carriage parts in use, and yet it
is a piece of workmanship calling for skill, care, and judgment. It must be strong and light to secure these results.
It is necessary to use the finest hickory for all the woodwork
except the side bars. For these I prefer lance wood or fine
grained white ash. In the absence of these, I recommend
hickory.

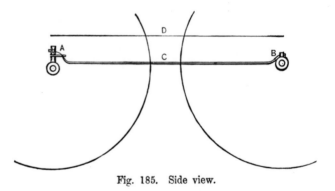

Fig. 185. Side view.

The axle beds have very little curvature, an upward sweep
of one-half to three-quarters inch being sufficient. This was
impossible a few years ago, when straight, wood perches were
used and the fifth wheel plates were placed under the perch.
Then the hight of the wheel governed the arch of the axle

beds, a low front wheel compelling a high arch to the front axle, and a high front wheel a sunken center, in order to get a level perch. The couplings now used, front and back, in addition to allowing the perch to hang low in order to be out of the way of the cross springs, makes the leveling of the perches an easy matter, and one almost independent of the sweep to the axle beds.

In laying out a carriage such as shown by Fig. 185, wheels three feet eight inches and three feet ten inches, bottom of body two feet four inches from the ground, first strike the front hub center and measure back from that point the length of the body, which for full size should be four feet two inches, and for a one-man body four feet, and set the center for the back hub. Next strike line *D*, the bottom of the body; then draw line *C*, the perch, six inches below line *D*. The ends *A B* being metal coupling, with which the carriage part maker can use almost any form of axle bed, but one having an upward curvature of five-eighths to three-quarters of an inch, is the most graceful. If double perches are used, the level must be retained, but the base line of the perches must start from a point midway between the center of the axle and the end, at the point indicated by *A*, Fig. 186.

Fig. 186. Back axle.

Fig. 187. Front axle.

Fig. 187 shows the form of the front axle bed and the head block. The front bed should be one and a half inch deep through the center and three-eighths inch at the end. When the head block is used as shown by Fig. 187, the side bars are hung upon half elliptic springs. In this case the head block at the center should measure full one and a quarter inch deep and five-eighths inch at the fifth wheel bearings. In many carriage parts the short head block is dispensed with, and a bolster and head block combined, as shown by Fig. 188, is substituted. In this the center bearings must correspond with those of the axle bed. The end bearings *A*, Figs. 188 and 189, when the side bars are clipped on, must be three-quarters inch square. The fifth wheel should be no smaller than eight inches in diameter. A similar bolster, Fig. 189, is sometimes used at the back axle. It does not differ from the front bolster except at the bearings.

Fig. 188. Bolster and head block.　　Fig. 189. Bolster for hind axle.

The side bars have very little sweep, as the bearings are near the ends instead of at the center, as formerly. No special provision is made for the bearings, as the cross springs are clipped on and the distance varies in accordance with the kind of spring used. The side bars should be one inch thick for a full sized body, tapered to seven-eighths of an inch at the ends, one and a quarter inch deep at the center and seven-eighths of an inch at the ends.

For a one-man body the bars should be seven-eighths inch thick at the center and three-quarters inch at the ends, one and an eighth inch deep at the center and three-quarters at the ends. In rounding up leave the full width of the wood on the bottom, and round up to a cone form.

Many of the light side bar carriages now made dispense with the perch, using some one of the patented fifth wheel couplings at the front and clipping the side bars to the axle at the back axle. I do not advise the making of this except by expert carriage part makers.

Carriage Parts for Elliptic Springs.

The perch carriage for elliptic springs, more than any other, is the one that enters into general use. The principle of construction is the same in each, differing mainly in minor points, such as weight, form of perch, &c. The light perch carriage part is apparently so simple that almost any woodworker feels capable of making it, and as a result a very large percentage are not properly constructed, and the vehicles have an increased friction equivalent to thirty or forty per cent over what they should have.

If the woodworker will observe a few well defined rules he will be able to overcome the difficulty caused by increased friction, even if his taste and judgment fail to lead him to artistic outlines. In the proportioning there are rules of leverage, and combinations of wood and metal which should be studied. They are outside of the province of these plain articles, but they are worthy of research. There is one point, however, that must not be overlooked in the construction of carriage parts for light vehicles—elasticity. It may be agreeable for a builder of a light buggy to say that his axle will not spring between shoulders, but if they are perfectly rigid, a penalty is paid in the extra strain thrown upon the axle arm at the collar, and broken axles are the result of rigidity. Excessive elasticity is equally objectionable, producing a springy axle between shoulders, and throwing the wheels out of tread. The happy medium between these is an axle that has sufficient elasticity to break the shock of concussion between the shoulders and enough of rigidity to return to and retain its original form when the force of the blow has been expended.

In many cases the form of the body controls that of the beds, but there are general forms which cover the majority of bodies. Thus a drop front phaëton, at the lowest point at the back end, is from six to seven inches higher than the lowest point at the extreme front end, the bottom or foot

rest falling six to nine inches below a straight line, drawn
from these points. The curvature thus established forms a
guide line for the perch, and as there must not be less than
six inches between the hollow of the body at its lowest point
and the top of the perch, serves as a guide for the drop of
the front bed.

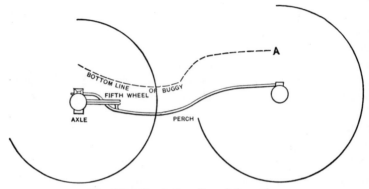

Fig. 190.   The bottom line of the rocker.

The side elevation shown by Fig. 190 indicates a form for
a bent perch, which serves to illustrate the rule governing the
construction; but the carriage part maker is compelled to
change the forms of perches to suit the general outline of
the body. The bottom line of the rocker is indicated by the
line A, Fig. 190. If a more sharply defined outline is used
on one with a square foot rest, the form of the perch must
be changed to conform to the body. The placing of the fifth
wheel above the perch is rendered necessary at the present
time because of the demand for low-hung bodies. In no
case should the perch and body be less than six inches apart
when the body is not loaded. The length of the perch is
determined by the length of the body.

For all drop front bodies there should be at least three
inches in the clear between the front end and the spring
bar. The back axle should be so placed that its center and

the back end of the body at the top back corner of the quarter shall be on the same perpendicular line. The ends of the perches should be on parallel lines for a space not less than four inches. This secures perfect parallel tenons. Between these points all the sweeps are to be made. Bent perches, when the desired shapes can be obtained, are the best; but if these cannot be had, sawed perches of fine, close grained hickory or white ash should be used. There is a large variety of fifth wheel couplings and perch irons on the market from which the desired end forms may be selected, but all the center of the perch must be of bent or sawed wood.

To determine the form of the axle beds, ascertain the hight of the wheels and the exact location of the perch, as previously described. Locate the fifth wheel on a parallel line running through the center of the arms, and draw a line above this for the bearings of the fifth wheel, the space between the two lines to be determined by the thickness of the fifth wheel plates. Strike another line for the head block spring bearing, two and a quarter inches above the top fifth wheel line, and another as an extreme bottom line for the bed, making the bed two and a half inches at the center. These drafts (the side view as Fig. 190, and the end views

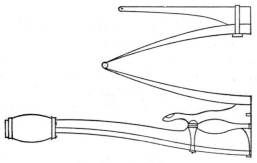

Fig. 191.   End view.

as Figs. 191 and 192), give a positive guide for the carriage

maker from which to make his patterns.   To make a pattern
for the front bed, procure a half inch board of sufficient
length and about five inches wide.   First ascertain the length
of the bed, as follows: Suppose the track to be four feet
eight inches outside to outside, the hub six and a half inches
long, deduct from the track width the distance from the
face of the spoke to the back end of the hub, on each hub.
Suppose this to be seven inches in all, the length of the bed
will be four feet one inch.   Next draw a cross line at the
center, as indicated by O, Fig. 193 ; then lay off the fifth
wheel bearings.   If the fifth wheel is twelve inches, strike
the outside lines for the bearings, six and an eighth inch each

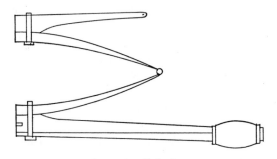

Fig. 192.   End view.

side of the center, and inside of them strike other lines, allowing a scant eighth inch more than the full width of the
fifth wheel plate.   Then divide up the board by a series of
cross lines, as shown by Fig. 193.   Strike the parallel line
A for the top of the fifth wheel bearings and the bottom of
the hub at the ends.   Then with a large compass the stationary point on a continuation of the line O, set so that
the movable point will intersect line O and an indication
line two and a half inches below line A on O, and line 7
where it intersects line B, a line that represents the bottom
of the axle at the shoulders.   Strike this sweep, and then
without changing the spread of the compass, set the station-

ary point on an extension of line 11, at a point where the movable point will intersect lines *B* and 7, and strike the forward sweep at line 11. From 11 to 12 the bed is straight.

These compass sweeps, when correctly made, give a good,

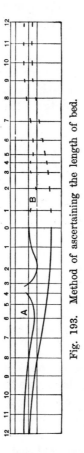

Fig. 193. Method of ascertaining the length of bed.

easy concavo-convex bottom to the bed. The workman will understand that there is no arbitrary rule governing this sweep, as tastes differ in this regard, but as the compass can be used to such an advantage both as to time and correctness, it is a good plan to use this form of obtaining sweeps whenever possible. Having established the bottom line sweep at one end, space off on the cross lines the corresponding distances on the respective lines at the other end, as indicated on the unfinished end of the sketch. The top lines between the bearings and the ends should be about as shown by Fig. 193, starting in by a short sweep and diminishing slightly to cross line 9, and graduating more sharply from 9 to the end, the latter to be a trifle deeper than half the depth of the axle at the collar, say a half inch for a seven-eighths inch axle. The sweep between the fifth wheel bearings should be

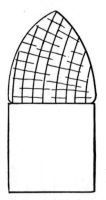

Fig. 194. The axle bed rounded up.

easy, showing as much of an opening as possible without weakening the bed. The back axle bed should be nearly straight on the bottom. A curvature of three-quarters of an inch is sufficient. The other proportions are about the same as those of the front bed.

The head block is the next pattern to be made. Strike a center line for the king bolt, and cut the underside between the bearings to the same form as the top of the axle bed. Strike a parallel line with the fifth wheel bearings two and an eighth inches above it, and mark off three inches on each

side, giving six inches for the spring bearing. The form of
the scroll is a matter of taste. The form of it controls the
general line of the top, and the thickness of the block at the
bearings should not be less than seven-eighths of an inch.
Set the mortise for the perch a trifle below the center of the
block, after deducting the curvature for the spring. When
rounding up the axle bed, strike a center line on the top,
and round up as shown by Fig. 194. If the bottom corners
are cut off a trifle, as shown, it will give a neat finish, and
there will be no cracking of paint to show between the wood
and iron.

Fine, second growth hickory is by all odds the best wood
for axle beds and perches for light work. White ash follows
next in value, and after it prime white oak.—*By* W. N. F.

Carriage Parts for Heavy Express Wagons.

Heavy express wagons are invariably made with platform
carriage parts for the front and hung upon heavy springs at
the back. These carriage parts are models of strength and
simplicity. Every piece of wood or iron in them is there for
use, not ornament, and nothing is omitted that will contribute
in any way to strength or utility. A number of patterns are
used, differing mainly in minor points, and so nearly alike
that to the casual observer they are all as though of one
model. The timber used is the finest of second growth white
ash, both bent and sawed. The former is the most expensive;
but where the bend is considerable, the increased strength
more than compensates for the extra cost. Full circle fifth
wheels are used in all cases. These should be of iron, not
narrower than one and a half inch, using half inch flat for
the bottom circle and half inch half round for the top circle.
The springs are of two to two and a half inch steel. The
width of the fifth wheel plates and the spring plates must
be settled before the carriage part maker can put up his
work.

In all cases there should be a full drawing to work to,

The absence of the drawing often leads to little errors which must be corrected by the blacksmith, and the latter is often blamed because of these defects when the fault is wholly with the carriage part maker.

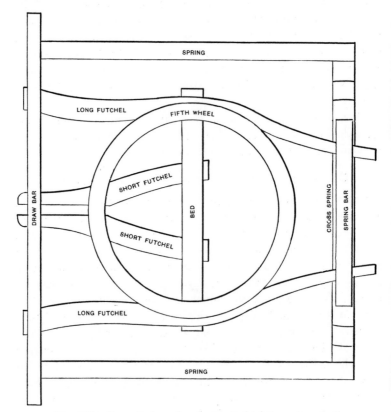

Fig. 195.   Ground plan of a short-pole futchel carriage part.

The simplest platforms are the best, and I have selected two patterns to better illustrate the essential points. Figs. 195 to 202 represent one pattern, and Figs. 203 to 210 another, Fig. 211 showing an elevation of the latter. But in reality the difference is so slight that it gives an equally good idea of the former group.

Fig. 195 shows the ground plan of a short pole futchel carriage part, with bent outside futchels, showing also location of side and cross springs.

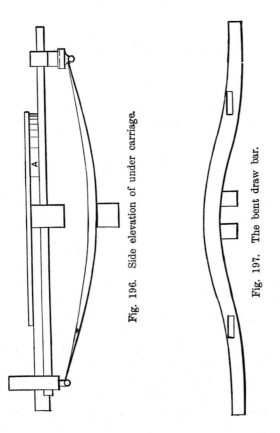

Fig. 196. Side elevation of under carriage.

Fig. 197. The bent draw bar.

Fig. 196 gives a side elevation of the under carriage, with spring resting upon the top of the axle.

Fig. 197 shows the bent draw bar, with end of futchels and location of mortises. Some workmen prefer putting the mortises on the line of the bottom of the draw bar, as the wood bar is weakened less than when the mortises are cut as shown, but if the workman is not careful, there is a likelihood of the long futchels being thrown out of line.

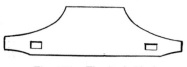

Fig. 198.   The back block.

Fig. 198 shows the back block which performs the double part of spring block and head piece to the futchels. The depth of this block is determined entirely by the arch of the springs and the spring couplings.

The bed piece must be two and a half inches wide by three inches deep at the center, tapered up to two inches at the ends, the top perfectly flat. As the king bolt passes through this bed, it must be very strong. The short futchels are two and a half inches thick, one and seven-eighths inch wide at the front end and two and a quarter inches at the bed, the faces being sixteen inches long. The ends are tenoned through the bed with seven-eighths inch tenons. The side futchels are two inches wide at the draw bar and one and a quarter inch at the spring block, the taper being gradual. They are one and seven-eighths inch deep front of the bed and one and a half inch back. The beds and the futchels are lapped together, the lap being cut in from the top of the futchels and the bottom of the bed, leaving the end of the bed full size and projecting at least one and a half inch beyond the futchels. The spring block must be full width of the spring plates at the spring bearing, and not less than one and three-quarters inch at the top. The draw bar is bent, so as to pass over the top of the ends of the short futchels, to which it is secured by bolts.

The upper carriage consists of three cross bars running in

the direction of the lower bed, and an upper bed crossing at right angles with the cross bars. These are all shown, together with the upper fifth wheel plate, by Fig. 199. The front and back cross bars take the sweep of the wheels in the center, as shown. They may be sawed if preferred, as

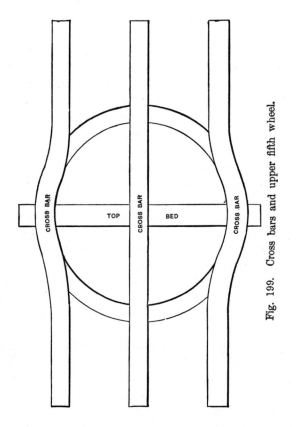

Fig. 199. Cross bars and upper fifth wheel.

the strain on them is not in a direction that would weaken them to an appreciable extent. The center cross bar is straight. These bars should not be thinner than two inches.

Their depth is determined by the hight of the front wheels, as the body rests upon them, and it must be so high as to allow the front wheels free passage under it, under all circumstances.

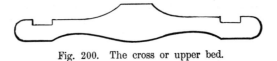

Fig. 200.   The cross or upper bed.

The cross or upper bed, Fig. 200, should be of two inch stock, not less than two and three-quarters inches deep in the center and two inches at the ends.   In this form of upper carriage, front and back bars are left full depth the whole length of the fifth wheel bearing, and the upper bed is lapped to the underside, the laps being cut as shown by Figs. 200 and 201.

The center cross bar is cut away so that its underside at the middle rests upon the center of the upper bed, the king bolt passing through both.   The ends and bars, at all points where they bear upon the fifth wheel plates, are bolted with countersunk head bolts firmly to the fifth wheel plates.

A circular block serves as a rest for the back of the lower fifth wheel plate, as indicated by *A*, Fig. 196, the front resting upon the short futchels and bolted thereto.   An iron brace extends from the underside of the bed to the center of the circle, and having a T head, serves as an additional support.

The ground plan of another form of carriage is shown by Fig. 203.   It will be noticed that while this has the same proportions, it differs in having all the futchels extending through to the spring block, greatly increasing the strength back of the bed.   This is used for the heaviest class of carriages, and is found to give all the support necessary for the heaviest kind of work.   The bed is two and three-quarters by three inches.   The center hounds are two and a half inches deep front of the bed and one and three-quarters inch back of it, the reduction being entirely from the underside.

The futchels pass through mortises in the beds, the top being flush with the top of the bed itself. The back ends also pass through mortises in the spring block. By being formed in this manner, the lower plate of the fifth wheel has a level bearing upon the bed and the back and front of the

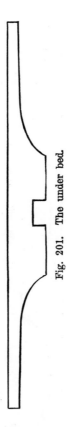

Fig. 201. The under bed.

center futchels, without being blocked up. The tenons through the spring block are one inch deep.

The outside futchels are straight forward of the bed, bending in from that point to the spring block. They are ten-

oned through the draw bar and spring block and lapped from
the underside to the bed, leaving the end of the bed to be
finished as in Fig. 195.   These should be two inches wide
at the draw bar and bed, tapering from the bed to one and
a half inch at the spring block.   They are two inches deep

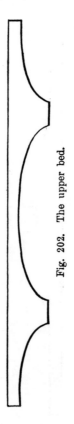

Fig. 202.   The upper bed.

at the front and one and a half inch at the back ends.   The
spring block must be full thickness of the spring plates, narrowed up at the top to one and a half inch.   The draw bar
is sawed out at the center, being cut high enough to rest
upon the futchels.   Use two-inch stock, leaving the bar two

inches square at the ends and two and a half inches deep in the center. Round block bearings may be placed between the lower fifth wheel plate and the outside futchels.

Fig. 205 shows the spring block—side view. Its depth, as stated regarding that of Fig. 198, must be governed entirely

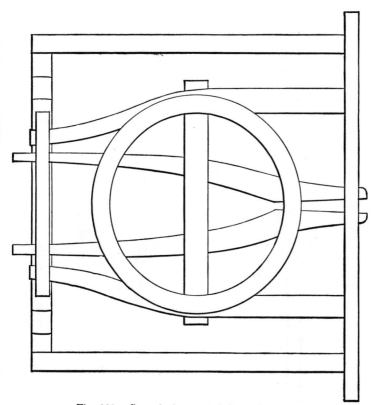

Fig. 203. Ground plan second form of carriage.

by the curve of the springs and the length of the couplings.

Fig. 206 shows a ground plan of the top carriage. With it all the cross bars are straight. They must be fully two inches thick.

Fig. 207 is a side elevation of the upper bed, which crosses the three bars and to which it is bolted. The front and back cross pieces are cut away as shown by Fig. 208, the arch being such as to carry it over, but snug against the top of the upper bed, to which both bars are bolted.

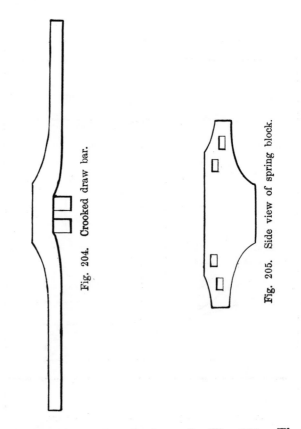

Fig. 204. Crooked draw bar.

Fig. 205. Side view of spring block.

The center cross piece is shown by Fig. 209. The center laps upon and into the center of the upper bed, as shown by Figs. 195 and 199, and is cut away in the center at the top and between the lower bed and the fifth wheel bearing on the underside. So far as the upper carriage is concerned,

they may be used with either lower carriage, it being a matter of choice.

In finishing up the various pieces there are different styles,
such as full chamfers, corner beads—that is, beads on chamfers and edge beads; beads run along the edges on the sides.

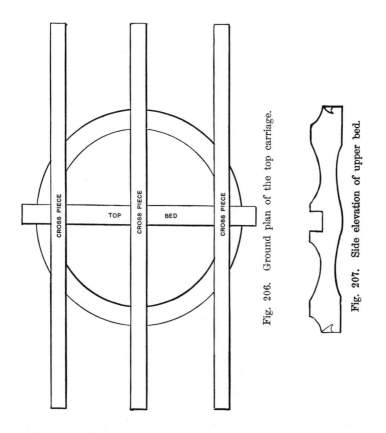

Fig. 206. Ground plan of the top carriage.

CROSS PIECE TOP CROSS PIECE BED CROSS PIECE

Fig. 207. Side elevation of upper bed.

This latter is the simplest, and is neat, as no attempt is made
at display in finishing the pieces. In all cases where the
pieces lap together, the end of one piece must be left full
size, to give a neat finish, and the style of finish must tally

with that of the sides of the various pieces; but all scrolls
or carvings are superfluous.

Fig. 210 gives a full side elevation, showing all parts together. It is a good plan, just as soon as the woodwork of

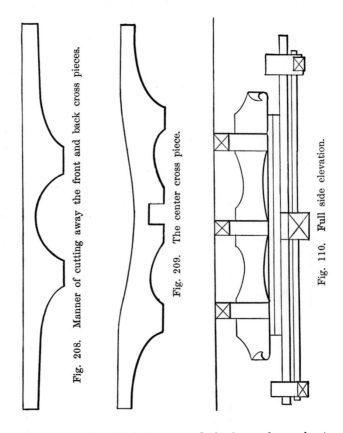

Fig. 208. Manner of cutting away the front and back cross pieces.

Fig. 209. The center cross piece.

Fig. 110. Full side elevation.

a carriage part is finished, to soak it for a few minutes in
warm raw linseed oil, placing the pieces where they can drip
after being removed from the oil. Do this before the carriage is put together.

Platform Carriage Parts.

Platform carriage parts for pleasure carriages are made in an almost numberless variety, but the principles governing their construction are embodied in a few forms, modifications of which constitute the majority. These changes are due to two causes: First, the absolute necessity of constructing a carriage part that will harmonize with the body; secondly, one that, while harmonizing, will at the same time support the body properly and give the requisite sweep of the axle, to permit the wheel turning under without coming in contact with the body; and, thirdly, one that is adapted to one horse, two horses, or a combination that may be adapted to either. A few years ago this last consideration was an important one, but of late it has fallen into disuse.

In considering the principal varieties, I will begin with the pole carriage, better known as the swivel futchel carriage, as

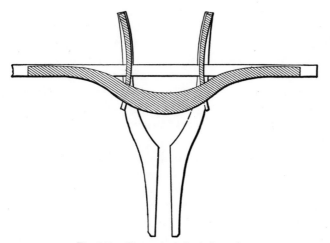

Fig. 211.   The swivel futchel carriage.

shown in Fig. 211. The upper and lower carriage are shown together, the upper being indicated by shade lines, the lower

in outline. The lower section consists of a straight bed and
two sawed futchels. The upper section is also of three pieces,
a bent bed and two short bent or sawed futchels. In addition to these, there may be thin sawed circles to give finish
and support at unequal bearings to the fifth wheel plates.
These correspond in circle to that of the iron plates, and in
thickness are governed entirely by the space to be filled to
secure a level wheel. The front view of the beds is shown

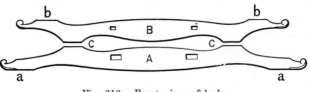

Fig. 212.   Front view of beds.

by Fig. 212, *A* the lower, and *B* the upper bed. *a a* of the
lower bed indicate the spring bearing bearings, *b b* of the
upper bed the body bearings, *c c*, between the two, bearings
of each, for the fifth wheel. The mortises in each represent
those for the respective futchels. The length of the lower
bed between *b b* must be governed by the length of the axle.
This varies, as in case of vehicles for city use. No attempt
is made to track the front axle. It will be four to eight
inches shorter than the back, according to the cut-under of
the body on the sweep of the top bed, though the latter
should be subject entirely to the situation of the cut-under.
But it is not in all cases, as some builders prefer a deep
sweep and others a flat one to the top bed. It follows therefore that all points must be worked in unison. The depth
of the beds between the fifth wheel bearings and the spring
and body bearings must be determined by the hight of the
wheels and location of the foot rest of the front. The distance between the bearings *b b* represents the width of the
boot from outside to outside, at the point of attachment. In

determining the space between *a* and *b*, allow for the thickness of the fifth wheel plates. These vary from three-eighths to five-eighths inch each, according to the weight of the vehicle. It is desirable that the bearings *a* and the center of the bed *A* be on a straight line, as are also the bearings for the fifth wheel plates and the center between these. Where the two beds are straight, the lower should be a trifle the deeper; but where the bent top bed is used, the two are of the same dimensions at the bearings and at the centers. Until within a few years ago, the top bed, no matter what its sweep was, was sawed out, as it was found difficult to bend such heavy pieces of timber, and more difficult to keep the bed in shape after it was worked out. These troubles no longer exist, and as every dealer in carriage materials carries bent beds in stock, there is no excuse for using the weak sawed bed.

The object of this bent bed is to carry the king bolt forward of the natural center, while allowing the bearings of the fifth wheel, which are the real supports of the carriage, to be directly on a line with each other. By thus placing the king bolt forward of the natural center, the front of the body can be shortened without interfering with the turn-under of the front wheels; or where it is not desirable to shorten the body, the carriage part can be placed further back than it could be were the two beds straight.

The bent beds on the market are generally one and three-quarters inch thick and from two to six inches deep, having a sweep of two to nine inches. The sawed futchels for a carriage of medium weight should be one and three-quarters inch thick, one inch wide at the front ends, two and an eighth at the back of the pole plate, one and a quarter by seven-eighths at the bed, and one by seven-eighths at the back end. For ordinary use, the pole opening should be three and a quarter inches at the front end of the futchels. This will allow for a three-inch pole after the plates are on the face of the futchels.

The sweep of the under and lower side of the beds between the bearings should be easy, and as full as possible, consistent with the strength of the beds. In finishing, before cornering, a slight rounding of the beds on front and back adds to the neatness of their appearance.

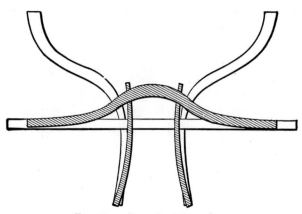

Fig. 213.   Open futchel carriage.

The open futchel carriage, Fig. 213, is the popular carriage for a one-horse vehicle. The upper and lower parts are designated by shaded and plain outlines, as in Fig. 211. In this the futchels of the under carriage are bent. The only straight piece in this carriage is the lower bed. These bent futchels, like the bent beds, can be bought ready for use, better bent, and of all desirable shapes, than when made at the carriage factory. These futchels constitute the main difference between the two carriages shown. The carriage is, however, much lighter throughout, being for a one-horse vehicle. The general shape of the beds, front view, is the same as those of Fig. 212, differing in proportions and location of futchels only. With this style of carriage the shafts are separate, the ends being made to fit between the two plates on the sides of the futchels, and which extend far

enough beyond the wood to insure a safe support to the
shafts.

The futchels to the under carriage should be about one
and three-eighths inch thick by one and a quarter inch wide
at the front ends, tapering gradually in width to one inch
wide at the bottom, one inch by seven-eighths at the shoulder,
and seven-eighths by three-quarters at the back end. The
upper futchels should be an eighth of an inch wider at the
back than at the front ends, and three-quarters of an inch
thick. The bed at the center on the top should be an eighth
of an inch thicker than at the ends. The other proportions
are determined by the requirements of the body and the
wheels.

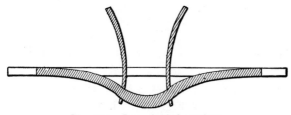

Fig. 214.   Iron shackel carriage.

The iron shackel carriage, Fig. 214, is the merest skeleton
of a carriage, and yet it is the one that can be and is adapted
to more uses than any other one style. There is no more
wood than is absolutely necessary to give securing points to
the iron work. The under bed is all there is of wood of that
part, while the upper bed and the two short futchels constitute the balance of the wood; yet it is ironed for a pole or
shafts as for an adjustable carriage which can be used for
either. The front view of the beds is the same as that
shown by Fig. 212, and all the rules governing the construction of these pieces are the same in both cases. Some of the
lightest carriage parts made are of this pattern, as are also
some of the heaviest. The fact of its simplicity may lead to

the idea that very little skill is required in its construction. This would be an error, as all its success depends upon the woodwork. The blacksmith uses it as a foundation for his work, and without a correct foundation the whole structure fails, and when the fore carriage of a platform vehicle fails, the whole is a failure.

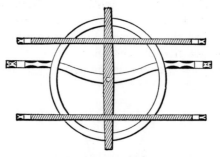

Fig. 215.   A cross head piece which acts as an upper bed.

An entirely different carriage part than those previously described is shown by Fig. 215. Like Fig. 214, its under carriage is of a single piece of wood, all the other parts being of iron; but that piece is bent like the upper ends of Figs. 211, 213, and 214, the upper carriage consisting of a cross head piece which acts as an upper bed, and the two parallel supports.

Fig. 216.   Front view of upper bed.

The front view of the under bed is shown by Fig. 216 and that of the supports by Fig. 217. In some cases a full circle of wood covers the top of the upper plate of the fifth wheel, but a lighter finish is given by the use of the round upper plate.

The cross on the upper bed is thick in the center, gradually tapering on the sides and top to the ends, with the parallel supports lapped into the bed as shown. The curvature of the parallel supports is determined by the hight of the wheel and the location of the boot front. The space which separates them is not arbitrary. Where the bend of the lower bed is greatest, it is necessary to place the front support nearer the king bolt than the back, in order to locate the carriage properly.

This carriage is ironed mainly for one horse, but it may be ironed for two equally well. As with Fig. 214, the woodwork is but the frame; all the working parts are of iron. It has never been a popular carriage in this country, but in England it appears to be a favorite, while it is also largely used in

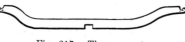

Fig. 217.   The supports.

France. The upper and lower carriages are designated as with those previously described.

In making carriage parts a draftboard is a necessity, and the carriage must be drawn out in full size, to show the ground plan of the two sections, the hight between bearings having nothing to do with the location of the futchels, fifth wheel, &c.

In working first dress up the beds to the required thickness and shape. Straighten the top and bottom lines, lay out and cut the mortises for the futchels, and then mark off the bearings. Dress up the futchels, and if time permits, leave the tenon portions a little full, and do not fit them up under twenty-four hours after the mortises and tenons have been cut. This will give the wood time to shrink and will insure a much better job than if finished up at the one time. The present fashion does not call for elaborate scrolls, but the ends must be finished neatly and in a uniform pattern. The corner bead or round may be used to finish all parts not plated, but a circle should be struck for all bolt heads, to insure their bearing snugly to the wood when finished.

All parts, when plated, or when the under sides are left flat, should be finished with a bead, the size to be in keeping with the weight of the carriage.

Ash is generally conceded to be the best timber for the carriage parts, particularly for the beds and heavy futchels; the lighter futchels may be of hickory. The short futchels, as a rule, have but little bend, and for them, in the absence of pieces bent expressly, there is nothing more convenient than a good hickory felloe. It is not necessary to cut one that could be used on a wheel, as there are always enough with slight defects, which unfit them for the wheel, though the quality of timber may be all right.

Platform Gear for a Light Delivery Wagon.

All the better grades of delivery wagons are hung on platform gears, as they can be hung to turn in a much shorter circle than when hung on a perch carriage. There was a time when the blacksmith looked on a platform gear as a part to be made only by the most expert workman. That day, thanks to the trade journal, is past, and the man who now professes to be a journeyman, belies his claim if he, as a woodworker, cannot make a platform carriage part, or as a blacksmith, an iron one, when he has full instructions how to proceed in both branches.

Simplicity and strength are the two essential features, and the reader of a trade paper has good opportunities for comparing the simplest with the most complex.

The carriage given herewith is one of the simplest made, and at the same time it is very strong. Fig. 218 shows the lower carriage complete. The center bar, which is the main connecting bar of the woodwork, is two and a half inches wide and two and three-quarters deep in the center, the ends

being one and three-quarters inch deep. The hounds are
apped in flush with the top.

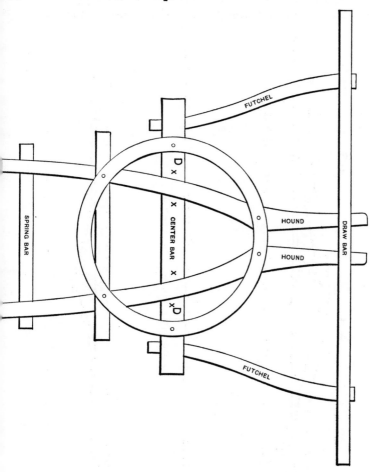

Fig. 218. The lower carriage complete.

The king bolt plate extends from D to D, and is securely
olted, the bolts being at X X X X. The futchels are mor-
ised through the center and through the draw bars. The

hounds are lapped to the spring bar and the wheel bar. The
spring bar is two and three-quarters inches deep in the center and one and three-quarters wide. The hounds are two

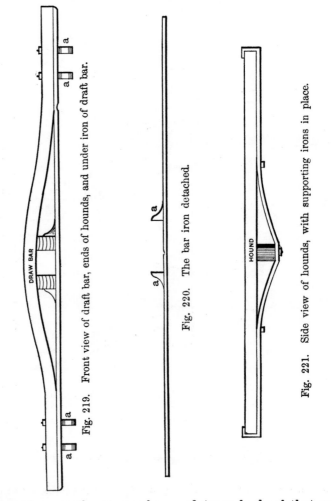

Fig. 219. Front view of draft bar, ends of hounds, and under iron of draft bar.

Fig. 220. The bar iron detached.

Fig. 221. Side view of hounds, with supporting irons in place.

inches deep at the center bar, and taper back of that point
to one and a half inch.

The fifth wheel is twenty-two inches in diameter, of one and a quarter by five-sixteenths inch iron, secured by countersunk bolts at the points indicated. The top carriage consists of three bars with their bearings directly over the points where the fifth wheel plates are secured. They are one and three-quarters inch wide, and their depth is determined by the hight of the wheels, as the body must be hung level.

The front view of the draft bar, ends of hounds, and under iron of the draft bar are shown by Fig. 219. *A A* represent the spring eyes. The simplest method of making these is to finish them with bolts and secure them by nuts on the top of the draft bar. If preferred, these eyes may be swaged on the iron, but they are no better and cost more when made in that way than when made as illustrated.

Fig. 220 represents the bar iron detached, the lugs, *A A*, being as supports to the ends of the hounds.

Fig. 221 represents a side view of the hounds, with the supporting irons in place, *A* being a thimble, one and a half inch long. The brace is of three-quarters inch oval iron, and the ends of three-quarters inch flat half-round. The side springs are of one and a half inch steel—five plates—four and a half inches set, forty inches long, with the hole set one and a half inch forward of the center. The cross spring is of one and a half inch steel, thirty-six to thirty-eight inches long—six plates.—*By* W. N. F.

Light Express Wagon Gears.

The light express wagon, though having one general style of body, is geared in a variety of ways, by which cheapness may be secured or the convenience of the vehicle increased. The cheapest gear is the plain double perch, shown by Fig. 222, the side elevation, and Fig. 223, the ground plan. In making this perch, the first point to be ascertained is the hight of the wheels. A popular hight is three feet two inches front, and three feet eight inches back. These hights permit the body being hung two feet ten inches from the ground, and admits the front axle turning, so that the wheel will strike a "rub iron" on the perch instead of rubbing against the body.

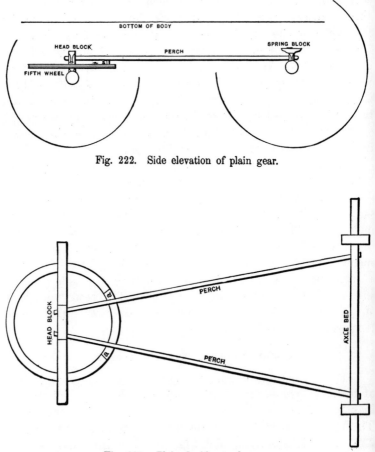

Fig. 222.   Side elevation of plain gear.

Fig. 223.   Plain double perch gear.

Having determined the hight of the wheels, lay off the back axle bed so as to give it an upward curve of one and a half

Inch on the under side, the shape shown by Fig. 224. Strike a parallel line intersecting the bed at the mortises *a a* on the inside. These points will give the bottom of the perch.

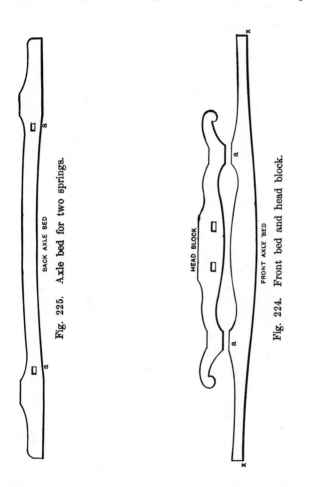

BACK AXLE BED

Fig. 225. Axle bed for two springs.

HEAD BLOCK

FRONT AXLE BED

Fig. 224. Front bed and head block.

Determine the distance from the center of the axle arm to the perch, and strike a parallel line full length between the axles. Make the gear for a seven-foot body five feet three inches long. The head block must be two and a half inches deep. Set the perches so that the tops are at the center, between the spring and the underside of the head block; then add to this the thickness of the two plates of the fifth wheel, which will be about three-quarters of an inch; this line will give the top of the front axle bed, from which the drop of the bed can be determined. To make this pattern, strike a parallel line touching the fifth wheel bearings, as shown by *a a*, Fig. 225. Determine the distance between this line and the top of the axle, and strike a parallel line from points *x x* for the bottom of the bed. Make the bed through the center two and a quarter inches deep, and strike an easy sweep from that point to *x*, which will give a bed like that shown by Fig. 225. Frame the perches as shown by Fig. 223, cutting the shoulders on the undersides, leaving half the depth of the perches for tenons. The perches should be seven-eighths inch square. The fifth wheel block (*a*, Fig. 222), may be a segment of a circle, extending, as shown, from *a* to *a*, Fig. 223, or of two blocks located at the point where the perches cross the fifth wheel plate.

This gear is designed for three elliptic springs, and it is necessary to provide bearings for spring blocks, compelling the back bed to be formed at the ends, as shown by Fig. 224. The blocks should be about six inches long, shaped as shown on Fig. 222; the fifth wheel should not be less than two feet in diameter. Use prime, first quality, forest growth ash for the beds and head block, hickory for the perches. Bead the bottom edges of the beds and round the top to a full oval. Corner the perches, but do not cut away more than necessary to give a neat round, leaving the top flat, the full width of the bolt head.

Another style of gear for two springs is shown by Fig. 226. This is the old pattern "hound gear," which for years has been discarded except for very heavy wagons. It has lately come into use again, and is the most popular gear for two-spring carriage parts.

In laying out for this gear follow the directions given for the double perch gear, so far as the level of the perch and the position of the fifth wheel are concerned. The extension of the perch through the head block to the front of the fifth

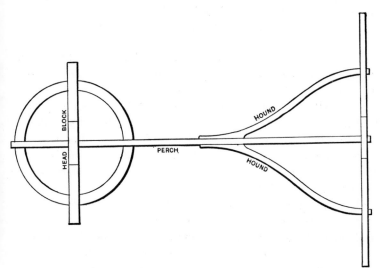

Fig. 226. Gear with perch and hounds.

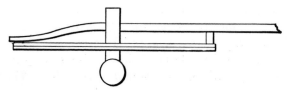

Fig. 227. Side view of fifth wheel and reach.

wheel, as shown by Fig. 227, answers a double purpose, being a support to the wheel and giving a finish in front of the head block. It necessitates the use of a larger mortise in the head block than would be used were the perch not extended. It also requires a heavier piece for the perch, or a short bend.

Fig. 228.   Back bed for reach and hounds.

The back axle bed, Fig. 228, also differs from that of the perch carriage, having the spring bearing at the center instead of at the ends.

The hounds should have a bearing of not less than nine inches at the perch, and be of a length that will equalize the length of the perch back and front of the bearings. They should spread well, as no other braces are used for the hind axle. The perch is one and a half inch square at the head block shoulder, tapering in width to one and an eighth inch at the back axle shoulder; the hounds are of the same depth as the perch, one and three-quarters inch wide at the back end of the bearings and one and an eighth inch wide at the back axle shoulders. The extension of the perch forward of the head block should be three-quarters inch deep and one and three-eighths inch wide at the head block, and a half inch deep and one inch wide at the front end at the fifth wheel plates. The back axle bed must be of timber of the same width as the spring plates, the surfaces left square at the mortises for the shoulders. Unless the shoulders are boxed in, the top at the hounds must be left flat for the bolt heads or clips, whichever is used. Clips are preferable, as they do away with holes through the axle. When they are used, the tenons of the perch and hounds do not extend through the axle bed. The fifth wheel support block is two and a half inches in diameter, turned. Space off the perch and hounds for bolts, and strike compass circles for bolt heads—four in front of hounds and three back. The hound to each have four. Bead the under edge, and round up to an oval. Make the fifth wheel bearings of the head block one and an eighth inch square. Use the best quality of forest growth ash for all parts of the gear, and see that it is well seasoned.

Another gear is the platform. It is the most expensive of any, as it is also the most convenient for turning, but unless the body is hung very high, the front wheels must be low— not higher than two feet six inches. All the woodwork for this carriage part is for the front, except a small spring block for the cross spring, as the back axle is forged round between spring bearings, and the three springs constitute the entire back carriage.

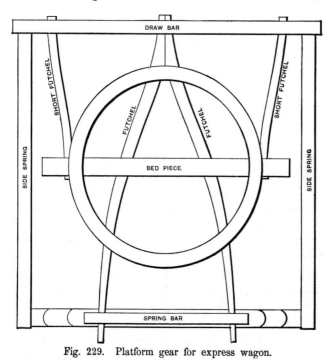

Fig. 229. Platform gear for express wagon.

Fig. 229 shows the ground plan of this carriage part, giving location of spring and fifth wheel as well as woodwork.

Fig. 230 is a side elevation of the same, together with a side elevation of the top carriage.

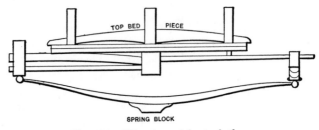

Fig. 230.   Side view of front platform.

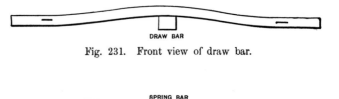

Fig. 231.   Front view of draw bar.

Fig. 232.   Short spring bar.

Fig. 231 is the draw bar, and Fig. 232 the back futchel bar and spring block. The bed piece projects three inches beyond the fifth wheel plates. It should be two and a half inches deep and two inches wide at the center, the ends tapered from the underside and the front and back to two by one and a half inch. The futchels are one and a half by one and an eighth inch at the front of the bed piece, and one by one and an eighth at the back, tapering to one inch square at the spring bar. The front end of the futchels are thrown up enough to bring the top on a level with the top of the bed piece, thus securing a level bearing for the fifth wheel without "blocking." The short futchels which serve to connect the head piece with the draw bar are straight on top, one and a quarter inch deep, and one and a half wide; the ends are tenoned into the draw bar and head piece. The draw bar (Fig. 231), has an upward bend, which will bring its underside on the top of the futchels. This is strengthened by a truss iron, fastened at the ends of the draw bar and extending under the futchels, bolted at each point. The draw bar should be two and a half inches wide and one and three-quarters deep. The shaft clips are attached to the bar just outside of the futchels. The spring bar (Fig, 232), serves to combine the spring and futchels. It must be the full width of the spring plate at the spring bearing, and tapered to one and a quarter inch at the ends.

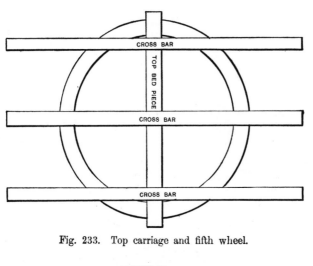

Fig. 233. Top carriage and fifth wheel.

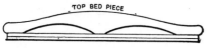

Fig. 234. Center bar and fifth wheel.

Fig. 233 shows a ground plan of the upper carriage, with the top bed piece and cross pieces in position. The top bed piece, Fig. 234, serves as a head block, but crosses the bed piece of the under carriage at right angles. To these two pieces are attached the king bolt and other necessary irons. The cross bar, Fig. 235, is cut on the underside so that the bearings rest on the fifth wheel plate at the points indicated, and the body bolted to them at the ends. The carriage must be made up level, leaving it to the blacksmith to place it true on the axle. The cross bars are regulated in depth by the hight desired for the body; they are one and a half inch thick. A lighter arrangement for attaching the top carriage to the body is to use turned supports, placing them at the points designated for the cross bars and bolting them to the body, the bolts passing through the center of the posts.

OUTSIDE CROSS BAR

Fig. 235.   Outside bar, showing bearings.

The timber for this class of carriage must be of the best white ash, close grained and tough. In finishing up, indicate the location for all bolt heads, and leave a flat surface for them. Bead all under edges with a scant quarter inch bead, and round up the sides, or finish the upper corners with a corner bead. The ends of the various pieces must be finished by a bead or with scrolls. The rounded end, beaded, makes a neat finish, and is more easily made than scrolls.

Many workmen fear to put up a platform carriage simply because of not understanding the general principle. The easiest way to acquire this is to make full-sized drawings, as directed. One day spent in studying out and making these drawings will give a better insight of the principles governing the construction of a platform carriage than a year's work after patterns and drawings made by another.

CHAPTER VIII.

Directions for Laying off the Frame of a Panel Seat Body.

RECOGNIZING the difficulty of giving instruction through printed and illustrated descriptions of methods of working where the details are as intricate as those of the geometrical rule—known among carriage makers as the "French rule"—without the aid of a teacher, no attempt will be made to give the general details of the rule. But in the following articles the working of the primary elements as applied to individual bodies will be given, which may serve to instruct the reader, and at the same time create an interest that will lead to a study of the rule in its entirety.

One of the simplest forms to which the rule can be applied is a low front, full seat body, such as that shown by

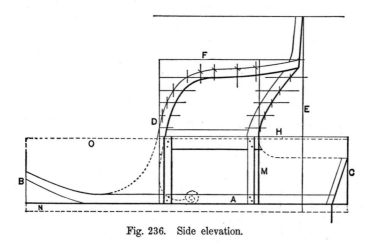

Fig. 236.   Side elevation.

Fig. 236. In it the seat is the most difficult part to work, being framed up in the manner of a full panel job, the body proper being paneled in the same way as the ordinary buggy. In laying off the draft, strike the base line *A ;* then lines *B* and *C*, representing the full length of the body; then strike the perpendicular lines *D* and *E*, and the horizontal line *F*, which, together with the portion of the base line *A*, between where it is intersected by *D* and *E*, constitutes a square, within which is contained the seat, the only part of the body not framed square. No dimensions are given, as it is presumed that the draftsman has those all decided before making his working drawing.

The top line of the body, *H*, is next laid off; then line *M*, giving the depth of the seat frame. With these lines all cardinal points are established, and the outlines of the seat can be laid out, completing the elevation view of the body.

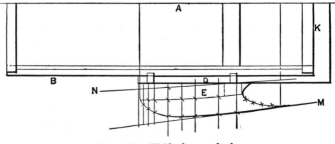

Fig. 237. Half of ground plan.

The working plans, consisting of the bottom, Fig. 237, and the end, Fig. 238, are next drawn. For convenience' sake, I have drawn these separate from the body, to avoid too many lines, which might mislead the workman; but when drawn to full size, both should be drawn on the board with the side elevation. To do this without using an extra wide board, lay it on the draft so that the inside of the sill will be an inch below the base line *A*, Fig. 237, as indicated by dotted lines *N*, and the center line, as indicated by dotted lines *O*. The draftboard should be long enough to admit Fig. 238 being placed upon it, back of the body.

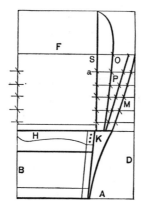

Fig. 238.   Half view of front.

For convenience' sake next lay off Fig. 238, by first striking lines *A*, *H*, and *F*, as continuations of corresponding lines on Fig. 236; then strike perpendicular line *B*, as the center line of the body, and measure off on line *A* half the width of the body on the bottom, and on line *H* half the width on the top, and strike line *K*, which gives the outside line of the body and the flare of the side.   Then measure off on line *F* the required width of the seat at the front corner, and strike line *D*, and on line *H* the width of the seat frame on the front edge, and from the points thus indicated, strike the line *M*, which indicates the front corner and flare of the seat arm; then line *P*, indicating the face of the seat arm.

The back of the seat is set up nearly square, one inch flare being the maximum.   The overhang of the frame at the back should be half that at the front.   To get the back line therefore, divide the space on line *H*, between *K* and *M*, and indicate on line *F* a point one inch wider than on line *H*, and strike line *O*, representing the outside line of the corner pillar; then measure off on line *H* the thickness re-

quired for the corner pillar at the bottom, and strike the
perpendicular line as the face line of the corner pillars, which
completes the outline of the back.

The next step is to prepare the ground plan, Fig. 237. To
do this, strike line *A* as the center; measure off from that
half the width of the body, as indicated on line *A*, Fig. 238,
and strike line *B*, the outside line of the sill; then obtain
the width on line *H*, Fig. 238, and strike line *D*. representing the flare of the body at the top. Next strike line *E*,
the outside edge of the seat frame, the points being those
obtained from Fig. 238. Then continue lines *B* and *C* as
the extreme length of the body, and line *K*, the edge of the
end bar. Lay off the seat arm by the widths obtained on
line *a*, where it intersects line *M*, and line *F* where it intersects line *O*, Fig. 238, and strike the line *M*, which represents the outside straight line of the flare of the arm at
the top. This completes the draft, so far as general outlines
are concerned, and the drawing is ready for indicating the
points for pricking off.

Fig. 239.   Half view of back end.

The first step is to strike a series of lines, horizontal and
perpendicular, as designated by those on the sketches, all to
be drawn to intersect the outline at the same points throughout. Next establish the turn-under and side sweeps, and

prick off the back from line S on line O, and the front of seat arm from line P. Strike line N, Fig. 237, as the contract line of the seat, and from it strike off the sweep of the seat from E. Fig. 239 shows in outline the back when framed up and molded, the panels being grooved in.

The general principles detailed in this article can be followed by any fairly well informed workman on bodies where a part is square and another part curved.

Cabriolet.—How to Frame and Lay off the Body.

The cabriolet is the representative body of the class known as half top work, embodying as it does all the points of a full swell quarter, a framed boot, and contracted rockers. It is looked upon by bodymakers as one of the most troublesome of all small panel bodies. In all cases where properly built, the front end is contracted, the amount of contract varying from eight to fifteen inches. This requires careful work, as the boot should stand square and the width be the same back and front. Bodymakers are not always particular about this, as it is easier to frame the rockers flat and create the contract by using a shorter bar before than behind. When this is done, the top of the boot is widest at the back, and the neck lines straight and ungainly. In this article the working drawings will illustrate the two methods of framing.

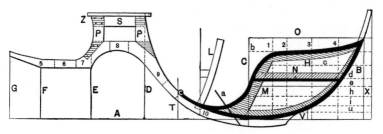

Fig. 240. Side elevation.

Fig. 240 shows the side elevation, giving framework of back

quarter and boot complete. In preparing this, draw base line A; then upright line B, as the end line of quarter at the arm rail; then line C, representing the front edge of the seat D; then back of the boot E—front of boot, and in this body, the back end of the heel board;—F the front of foot board, G the end of bracket, T front end of bottom side, and V the back end of the rocker; also the location of the back cross bar. Next strike line O, the top of the quarter at the arm rail X, the extreme back line of the corner pillar, and Z, the top line of the boot. Lay off the back quarter as shown in the square bounded by lines A, B, C, O, and T. In this case the bottom side is bent, and forms the corner pillar as well as the bottom side. The front pillar M is cut straight on the back. The foot is wide and laps onto the bottom side, showing a joint as per line a, which is the shortest joint that can be made. The arm H laps upon the upright, where lines 1 and b intersect. The quarter rail N is used where the lower part of the quarter is left open. It is framed onto the front and corner pillars so that the end makes a clean finish against the outside moldings. When the quarter is full paneled, this rail is not used, but two long strainers take its place, extending from the arm H to the bottom side. The rocker is composed of five pieces—5 the bracket, 6 the foot piece, 7 the front of riser, 8 the top of wheelhouse, 9 the neck, and 10 the drop piece. The wheelhouse piece 8 may be dispensed with, and the pieces 7 and 9 cut long enough to splice together and complete the full length. It requires a little more timber to cut these pieces long, but by so doing there are fewer joints and less labor. The boot is composed of the two uprights P and the top bar S. The location and form of all the joints are shown. These are all covered with the boot panel, and the outside shoulders must be cut so that the grain of the panel will be as nearly as possible at right angles with the joints of the frame.

Having the elevation fully laid off, prepare the ground or

working plan, Fig. 241, by first striking line *A*, as the center of the body; then determine the width of the body on the seat rail *B*, from the center to the outside of the pillar. Deduct from this the thickness and the turn-under of the pillar; then strike a pencil line from the point thus obtained

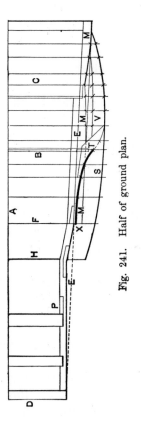

Fig. 241.   Half of ground plan.

back to line *C*; then strike the line *D*, corresponding with line *G*, Fig. 242. Measure off on it the required width, and strike line *E*, the face of the rocker. If the contraction is made by simply contracting the front end and working the rockers square, the contract will be at line *H*, and a new contract line must be drawn between *F* and *H*. Next lay off the bottom side *M;* then determine the flare of the pillar, as shown by *L*, Fig. 240. Select a sweep for the side, and strike line *S*. Lay off the pillar *T* and quarter arm *V*, and the drawing is ready for the pricking marks.

To prick off, strike a series of horizontal and perpendicular lines, as indicated by 1, 2, 3, and 4, and *b, c, d, e, h, i,* and *u*, Fig. 240. Continue the perpendicular lines across Fig. 241, and strike intermediate lines, to bring the prick marks closer together. The body is then ready for pricking off. The cross lines following the arm rail and pillar give the outside points, those on line *V* the quarter rail, and on *M* the bottom side and corner. The length of all the bars is shown on the board—1 the bracket bar, 2 the toe, and 3 the heel bars for the front, one on line *F* for the front of the body and the back bar *C*.

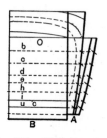

Fig. 242.   Half of back end.

Fig. 242 shows half the back with prick points indicating the corner and arm pillar, the dotted lines showing the molding. This also gives the length of the back rail, the index lettering giving corresponding lines to the parallel ones on Fig. 240.

With this plan before the workman, he should be able to lay off any body of this general character.

Constructing a Brougham Body.

The brougham is looked upon by bodymakers as one of the most intricate vehicles that they are called upon to build. While it does not belong to the primary branch of the business and requires a knowledge of the French rule to enable the workman to construct the body, yet this book would not be complete did it not indicate in some practical way the degree of perfection that the art of carriage making has attained. A plain pattern has therefore been selected, more with a view to exemplifying the work than to giving an outline of a body to be followed.

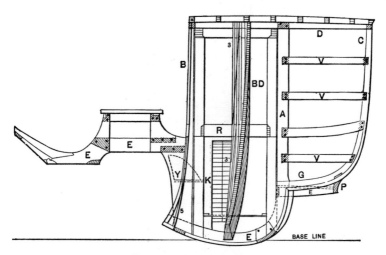

Fig. 243.   Side elevation.

Figs. 243, 244, and 245 show a working drawing, with all general details, in a much more complete manner than it is usually laid out by the foreman or draftsman. All minute details, however, are important, as the bodymaker is responsible for the perfect construction of the body, and in the absence of the minor points being laid down, he may easily omit some matters that should claim his attention.

In a perfect draft the rockers conform in their general
shape to the form of the roof or top rail *B*, as indicated by
Fig. 243, a full side elevation view. The three pillars of a
brougham are secured at the top by the roof rail, and as the
bottom frame is shaped to receive the bottom ends of the

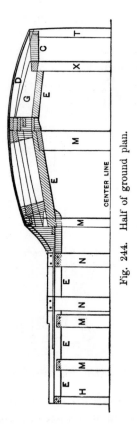

Fig. 244. Half of ground plan.

pillars, it naturally follows that the hinge and lock pillars
should both be worked by the same pattern; also that both
should have the same inclination, and that the faces should
be parallel. The corner pillar, as shown by Fig. 244, which

gives a view of half of the back, must be perpendicular from the back bar X to the top. The rocker E, in the doorway, Fig. 243, must be contracted to harmonize with the roof rail D, in order that the door bed will be perfectly square, relieving the door from strain or twist, a matter of great importance, as the glass frames in the door must run in parallel grooves; otherwise they will bend and not run smoothly.

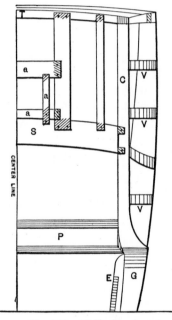

Fig. 245. Half of back end.

When the door is hinged to the pillar A, Fig. 243, it must shut on pillar B, touching its entire length, in order to prevent rattle. Formerly the bodymaker was required to give at least a quarter twist to the door, so that the top would strike before the bottom, and the twist was depended upon to hold the door firm. With the door framed square, small buttons of rubber are secured to the face of the rocker E, and thus cause the bottom to come in contact with the rubber pad, while the top is an eighth of an inch away from its bearing. The size of the hinge pillar is determined by the concealed hinge and the space required for the glass frame, or two frames, if stable shutters are used.

In building a body the first thing to do is to inspect the patterns, and to test them by the draftboard. Patterns will change their shape—little perhaps, but that little is enough to cause a great deal of trouble where so much depends on perfect accuracy, as bodymaking by the French rule does. One standing pillar must be drawn, the lines for the shoulders for the roof rail, the location of the arm and belt rails, and the shoulder line for the top of the bottom side G, Fig. 243. These lines must be drawn to the proper angles. All other patterns should be looked after and treated in the same manner, as it will save time later on, when it is less convenient to make the necessary corrections. Next examine every piece of stock; see that it is all as it should be, both as to size and quality.

All bodymakers do not follow the same routine in working, but preference is given by many to begin with framing the boot, and the stock is dressed up first. All joints and laps are then cut, care being taken that wherever possible the outside joints are so laid off that they may be nearly if not quite at right angles with the grain of the panel. When this is done, there is very little liability of panels being checked after they are glued on.

In this body the boot is vertical and without contraction, but the panel should be a half inch thick and finished up slightly rounding in every direction. The piece 3, on pillar $B\ D$, between the pillar and the rocker K, takes the vertical direction of the boot on one of its edges, and the inclination of the coupé pillar on the other. This piece is afterward covered with a quarter inch whitewood panel, line 5, Fig. 243. This panel is grooved under the front moldings of the coupé pillars. The piece 3 is glued and screwed to the coupé pillar, and the panel glued and clamped into its place with the top edge inserted into the groove in the cross rail, which has a molding worked on its lower edge to correspond with that of the door rail *R*. This panel is completed with the pillars before the frame is set up. The coupé pillar laps over the rocker *E* three-eighths of an inch. The piece 3 therefore is the thickness of the rocker at the bottom. The middle sketch *B D*, Fig. 243, shows the full outline of the coupé pillar, the sweep of the front edge as boxed out, and the outside or main line of the pillar, together with the blocking up piece 3, the rocker *K*, the top and bottom lines, tenons, &c., so plain as to require no further description.

The hinge or standing pillar *A*, Fig. 243, is lapped over the rockers three-eighths of an inch, with the shoulder on line *G*. Three-eighths of an inch is taken from this pillar above, and another three-eighths below the belt, to accommodate the upper and lower panels. The molding is worked upon the pillar, which is also grooved to receive the quarter panel, concealing all joints to the bottom line. The bottom side *G* is secured to the pillar by a tenon and mortise joint. The rabbet a quarter inch deep and one and a half inch wide, a corresponding offset being left upon the hinge door pillar, the purpose of which is to exclude the dust.

The roof rail *D*, Fig. 243, has a round on its top edge, between the ends, of three-eighths of an inch. The ends are tenoned into the corner pillar and the coupé pillar *B D*, and secured by pins. Three-eighths of an inch is taken off the roof rail from the standing pillar *A* to the corner pillar *C*, which space is filled by the quarter panel. The corner pillar is dressed off three-eighths of an inch from the top rail down to the belt rail, and the same amount off the back down to the cross bar *S*, Fig. 245.

The framework *a a a* of the back glass, Fig. 245, is of whitewood, one inch thick, and framed together as drawn. The back rail *S* is framed into the corner pillar with two tenons. Its lower edge is rabbeted to receive the lower back panel, the top back panel covering the joints and finished to show a molding. The top cross rail T, Fig. 245, is tenoned into the corner pillar, as shown by the ground plan, Fig. 244. It is rabbeted to receive the roof rail.

The line Y, Fig. 243, indicates the location of the turn-down seat, when down; the dotted lines show its position when up and out of the way of the front drop light. The space below the glass frame is fitted up for a package holder.

The ground plan, Fig. 244, shows all the pieces, the lettering corresponding with that on the same pieces in Figs. 243 and 245; also the top and bottom bars of doors and pillars. The bars M are all connecting cross bars. H is the toe bar, and N N the seat frame bars. The strainers V, Figs. 243 and 245, are of whitewood, three-quarters of an inch thick. The back between the ends of the rockers P is closed by a whitewood bar, worked out to the required shape.

CHAPTER IX.

Practical Wheel Making.

In these days when there are so many wheel factories, it may seem a waste of time for the woodworker to read up on the art of wheel making. Yet inquiries received, convince me that the subject is one of interest to a large number of workmen, and that discussion, brought about by the publication of essays, leads to good mechanical results, besides tending to stimulate thought and study.

In order to treat the subject thoroughly, I will begin with the rough rived spokes, notwithstanding so many are bought turned. Unless the workman thoroughly understands the superiority of the rived spoke over the sawed one, and the advantages from having the spoke made with the layers in a certain position, he will not be able to judge of the quality of the goods he is purchasing, neither will he be able to understand why one wheel, to all appearance as good as another, is vastly inferior when it comes to wear. There is also much misunderstanding regarding the value of red and white hickory.

The rived spoke is the only one that should be used, but owing to the cutting of small trees, there are a large number of sawed spokes on the market. These sawed spokes have the same end appearance as the rived, but an examination of the sides will show the cut off grains, knurls, &c. In some instances the timber is free from defects, and the fibers run straight, so that when sawed very few irregularities are apparent. There is, however, no material advantage in sawing, except where the logs are eight inches or under in diameter, while the disadvantages are very great, the main one being the inclination to spring both before and after being rounded. A sprung spoke may be straightened so that when put into the wheel the injury may not be apparent, but it will eventually assume its former bend. Rived spokes may spring if not properly piled, but the liability is much less than that of the sawed spoke; and even if they do spring a little, there is sufficient timber left to straighten them without bending, and when rounded up there is no danger from springing, unless they are improperly piled or are unevenly seasoned.

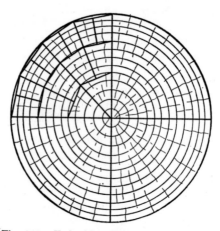

Fig. 246.   End of log showing quarter lines.

Fig. 246 shows an end view of a log with the quarter lines and one-quarter laid off split. In all cases the "bolt" is widest across the layers and thinnest on the edge nearest the heart. Split in this way the ring layers are in the position to secure the best results, and the "bolt" has all the lengthwise fibers running straight. A knot or other irregularity is sure to be developed.

In many small shops where repairing is an important part of the business, it is necessary for the workman to know how to dress and round up spokes, a branch of the business that few learn nowadays. The old-time wheelmaker gave much attention to this part of the business, and his method of working has not been improved upon. With him the ax and chopping block were important auxiliaries. He began work by hewing off the heart side to the width required for the face of the spoke, and then straightened up the sides as

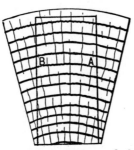

Fig. 247. How the "bolt" should be marked for spoke making.

shown by lines *A* and *B*, Fig. 247. By this course he maintained the layers of the wood in the most desirable position, and was able to work out the few irregularities in the fibers while preparing the "bolt" for dressing to the proper proportions, the latter being a point not to be overlooked. It is also a subject on which there is much difference of opinion.

Custom regulates the purchasing measurements of a spoke by the length of the mortise to be filled. Thus a one-inch spoke has a tenon one inch deep on the line of the shoulder. There is no established law as to the proportionate width of the face. It may vary by being from ten-sixteenths to thirteen-sixteenths, these measurements representing the extremes for a light spoke. Eleven-sixteenths is a happy medium, one which gives the best results as to appearance and all the necessary strength. The end at the felloe is reduced about one-sixteenth below the thickness of the spoke at the face. The rule which governs most wheelmakers in the proportions of the felloe end is to make the depth a trifle narrower than

the tread of the felloe. Thus a three-quarter inch felloe for
a spoke eleven-sixteenths by one inch would require a spoke
ten-sixteenths by twelve-sixteenths. A spoke one and three-
quarters by one and one-quarter at the shoulder should measure one and one-quarter, the widest being the depth. With
heavy spokes. the depth increases an eighth of an inch to each
additional quarter inch above one inch. In squaring up, the
length of the spoke between shoulders must be determined
in order to secure uniformity, as all the reduction is made
on the back edge.

The spoke being squared up, the next thing is to cut the
tenons, the shoulders of which must be at right angles with
the face of the spoke, unless the spokes are to "stagger"
their full width. In that case, the angle of the shoulder can
be determined by drawing a line to represent the hub, and
one at right angles to represent a plumb spoke. Then measure forward and back at the base line to the extent of the
"stagger" and draw a new face line, which will give the
angle of the shoulder.

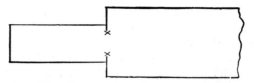

Fig. 248.   Common form of tenon and shoulder.

The common form of tenon and shoulder is shown by Fig.
248. In cutting it the spur cutter is employed to give a
smooth shoulder, and unless the workman is careful, the spur
will cut below the face of the tenon, as shown by the points
x x, which materially weakens the tenon when in the hub,
besides which it affords a lodgment for moisture, and sooner or
later rots the wood. This is proven by the fact that many
shipments of spokes sent to Australia were ruined by decay
at the shoulder, while all other parts were in prime condition.

Another objection to a square shoulder is the liability to check when the spoke is "set down." The concave shoulder shown by Fig. 249 is free from all the faults of the square shoulder, and with proper tools is as easily cut.

The width of the tenon is an important factor, the wider the better, provided the hub is not cut away to an extent to weaken it. The best rule I know of is to leave a fourth more wood between the mortises than is taken up by them. If the spokes are not to be used immediately, it is a good plan to leave the tenons a little full, to allow for shrinkage, to be afterward fitted up at the time of driving.

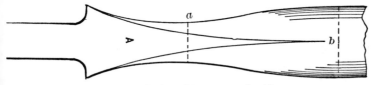

Fig. 249.   Spoke with concave shoulder.

Rounding is the next act. This calls for workmanship and skill. There is also a principle involved which has much to do with the wearing quality of the wheel.

The strength of a light wheel, one and an eighth inch spoke and under, depends upon elasticity, which must be properly distributed. Above one and an eighth inch spoke elasticity is likely to prove a weakness. A light wheel will yield when the rim comes in contact with an obstruction. If the spokes do not yield, the full force of the blow is thrown upon the rim, and through the rigid spoke to the shoulders at the hub. If between the rim and the hub, there is no point where the spoke can act quickly to take up the effect of the concussion. The full force of the blow will flatten the rim between the spokes or break the tenons. To overcome this, the spoke is lightened at a point about one and a half inch from the shoulders. This is technically known as the 'throat.' By being light at this point, an elastic cushion is formed, which, by yielding, breaks the force of the concussion before it reaches the tenon, and prevents damage. When the wheels are heavy, there can be no yielding, and the cutting away at the throat is but a matter of taste. The shape of the face *A*, Fig. 249, is also a matter of taste. Some prefer the long face, as shown, others a short one; but no matter which is used, the outline must be sharply defined.

Fig. 250. Shape of spoke   Fig. 251. Form of body of spoke   Fig. 252. Another form
at *A*, Fig. 249.   *b* at , Fig. 249.   of body of spoke at
                                                               b, Fig. 249.

Fig. 250 shows the shape of the throat at *A*, Fig. 249. Figs. 251 and 252 show two forms of the body at *b*, Fig. 249. In both the back is round. While the face of Fig. 251 rounds up to a sharp edge, the form of Fig. 252 is purely elliptical. Fig. 249 shows the throat, face, and body of a well-shaped inch-spoke reduced to half size.

The felloe end of the spoke is the weak end, notwithstanding the fact that it is not so recognized by wheel makers. There are two reasons for this; first, the amount of wood is necessarily small; second, the joints at the rim are exposed to moisture much more than those at the hub. Then too when the tire loosens from any cause, the rims work back and forth on the tenon—very little, it may be, but enough to crack the paint and to admit the moisture. The two difficulties to be overcome are to make a tenon that will be large enough to hold the rim without breaking, and yet small enough to leave a good bearing surface for a shoulder for the rim. If the shoulder is too narrow, the rim will settle. The rule observed by those who have given the matter attention, is to leave half of the width—a fourth on each side for shoulders. This makes the tenon a trifle smaller than half of the spoke at the end; but the proportion is as nearly perfect as can be, as shown by Fig. 253. The shoulders must be flat, or slightly tapered toward the tenon. If beveled outward, they act as a wedge and force the sides of the rim out.

The back taper of the tenon is next to be considered. Formerly it was thought that the back should he tapered to about a sixth the width of the tenon at the lower end, but experience has proved that the nearer straight the tenon is the better it is. It cannot be absolutely straight, as it is necessary for a slight wedging, in order that the grip of the wood may be decided enough to hold; but not more than a

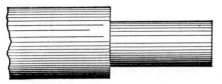

Fig. 253. Felloe end of spoke.

sixteenth of an inch is necessary to every one and a quarter inch of tenon. A gauge made to that taper will secure a good result, whether the spoke be less or more than one and a quarter inch.

The spokes being rounded and tenoned at the hub end, the next thing is driving, an operation that determines more than any one other act the durability of the wheel. First, in this connection, is the hub and the location of the mortises.

Fig. 254 shows a three and a half by six inch hub reduced to half size, the spokes dodged or staggered half an inch. It will be noticed in this that the front edge of the forward mortise and the back edge of the back mortise are equal distances from the end shoulders. This secures a perfect bal-

ance, as the bearing passes through the center of the hub.
For the sake of ornamentation, it often happens that too
much wood is cut away forward of the tenon. This is a mistake, as durability is sacrificed to appearance. The design
given herewith, Fig. 254, gives all the wood necessary and
furnishes a neat ornamental end. There is a prejudice in
the minds of many wheel makers against the machine mortised hubs. A more senseless objection could not be raised,
as it is out of the range of human ability for a human hand
to produce a number of mortises so uniform in size and shape

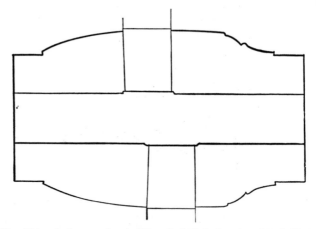

Fig. 254. A three and a half by six-inch hub reduced to half size.

as those made by a well arranged machine. Spokes should
be fitted at the time of driving, no matter how well they may
have been tenoned and beveled, as wood always shrinks after
each dressing off, and scarcely any two pieces will shrink alike.
In width the tenon should fit snugly, but not tight. To test
it, slip the corner of the tenon in the mortise. If it can be
pressed in by hand and thoroughly fills the mortise, it is
tight enough. I have already given directions for the proper
bevel of the back, but it will not do to make a bevel and
drive in the spoke without ascertaining whether the bevel to

the mortise is the same as that given to the tenon. If it is more, the 'mash' will be too great at the bottom; if too little, it will be too loose at the bottom. Fig. 255 illustrates the idea, but the bevel is exaggerated. It will be noticed that the bevel of the spoke does not fill the mortise until the spoke has entered the mortise four-fifths of its whole length, the dotted line *b* showing the point of contact. The dotted line *a* shows the amount of 'mash' given to the tenon when the spoke is driven down to the shoulder. If the end of the spoke comes in contact with the edge of the mortise at a higher point, the grains in the hub will be forced down as shown by Fig. 256. If the grains of the hub are extra

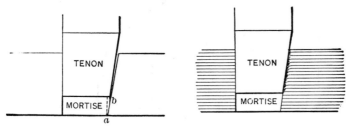

Fig. 255. How tenon should fit mortise.   Fig. 256.   Effect of forcing tenon into mortise that is too close.

hard, a part of the 'mash' is taken up by the spoke. This, if severe, disintegrates the grains, and the spoke will work loose in the hub much sooner than if the grains were intact. In preparing the spokes, the end corners of the tenon should be chamfered a little to prevent tearing the edges of the mortise.

One of the most injurious acts of the wheelmaker is the cutting away of the edges of the mortise to permit the shoulder 'setting down' snug to the hub. The corners should fit the shoulders of the tenons to give a firm bearing, as shown by *a a*, Fig. 257, but the careless manner in which this work is done more frequently leaves the shoulders as shown by *b b*,

Fig. 257, irregular in form and totally unlike any shoulder. The spoke set down catches on the edges and leaves a vacant space, or it is mashed down into the wood, working irreparable injury in both cases. In driving, insert each alternate spoke; then the intervening spokes, the bottom of those first driven being cut away as shown at *c c*, Fig. 257.

The dish necessary is one of the questions most in dispute. With light wheels very little is necessary. An eighth of an inch is enough; but it must be uniform. A skillful

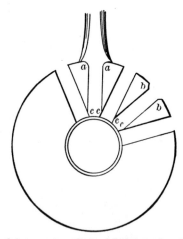

Fig. 257.   Proper and improper method of fitting spokes in hubs. *a a*, proper method; *b b*, improper.

driver will be able to set the spokes in without drawing them much, provided the mortises are correct, but drivers often pull or push the end of the spoke three or four inches before setting down, in order to face it into its proper place. A spoke so driven is battered and its hold on the tenon weakened. When driving, place the tenons near a warm pipe or stove, and use hot glue. For light spokes use a mallet, such as is shown by Fig. 258. The head should be about six inches long, two inches wide, and two and three-quarters inches deep. The handle should be twenty-eight inches long, and three-fourths by one-eighth of an inch thick, two inches from the head, and large enough to insure a good grip. A mallet of this kind gives a quick, sharp, elastic blow, which sends the spoke home without springing. A heavy head and a stiff handle will invariably spring a light spoke. When the spoke is heavy, the elastic handle is not so essential, but there are many drivers who use elastic handles even when driving heavy spokes, claiming that they can drive any spoke equally well and with less strain upon the arm. The mallet head should weigh about a pound and a half.

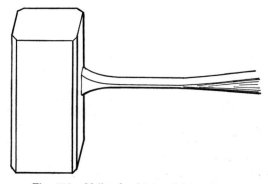

Fig. 258. Mallet for driving light spokes.

The sledge hammer has no place in the wheel shop, notwithstanding it is frequently found therein. A well fitted spoke, driven in hot glue, with a comparatively light blow, will hold much better than one battered down by a heavy maul.

Having the spokes properly driven, the rims are next to be considered. The proper proportions for a wheel with a one-inch spoke is seven-eighths inch tread, and about a sixteenth inch additional width on the underside. For heavier wheels for city use, the underside width is increased materially, as a narrow tread is preferable to a wide one; but there is no fixed rule as to the proportions.

Select fine, close grained timber for the rims. Prime forest hickory or ash is preferable to second growth, provided the grains are well knit together. One cause of rims splitting is the injury the wood receives when steamed for bending. If the timber is green and is steamed with very hot vapor, all the adhesive properties of the sap are destroyed, and during the process of bending the grains disintegrate. The injury is far less from this cause, under the end pressure method of bending, than under the old way of stretching the outer portions, yet the damage is too often a serious one. Grains thus separated when being bent, do not regain their former solidity, and the checks are sure to appear when the wheel is made up.

Boring the tenons on the spokes and the holes in the rims are very important operations, as they have an important bearing on the durability of the wheel. The hollow auger and brace in the hands of a careless workman will give tenons at a variety of angles and centers. Tenons bored in by machinery are always true, but it is not profitable for small shops to use machinery. A cheap but good frame can be made which will hold the wheel in an upright position and each spoke in turn in its correct place. The hollow auger is attached to a spindle which passes through two bearings, holding it in one position. The brace is fitted to the outer end of the spindle, and as it cannot change the position of the spindle, the workman cannot bore a crooked tenon. A stop properly adjusted regulates the depth of the bore.

The tenon must fit the hole in the rim, but not so tight as to require hard driving. The spoke should be cut level with the tread of the felloe, but not below it, if the rim is set down properly to the spoke shoulder. At the time of setting the tire, if the spoke tenon projects, cut off with a flat chisel, working from the face of the felloe and cutting flat across the spoke.

In dressing off the face of the felloe, be governed by a straightedge laid across, and dress the face true to the straightedge all around; then true the tread by making it at perfect right angles with the face.

Presuming that the wheelmaker has produced a good wheel in every respect, he should be allowed to say something about it when the blacksmith puts on the tire, as all his good work can be ruined in a few minutes by forcing on a tire that has too much draw, or which is too hot, or not true. All that the blacksmith should be allowed to do is to give "draw" enough to set the wood up without mashing, and the metal snug up to the wood. Extra heating, which chars the wood and requires a flood of water to cool, is injurious, as the best wheel can be made inferior in wear to a common one, if the tire of the latter is put on skillfully and that of the former burned and battered on.—*By* W. N. F.

CHAPTER. X.

Portland Sleighs.

THE class of light sleighs known as "The Portland," has become the standard in all parts of the country, being far more simple in construction than the panel or Albany sleighs; also much lighter, besides being, when properly made, the most comfortable of sleighs for light driving. The body is susceptible of many changes in outline without losing the general characteristics of the vehicle.

With this sleigh more than with any other, the tread of the runners and the stability of the front determines its value for comfort and speed. The full bend given to the runners of the Albany cutter is admired by most sleigh builders, and is used regardless of the fact that the outline is not in harmony with that of the body, besides unfitness in other respects.

When the full bend is used, it becomes necessary to load it down with iron braces, &c., to insure stability, otherwise there will be a trembling, which is imparted to all parts of the sleigh when in motion; at the same time the weight and leverage increases the liability of the sleigh riding over on its "nose," one of the most disagreeable faults in connection with sleighs.

Too many sleighs are built by the "guess rule," regardless as to whether the result will be right or wrong. If a draft-board is used and the outlines all plainly and correctly indicated, the builder can put up all upon the correct principle and maintain uniformity, a feature that contributes much in an economical point of view, particularly in the iron work.

In laying out the draftboard, give the runner as nearly as possible the bend shown by Fig. 259, the sweep to begin at *X*. Back of that point the line of the tread must be straight. Then strike a perpendicular line, as shown by the dotted line *A*, the base of which is on the line of this tread, three inches forward of the point *X*, where the bend begins. This line determines the position of the front end of the sill and the top of the front knee. Measure up on this line the hight required for the knee, say twenty-two inches, and strike a

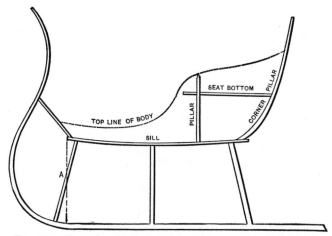

Fig. 259.   How the sleigh should be laid out on the draftboard.

line parallel with the tread of the runner. Measure back on this line three feet nine inches for the length of the sill. Next measure back three inches from the end of the sill; mark the point; then ascertain a point where the bend of the tread is two inches above the straight line, and strike a line from that point to the point previously indicated on the upper horizontal line. This will give the front of the forward knee. Then measure forward from the back end of the sill six inches, and strike a line from that point to the tread line, at the same angle as the front knee line, for the back face of the rear knee. Then strike a perpendicular line midway between the two outside lines for the center knee.

The sill should be made to drop about one inch at the point where it intersects the middle knee. Then set up the corner pillar, seat pillar, and bracket lines, the corner pillar to fall back of its base nine inches at the top rail, the seat pillar on a perpendicular line twelve inches forward of the end of the sill; the bracket line at an angle corresponding with a line starting at the front of the middle knee where it intersects the runner, passing over the end of the sill a half inch from the end to the runner. Next mark the outline of the top body, and the side elevation draft is ready.

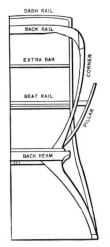

Fig. 260. Back elevation draft.

The back elevation draft should be made as shown by Fig. 260. If the draftboard is long enough, this draft can be put on at the back of the side elevation. As all the pieces are plainly indicated by name on the draft, no explanation is needed except for the width and for the knees. The seat rail is three feet four and a half inches between shoulders on the top line. The seat pillar being three-quarters of an inch deep, the back rail is three feet long; the dash rail is two feet six inches long over all; the bottom frame over all two feet four and a half inches. The length of the intermediate bars is determined by the location of the lines between the exterior points. The spread of the runners is three feet six inches.

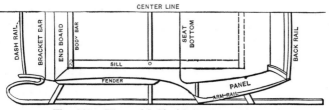

Fig. 261.   View of half of body from the top.

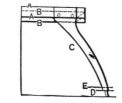

Fig. 262.   Plan for setting up knees.

Fig. 261, which gives a view from the top of half of the body, gives location of body bars, sweep of outside of panel location, width, and length of fender.

Fig. 262 gives the working guide for setting up the knees; *A A* top and bottom of back and front beams; *B B* top and bottom of middle beams; *C* the knee; *E* bottom shoulder of front knee; *D* bottom shoulder of middle and back knee.

In setting up the knees it is of the utmost importance that they maintain a straight line on the outside with the runner. To do this, the shoulders must be cut to accord with the bend of the sill and the cant of the runner. the center beam to drop to correspond with the drop of the sill, and the shoulder on the knee cut to that line. The front knee being shortened by the bend of the runner, the shoulder must be cut on a line as much above the shoulder lines of the other knees as the bend is above the straight line. The dotted line *B*, Fig. 259, makes this point clear. A draft made with one outline for the knees and the shoulders and beams, as located in Fig. 262, gives the workman not only the location of each shoulder, tenon, and mortise, but also the bevels of all but the front foot of the forward knee. The bevel of this can be got from Fig. 259.

The sills should be of good ash, seven-eighths inch thick and three inches wide, boxed out to leave a molding three-eighths inch deep. The back corner pillars, if bent, need not be more than three-quarters by one and a quarter when finished. If sawed, they should be three-quarters at the top and one and an eighth at the bottom by one and a quarter, boxed out to leave a molding, as shown by Fig. 260. The top back rail three-quarters by six inches, seat pillar five-eighths by three-quarters, seat pillar five-eighths by three-quarters, runners on the tread three-quarters inch and a half inch deep, tapering in depth to five-eighths inch at the dash rail; knees a half inch thick, finished as shown by Fig. 263. Side pan-

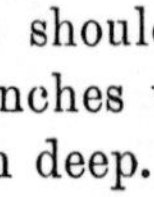

TREAD

Fig. 263.   How to finish the knees. 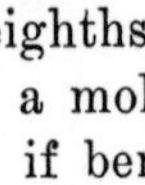   Fig. 264.   How layers of wood should be in runners.

els full three-eighths inch thick, back panel a quarter inch, top panel a half inch, bottom boards a half inch, dash panel a quarter inch.

To obtain the best result, the side panels should be steamed and bent over a form. If this is not done, the panel will flatten between the corner and seat rail pillar on the top line. There will also be a slight flattening forward of the seat rail pillar. Forms can be made of heavy plank, and if half a dozen sleighs are to be made, the time saved in fitting and setting up the side panels will more than compensate for the time spent in making the forms.

The sleigh should be set up on a platform, with cleats and top buttons to hold the runners in place, and the runners so firmly secured that they cannot move while the body is being put up.

Don't pin the tenons in the runner mortises, but make the mortise a trifle wider on the tread than on the top, and wedge in the tenon. More runners break at the pin hole than at any other point. Have the runners bent with the layers of the wood, as shown by Fig. 264. The wood will not only keep in form much better in this way than when bent with the layers extending across, but the liability to split will be greatly decreased.—*By* W. N. F.

Heavy Bob Sled.

For heavy lumbering and other purposes, where the loads to be drawn are of a bulky nature, and where the roads are

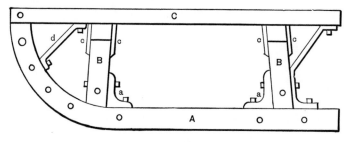

Fig. 265.   Side elevation of front bob.

uneven, the bob sled is superior to the single. Its advantages are twofold. First, they can be adjusted to different

lengths; second, owing to the shortness of the head, they
can be turned in places where it would be impossible to use
a long runner.

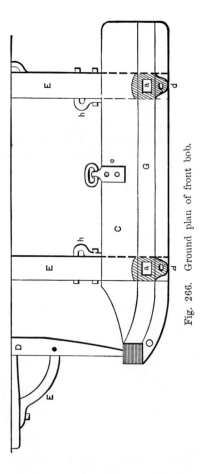

Fig. 266. Ground plan of front bob.

Again, compact form makes it possible to construct them
with great strength. The runners, *A A*, Figs. 265 and 267,
are best when made from natural white oak crooks. They
should be five inches deep and at least two and a half inches

tread. Three inches will be none too heavy, as it gives a better hold for the knee tenons. The knees, *B B*, Figs. 265 and 267, should be four inches thick, the same width of the runners at the bottom tenon, and six inches at the beam shoulder—the beams four by five inches. The fenders, *C C*, Figs. 265 and 267, three inches by ten and a half inches. The tongue bar, *D*, Fig. 266, four and a half by three at the center, and three inches square at the ends. The tongue five by two and a half at the whiffletree plate, and three by two at the bar. The tongue hounds, *E E*, Fig. 266, two and a half inches thick, three inches wide at the tongue bar, and ten inches long on the face at the whiffletree plate. The

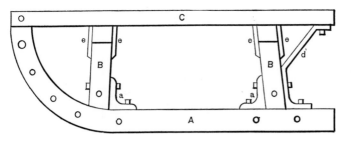

Fig. 267.   Side elevation of rear bob.

short tongue or coupling, bar *G*, Fig. 268, should be four inches by three at the center, and three inches at the ends, the hounds two inches thick, two and a half inches at the bar. The short tongue *H*, Fig. 268, three and a half by two and a half inches at the hounds.

Fig. 265 shows the side elevation of the front bob. The cast corner blocks *a a*, Figs. 265 and 267, are bolted to the inside faces of the knees and to the top of the runner. *C C* of the same figures, are beam plates, and *d*, of Fig. 265, is an extra brace between the rave and the runner, to give the required strength to overcome the strain from the pole, the

back brace in one piece for the support of the back and of
the runner and rave.

Fig. 266 gives a ground plan of the front bob. The runner has a tread of four feet six inches back of the bend. *C*

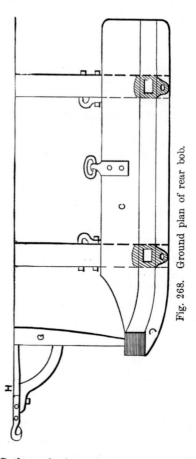

Fig. 268. Ground plan of rear bob.

is the fender, *D* the pole bar, *E* the beams. The dotted lines
show the location of the runners, *a* the mortises for the
stakes, *b* the stake plates, with holes *d* for the skid hooks, *e*
the clip and ring for skid chain. The top of the plate is

let in flush with the top of the fender, and the eye is placed below the lower side of the fender out of the way. *h h* are extra staples for skid hooks, chains, &c., *i* the coupling staple for securing the back bob.

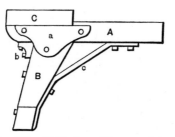

Fig. 269. Half view of beam and knee.

Fig. 267 shows a side elevation of the back bob, the tread of the runner *A* being four feet, or six inches shorter than the tread of the front bob. *B B* the knees, *C* the fenders, *a a* the cast corner blocks, and *d* the back brace. The blocks and braces are of the same models as those of the front bob. *e e* the beam plates.

Fig. 268 gives a ground plan of the back bob. The general construction is the same as that of the front bob, with the exception of the coupling pole *H*, which is short, and is provided with a hook for coupling.

Fig. 269 shows a half view of the beam and knee. *A* the beam, *B* the knee, *C* the fender, *a* the beam plate, *b* the beam block of cast iron, *c* the brace welded to the T-iron. The whole should be welded together.

Fig. 270 shows an outline section of the knee and beam, together with the form of tenons, &c. *A* the beam, *B* the knee, *C* the runner, *D* the fender, *E* the stake. The shaded section *a* represents the tenon which passes through the beam, with an upper end *b*, which extends through the fender. The stake tenon *C* passes through the fender and well down into the beam.

Fig. 271 shows the inside of the runner and beam with the T-iron, the front of which extends up to the top of the run-

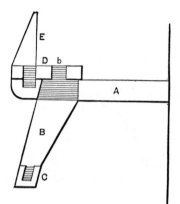

Fig. 270.   Outline of knee and beam, showing shape of tenons.

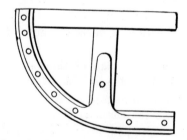

Fig. 271.   Inside runner and beam, showing T-irons.

Fig. 272.   View of top bolster.

ner, and is securely bolted thereto. The T-iron and brace should be in one piece, but as this manner of making up is more expensive than when the brace is separate, the majority of blacksmiths prefer to make them in two parts, as they are easier to fit.

Fig. 272 shows the extra bolster, with recess for stake and pin holes for iron pins, to prevent logs, &c., from moving. The underside of the bar is cut out at the ends so as to rest full length upon the top of the beam.

The shoes should be of steel. The cast shoes, with chilled faces, are cheaper, but not so reliable. The front should be of wrought iron, and heavy, not lighter than half an inch at the top of the runner. All runner plates on the inside should be secured by button head bolts on the outside and riveted to a countersunk hole, so as to give a strong, smooth finish.

Bob Sleigh.

The bob sleigh for general use possesses enough advantages over the single heavy sleigh to warrant its use for farm and light business purposes. It is more expensive, but buyers, as a rule, make no objection to the difference in the cost.

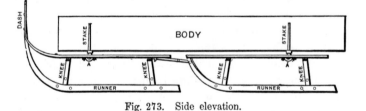

Fig. 273. Side elevation.

Fig. 273 represents the side elevation of a pair of bobs, made to accommodate a body eight feet long. The front bob has a wood dash, which gives a much better finish than when the body extends further forward. Formerly all runners of this kind were made from the butt log of the oak tree, the crook being from the root. Few sawed runners are made at the present time, as the bent are much cheaper and, as a rule, better.

For a medium weight sleigh, the runners should be one and three-quarters inch on the tread and two inches deep, the bend tapered to one and a half inch at the point where the rave is attached ; the knees one and three-quarters inch thick, full width of runner at the shoulder, and two and a half inches at the beam ; the beams one and three-quarters inch thick and two and a half deep ; raves one and a quarter inch thick and four and a half wide ; the front cut away from the inside forward of the beam, as shown ; fenders one and an eighth by one and a half inch square ; bolsters three inches deep at the center, tapered to one and three-quarters inch at the ends ; bolster stakes one inch thick and three wide at the bolster ; under bolsters three and a half inches square ; ends turned full size. The body should be made up on sills, three inches wide and one and a quarter thick, the sides of seven-eighths inch whitewood, ten inches high.

In framing, set the faces of the front knees one and a half inch forward of the point where the bend begins, and cant back two inches. Set the back knees four and a half inches forward of the end of the runners and cant forward one and a half inch. Lap the fenders flush with the top of the beams. Set the raves into the beams a half inch, and cut out an eighth of an inch on the rave. Set both upper bolsters on heavy under bolsters, the ends and bearings on the center supporting bars being turned so as to give a rock to the supports for the body. With these rocking bolsters all strain is removed, as the runners alone rock. The bolsters are supported at the ends by plates bolted to the under side of the raves and center bars placed six inches on each side of the king bolts, the ends secured to the beams. Plates of band iron are placed on the raves, as indicated by *A A*, Fig. 274, through which the bolts pass, which secure the bolster plates *a a*, Fig. 273.

Fig. 274 gives a ground view of half of the bobs as they

are attached, showing the tops of beams, bolsters, fenders, runners, and raves; also the bolster bearing plates.

Fig. 275 shows a half view of the back end, giving knee, beam, bolster, and stake. The usual track for bobs is three feet eight inches, but three feet ten is none too wide. In ironing the T-irons should be of heavy wrought iron, with-

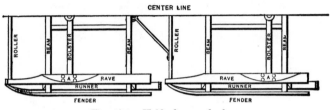

Fig. 274. Half of ground plan.

Fig. 275. Half end view.

out square corners at the bars. The dash is bolted to the extension of the runner. Aside from the T-irons, no iron work is necessary for the runners, but corner braces may be placed against the knees and runners. These are preferable to the long braces. Both draw bars revolve so as to allow a free movement of the runners.

Two-Passenger Sleigh.

A peculiarity in regard to sleighs is the tendency to adhere to one particular type for a period of years, and then changing to some other and making it the standard. About fifty years ago the Goold or Albany swell-body cutter became popular, taking the place of the O. G. back and front sleigh that had so long been in use. Twenty-five years later the improved Portland cutter became popular, and since then it has been the standard pattern. It has much to recommend it, particularly for speedy driving, but being, as it now is, made up in the cheapest possible manner from patterns precisely similar to the finest grades, the driving public are tiring of it. and builders are introducing new forms, hoping to catch the public favor. As yet nothing has come up that has met with general approval. One of the latest is illus-

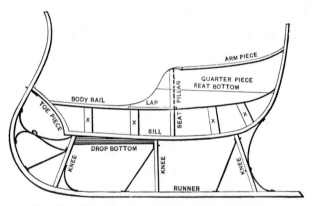

Fig. 276. Side elevation of a late design in sleighs.

trated by the side elevation, Fig. 276, the ground plan, Fig. 277, and the back, Fig. 278. It embodies many of the advantages of the Portland, with some of the beauties of form of the Albany. Its construction is more simple than the Albany, but not as much so as the Portland. The body is low down, the sides moderately deep, the track is three feet four inches from outside to outside, the body on the sills two feet ten inches, the runners one inch deep, seven-eighths of an inch tread, knees three-quarters by seven-eighths inch at the runner and three-quarters by one and a quarter at the beams; beam three-quarters by one and a quarter;

sill, which is bent, three-quarters by two inches; body rail three-quarters inch square; quarter piece ten and a half inches deep at the seat pillar; arm piece five-eighths of an inch thick and two inches wide at the front, rounding off flush at the corner pillar.

Frame the center beam fourteen and a half inches above a line parallel with the bottom line of the runners, and the back and front as much above as will accommodate the sweep of the sill. A diagram, such as that shown by Fig. 280, should be drawn, by which the knees are framed, as they should describe parallel lines from the runner up, no matter what the position of the beams. The runners may be framed to a face line following that of the knees, or the tenons may

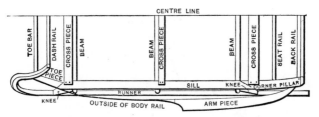

Fig. 277. View of half of ground plan.

be cut as shown by Fig. 280. The latter will give the runners a square tread.

In framing, set up the knees and beams, and lay them together to see that the tenons are all on line. Next put on the runners and test the frame as to its accuracy, correcting all joints. Then take the frame apart, and finish up the edges; round the outside of the knees to a slight oval, leaving the back full width. Slightly round the top of the runners; groove above the toe rail for the dash panel; mortise for the toe rail, dash rail, and toe piece before rounding. Then glue up the knees and beams, and when the glue is set, glue up the runners and secure them in timbers grooved to receive the runners and placed on parallel lines, and the exact width of the tread required apart. When the runners are in place, fasten them by means of set screws, so that they cannot slip in any direction. See that the beams are in the exact position in which they are to remain, and secure them firmly by cleats. The frame is then ready to receive the body. First set up the sills, and box in on the under-

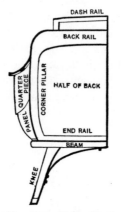

Fig. 278.   Half of back.

side an eighth of an inch. If it is necessary to draw in the top of the back, provide for this by cutting away enough on the inside of the boxing. Set up the toe pieces, lap the sills to the bottom edges, and cut stub tenons on the tops. Fasten these in their places, but do not glue them.

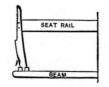

Fig. 279.   Tenoning seat rail.

Mark off and frame up the seat rail pillars, as shown by Fig. 279, giving them a turn-under of about two inches.

Frame the back and bottom rails, making the tenons on the rails in both cases. Frame the rails flush with the outside of the corner piece. Next lap the body rail to the quarter piece, as indicated by the dotted line on Fig. 276. When the glue is set, dress up the quarter and rail to the required thickness and width. Then secure it in position by thumb-screws, and mark off the laps and tenons.

When the frame is all put together and squared, remove the cross pieces, loosen the sills from the beams, and dress off the outside to the required sweep. Take all apart; gauge off and dress up the moldings, and groove for the panels. Then glue the sills and toe pieces together, set them up and glue and screw the sills to the beams. Next set up the back and put in the panel; set up the seat pillars and seat rails;

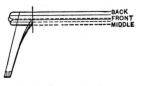

Fig 280.　Method of tenoning knees and beams.

then the quarter piece and body rail, and fit in the strainers. When the strainers are fitted, fit and put in the panel. Owing to the bend, this panel is best if of white basswood, three-sixteenths of an inch in thickness. Use white lead instead of glue for the panel groove. Glue the rails together and secure the quarter pieces to the seat rail pillars by screws from the inside, being careful not to allow the points to go through the outside. The sunken bottom may be used or not. If used, the side pieces are screwed to the inside of the sills. The bottom board, which should be half an inch thick, is nailed in. After the sides are set up, panel and glue up the dash. When the glue is set, remove the runners from the grooves, turn the sleigh over and nail in the bottom boards. Clean off the outside, fit in the seat board and a back piece to protect the panel, or, what is better, line the back on the inside and finish the inside smooth for painting. The bottom quarters may be lined in the same manner if desired.

Light sleighs, if properly made, require very little ironwork. Fig. 276 illustrates the necessary side irons, and Fig. 278 the form of brace for the backs of the knees. These braces may be made up with the strap forming one piece of the T-irons, or they may be separate and bolted to the latter. One point of vital importance is the location of the shaft eye. If this is placed too high up, the runners will bear heavy on the bend at the front knees; if too low, the reverse will be the case, and the heel will take the strain. The latter is a worse fault than the former, as the weight all being at the back end, the fault is aggravated by the load.

Use soft caststeel shoes, about three-eighths of an inch thick, narrowed on the tread about an eighth of an inch.

In painting use bright but harmonious colors. Trimming is a matter of choice, except with the cushion, but it should never be nailed in as in carriages; on the contrary, make up all side and back squabs on heavy backs, and secure by knobs or buttons, placed where they will not come in contact with the rider. Make up the fall and cushion together. Use a heavy piece of felt for the covering to the bottom. Bind the edges with leather, but do not fasten it in.—*By* W. N. F.

Square Box Sleigh.

For general use the plain box sleigh is the most convenient pattern in use, answering as it does for pleasure and light business purposes. The most desirable size is one which admits of the use of two seats, and yet not so large as to be ungainly in appearance when one seat only is used.

Fig. 281 gives a side view of a sleigh of this character. The entire length of the runners from the front of the dash post to the back end of the runner at the head should be six feet six inches. The body should be four feet ten inches long on the top line, the flare of the end being two and a half inches each. The runner should be of fine white oak, one and an eighth inch on the tread and one and a quarter inch deep, tapering the end at the point, from the top side where the rave meets the runner, to seven-eighths of an inch.

If long runners are used, the tops may be continued up and form dash posts, but it is cheaper to continue the front plates to the runner up to the required hight for the dash, and use a strip of seven-eighths inch band iron for an inside stay, the rivets passing through the straps and dashboard, securing all firmly together.

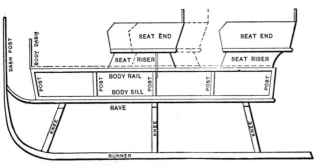

Fig. 281. Side elevation.

The raves should be five inches wide and one inch thick. This will furnish sufficient space for a support to the body, after allowing for an outside projection sufficiently wide to act as a step.

Frame the knees so that from the top of the rave to the tread of the runner, in a perpendicular line, will be fourteen inches over all. The knees should be one and an eighth inch thick and one and an eighth wide at the runners, and one and three-quarters at the beam, if iron braces are to be used. If knee plates only are used, the knees should be two and an eighth inch at the beam. The beams should be one and an eighth inch thick, two and a quarter deep, and of sufficient length to allow for a projection of three inches outside of the knees at each end.

The body panel should be nine and a half inches deep, the side frame for the panel eight inches high over all. This will allow the panel to extend a half inch above the top rail, forming a side guard for the seat riser. The long dash line on Fig. 281 indicates the top of the panel. The body rail posts and sills are all seven-eighths inch square. Frame the body so that the inside faces of the posts will come flush with the inside edges of the raves.

In framing up the knees set the front of the front knee at a point where the bend of the runner rises one and a half inch above the parallel line of the tread. This will serve

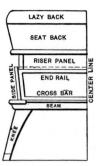

Fig. 282.   Rear view of square box sleigh.

to stiffen the runner at the point where the contact with obstacles on the road is likely to be most severe. Set the back knee with the back face sixteen inches from the end of the runner, giving it the same cant as is given to the front knee. Set the middle knee midway between the two. Do not mortise entirely through the runners for the knee tenons. A quarter to three-eighths inch of solid wood under the tenons will protect the mortise from the water which is sure to work in between the shoe and the runner, and which is the cause of so many runners, or tenons to knees, breaking. The little gain from the tenon passing through the runner is more than offset by the protection given by the solid wood.

In framing the knees into the beams, be careful to retain the one plan to all the knees; and as in this the top line is straight, the shoulders to the front knees must be cut high enough to equalize the rise of the runner, making the front knee shorter than the back.

The seat risers are of ash, three-quarters inch thick, and deep enough to lift the seat bottom twelve inches above the top of the rave, measuring from the top side of the seat frame. If the risers are canted in a half inch, it will have a tendency to give greater firmness than when set up straight. The riser of the back seat is cut away at the back end in order to allow the seat being set back enough to give leg room between the two seats.

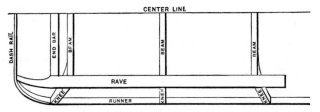

Fig. 283. Half view of ground plan of square box sleigh.

The seat ends are cut six inches high and flared two and a quarter inches. They and the back panels are set upon the seat frame, the edges of the latter being rounded.

The lazy backs are eight inches high. They may be stayed by arm rails or corner irons. The dotted lines at the front seat show the location of the seat when one seat only is used. The perpendicular dotted lines under the seat indicate the location of a weather board, which is hinged to the underside of the seat frame and hanging down against the center board, which is fastened to the two center pillars, dividing the body into two sections. When the front seat occupies the front position, this board, being hinged, effectually closes the space between the seat and bottom of the body. This board and the closing of backs of the back seat risers is a small matter, but it promotes comfort by excluding the wind.

Fig. 282 gives a view of half of the back, showing the position of the rave as it is let into the beam; also the panel, shape of lazy back, and the inside of the knee. It will be seen by this that the rave and the bottom boards, which rest on the beams, are flush on the top, and that the beam projects beyond the knee enough to give a firm support to the rave.

Fig. 283 presents a half view of the ground plan. A back bar may be framed across, connecting the rave, if desired, but it is not absolutely necessary, as the bottom boards effectually close that part of the sleigh.

In finishing up, leave the knees full thickness on the inside, and round up so as to leave a half inch flat on the outside. Round the tops of the runners slightly. Round the edge of the raves as shown by Fig. 282. Chamfer the inside corners of all parts of the body frame. Round up the inside edges of the seat ends, and finish all parts smooth, so that they can be painted. Secure the body to the raves by means of strap bolts and thumb nuts.

END OF VOLUME TWO.

INDEX.

VOLUME I.

Practical Blacksmithing.

Is a new book compiled from practical articles which have appeared from time to time during the last few years in the columns of "THE BLACKSMITH AND WHEELWRIGHT."

Volume I. relates to **Ancient Blacksmithing,** and gives illustrations with descriptions of some ancient tools ; tells how **Hammers Should Be Made** ; gives **Plans of Blacksmiths' Shops,** and a variety of plans of **Forges,** and the best way to build **Chimneys.** Illustrations with descriptions of a great variety of **Tongs, Hammers, Punches and Cold Chisels** are given.

Two prize articles on **Blacksmiths' Tools,** which have appeared in "THE BLACKSMITH AND WHEELWRIGHT," are printed in full.

There are five chapters in the book, each complete in itself.

Chapter 1 treats of **Ancient and Modern Hammers.** Chapter 2, **Ancient Tools.** Chapter 3, **Chimneys, Forges, Fires, Shop Plans, Work Benches,** etc. Chapter 4, **Anvils and Anvil Tools.** Chapter 5, **Blacksmiths' Tools.**

There is no book like it in the language; in fact a work on blacksmithing has never before been published in this or any other country. The book is bound in extra cloth with ink side stamp and gold back, and will be sent, *postpaid,* to any part of the country on receipt of price, **One Dollar.** Address

M. T. RICHARDSON, Publisher,

84 and 86 Reade Street, **NEW YORK.**

VOL. II.

Practical
- - Blacksmithing.

Chapter 1 treats of **iron** and **steel**, their antiquity and great useful-ness, the strength of **wrought iron** and **steel**, the **rotting** and **crystal-lization** of **iron, heating steel, testing iron** and **steel**, with illustra-tions ; treatment and **working of steel ; hardening steel**, with illustra-tions ; how to **select good steel ; restoring burnt steel ; cold ham-mering iron.**

Chapter 2 treats of **bolt** and **rivet clippers**, giving several ways of making these tools, accompanied by numerous illustrations.

Chapter 3 treats of **chisels** and **chisel shaped tools**, and is elaborately illustrated. Tells how to make all kinds of chisels, including clipping and cold chisels.

Chapter 4 treats of **drills and drilling**, tells how to make several styles of drill presses, each plan being accompanied by one or more illus-trations. It also tells how to make and temper stone drills, and gives many hints about drills in general. There is an article on drifts and drift-ing.

Chapter 5 treats of **fullering** and **swaging**, giving the principles of fullering. This has numerous illustrations.

Chapter 6 treats of **miscellaneous tools,** and gives the principles on which edged tools operate, and hints on the care of tools, tongs for bolt making, home-made fan, how to make a pair of pinchers, handy tool for holding nuts, and handy tool for countersunk bolts, how to make clinch-ing tongs, tongs for holding ship lays, accompanied by illustrations.

Chapter 7 is a continuation of **miscellaneous tools.** It tells about the shapes, with illustrations, of **lathe tools, useful attachment to screw stock dies,** wear of screw threading tools, tool for wagon clips, false vise jaws for holding rods, making spring clips, handy tools for mak-ing joints, tool for holding bolts in a vise, tool for making singletree clips, tool for making dash heels, mending augers and other tools, attachment to a monkey wrench, handy tool for finishing seat rails, tool for putting yokes on clips, how to make a candle holder, making a bolt trimmer, mak-ing a spikebar, how to make a tony square and easy bolt clipper, tool for pulling on felloes, a handy clincher, a bolt holder, making a cant hook, making screw boxes for cutting out wooden screws, mending a square, crane, an improved swage block, repairing augers, clamp for holding countersunk bolt heads, clamp for framework, tool for holding bolts, hints about callipers, vise attachment, a bolt set, a home-made lathe. The descriptions of the way to make all these different tools are accompanied by illustrations.

The price of this volume, in extra cloth binding, the same as Vol. I., to wit—**One Dollar,** and a copy will be sent to any address on receipt of price. In ordering be particular to specify that you want *Vol. II. of " Practical Blacksmithing."* Address

M. T. RICHARDSON, Publisher, 84 and 86 Reade St., N. Y.

VOLUME III.

Practical Blacksmithing.

It has been our aim in compiling Volume 3 of PRACTICAL BLACKSMITHING to make it even more interesting and instructive than the two previous volumes. We have given in detail, directions, accompanied by many illustrations, as to how to make the tools most useful to blacksmiths.

CHAPTER 1—Treats of Blacksmiths' Tools ; the preservation of same ; Bench Tools ; Tongs ; Tools for Farm Work ; Tools for holding Plow Bolts ; Tools for holding Plow Shares, etc.

CHAPTER 2—Gives various illustrations of Wrenches, and descriptions for their use.

CHAPTER 3—Gives illustrations and descriptions for Welding, Brazing, and Soldering.

CHAPTER 4—Describes the various uses of Steel ; Tempering, Hardening, Testing, etc.

CHAPTER 5—Illustrates and describes Hand Forgings.

CHAPTER 6—Illustrates and describes the making of Chain Swivels.

CHAPTER 7—Treats on various points on Plow Work, with illustrations.

The price of this volume, bound uniform with Volumes I. and II. is $1.00, and a copy will be sent to any address on receipt of price. In ordering be particular to specify that you want VOL. III. OF PRACTICAL BLACKSMITHING.

M. T. RICHARDSON, Publisher,

84 and 86 Reade St., New York.

VOLUME IV.

PRACTICAL BLACKSMITHING.

This volume completes the Series of Four Volumes. Like its companion volumes, it is handsomely printed with clear, large type on good paper and contains over 200 illustrations.

CHAPTER I.—Is devoted to **Miscellaneous Carriage Irons, Hammer Signals, etc.**

CHAPTER II.—Tells about **Tires, Cutting, Welding, Bending and Setting.** How to make a Tire Heating Furnace.

CHAPTER III.—Treats of **Setting Axles, Axle Gauges and Thimble Sk ins.**

CHAPTER IV.—Tells about **Springs.** How to make and reset. Different ways of Welding.

CHAPTER V.—Describes **Bob Sleds.**

CHAPTER VI.—Treats on **Tempering Tools,** including **Mill Picks, Drills, Taps, Di··s, Knife Blades, Chisels, Axes, Hammers, etc.**

CHAPTER VII.—Gives proportions of **Bolts and Nuts, f rms of Heads, etc.**

CHAPTER VIII.—Treats of **Working S'eel, Welding, and Case Hardening.**

CHAPTER IX.—Gives Tables of **Iron and Steel,** including size of iron, and different forms used by **Carriage, Wagon and Sleigh Makers.**

It is bound in extra cloth, with ink side stamp and gold back, and will be sent postpaid to any part of the country, on receipt of **ONE DOLLAR.** In ordering be particular to state that you want VOLUME IV. of PRACTICAL BLACKSMITHING. Address,

M. T. RICHARDSON, Publisher,

84 AND 86 READE STREET,

NEW YORK.

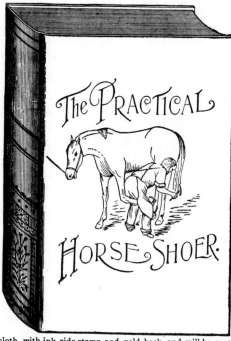

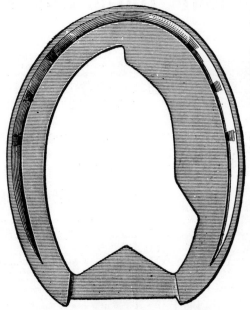